Chinese Religion

Chinese Religion

An Introduction

FIFTH EDITION

Laurence G. Thompson

Professor Emeritus
East Asian Languages and Cultures
University of Southern California

Wadsworth Publishing Company
I(T)P™ An International Thomson Publishing Company

Belmont • Albany • Bonn • Boston • Cincinnati • Detroit • London • Madrid
Melbourne • Mexico City • New York • Paris • San Francisco
Singapore • Tokyo • Toronto • Washington

Religion Editor: Katherine Hartlove
Editorial Assistant: Jessica Monday
Production Editor: Jennie Redwitz
Managing Designer: Stephen Rapley
Print Buyer: Barbara Britton
Permissions Editor: Bob Kauser
Copy Editor: Adrienne Armstrong
Cover Designer: Cloyce Wall
Cover Photo: Tony Stone, World Wide Ltd. (ISW) Beijing, China
Compositor: Joan Olson/Wadsworth Digital Productions
Printer: Malloy Lithographing, Inc.

*This book is printed on
acid-free recycled paper.*

For more information, contact Wadsworth Publishing Company.

Wadsworth Publishing Company
10 Davis Drive
Belmont, California 94002, USA

International Thomson Editores
Campos Eliseos 385, Piso 7
Col. Polanco
11560 México D.F. México

International Thomson Publishing Europe
Berkshire House 168-173
High Holborn
London, WC1V 7AA, England

International Thomson Publishing GmbH
Königswinterer Strasse 418
53227 Bonn, Germany

Thomas Nelson Australia
102 Dodds Street
South Melbourne 3205
Victoria, Australia

International Thomson Publishing Asia
221 Henderson Road
#05-10 Henderson Building
Singapore 0315

Nelson Canada
1120 Birchmount Road
Scarborough, Ontario
Canada M1K 5G4

International Thomson Publishing Japan
Hirakawacho Kyowa Building, 3F
2-2-1 Hirakawacho
Chiyoda-ku, Tokyo 102, Japan

Library of Congress Cataloging-in-Publication Data

Thompson, Laurence G.
    Chinese religion : an introduction / Laurence G. Thompson.—5th ed.
        p. cm.—(Religious life in history series)
    Includes bibliographical references and index.
    ISBN 0–534–25536–1 (pbk.)
    1. China—Religion. I. Title. II. Series.
BL1802.T5 1995
299'.51—dc20   95–10344

This book is dedicated to the memory of my Teacher—
Ch'en Shou-yi
   Analects IX.10.2

to the memory of my friend and guiding light of this series—
Fred Streng
   Analects VI.2

and to a colleague who has done much to move forward studies of
Chinese religion, including my own—
Gary Seaman
   Analects II.11

Contents

Foreword

The Religious Life in History Series was founded in for by the series founder J. Harold Stern. With he contributed the particulars were most to update the scholarship at many the present areas of material there effective in specific areas. These efforts will continue the introduction through the publication of special editions we are now planning new volumes in the series. But the most of this series now introduces the same new its beginnings We hope that readers will find these volumes more than in the most specific and series and areas to that people have in understanding the same text editors

The Religious Life in History Series introduces the richness and diversity of religious thought, practice, experience, and institutions as they are found in living traditions throughout the world.

Some of the religious traditions included in the Religious Life in History Series are defined by geography and cultural arenas, while others are defined by their development across cultural and geographic boundaries. In each case, however, the introductions seek to take full account of the variety within each tradition while keeping in sight those common traits and patterns that allow us to distinguish a particular religious tradition from others. Moreover, as a set of introductions to quite different religious traditions, the series naturally invites comparison between different ways of being religious and encourages critical reflection on religion as a human phenomenon in a broader sense. Thus, besides volumes on different religious traditions, the series also includes a core book on the study of religion, which is intended to aid the kinds of comparative inquiry and critical reflection that the series fosters through its introductions to religion in particular cultural and historical contexts.

The basic texts in the Religious Life in History Series all provide narrative descriptions of a religious tradition, but each also approaches its subject with an interpretive orientation appropriate to its focus. Some traditions lend themselves more to developmental studies, while others benefit more from topical studies. This lack of a single interpretive stance in the series is itself instructive. It reflects the interpretive choices made by the different authors, choices informed by a deep knowledge of the languages and cultures associated with the religious tradition in question. It displays as well the methodological pluralism that characterizes the contemporary study of religion. But perhaps most importantly, it can also serve as a useful reminder that what is considered religiously important in one context may not be so in another; indeed, what is seen as religious in one culture may not be so regarded elsewhere.

Most of the basic texts in the series have a complementary anthology of reading selections. These include translations of texts used by the participants of a tradition, descriptions of practices and practitioners' experiences, and brief interpretive studies of phenomena important in a given tradition. In addition, each of the basic texts presents a list of materials for further readings, including translations and more in-depth examination of specific topics.

The Religious Life in History Series was founded more than two decades ago by Frederick J. Streng. While he was editor of the series, continuous efforts were made to update the scholarship and make the presentation of material more effective in each volume. These efforts will continue in the future through the publication of revised editions as well as with the addition of new volumes to the series. But the aim of the series has remained the same since its beginnings: We hope that readers will find these volumes "introductory" in the most significant sense—as introductions to new perspectives for understanding themselves and others.

Charles Hallisey
Series Editor

Preface

It is now a quarter of a century since Fred Streng invited me to write an introductory text on religion in China for his new series, *The Religious Life of Man*. The process of producing such a text, and the book of readings that supplemented it, resulted in a whole new career for me in the field of Chinese religious studies, which seemed to offer great opportunities to a Sinologist. I have always been deeply grateful to Professor Streng for this opportunity and the results to which it has led. This fifth edition of *Chinese Religion: An Introduction* may serve in small measure as my tribute to his friendship and counsel.

In the new edition the following specific changes have been made: presentation has been improved by a number of small corrections; some of the illustrations have been replaced and a few added to help the reader; the Selected Readings, which in the nature of the case tend to go out of date with new scholarship in the field, have been revised and increased; and above all, a new chapter, Traditional Chinese Religion as Means of Coping, has been incorporated. It is hoped that the material in this chapter will serve as a convenient synthesis of the material earlier presented in the analytical chapters, and thus as a kind of summary overview.

As in the past, expert readers—this time Randy Nadeau of Trinity University and Willard Johnson of San Diego State University—have provided thoughtful and helpful comments in the effort to improve the book. To them, as to all previous reviewers, I express thanks (as well as apologies for suggestions regretfully not incorporated in the new edition). As in every version of this book I have the pleasant obligation to affirm that the original (and continuing) inspiration for the approach taken is the seminal work of C. K. Yang, *Religion in Chinese Society* (1961). It is a source of satisfaction to learn that that indispensable book has recently been reprinted and made available to new generations of students.

Laurence G. Thompson

Acknowledgments

The author is indebted to the following for permission to reprint copy-righted material:

Brigham Young University, Religious Studies Center, for permission to reprint from p. 140 from Spencer J. Palmer, ed., *Deity and Death*, 1978.

Thomas Y. Crowell Company and George G. Harrap & Company, Ltd., for permission to reprint from H. Maspero, "The Mythology of Modern China," in J. Hackin et al., *Asiatic Mythology*, p. 340.

Isis for permission to reprint from pp. 67ff. from Homer H. Dubs, trans., "The Beginnings of Alchemy," vol. 38, 1937, and from pp. 255 and 260f. from L. C. Wu and T. L. Davis, trans., "An Ancient Chinese Treatise on Alchemy Entitled Ts'an T'ung Ch'i," vol. 18, 1932.

The London School of Economics and Political Science for permission to reprint from p. 161 from Alan J. A. Elliott, *Chinese Spirit Medium Cults in Singapore*, 1955.

Monumenta Serica for permission to reprint from pp. 9f., 158ff., and 209ff. from E. Feifel, trans., "Pao P'u Tzu," vol. VI, 1941.

Mouton & Co., Publishers, for permission to reprint from pp. 25f. from Ch'ü T'ung-tsu, *Law and Society in Traditional China*, 1961.

John Murray (Publishers), Ltd., for permission to reprint from pp. 86–89 from Peter Goullart, *The Monastery of Jade Mountain*, 1961, and from p. 43 from Richard Robinson, *Chinese Buddhist Verse*, 1954.

W. W. Norton & Company, Inc., and Walter M. Whitehill for permission to reprint from pp. 9ff. from Chiang Yee, *A Chinese Childhood*, 1963.

Princeton University Press for permission to reprint from pp. 310ff. and 319f. from Kenneth Ch'en, *Buddhism in China: A Historical Survey*; © 1964 by Princeton University Press; Princeton Paperback, 1972.

Arthur Probsthain, Publisher, for permission to reprint from pp. 10–11 from John Steele, trans., *I Li*, vol. II, 1917.

The Smithsonian Institution for permission to reprint from p. 154 from David C. Graham, *Folk Religion in Southwest China*, 1961.

South China Morning Post, Limited, for permission to reprint from pp. 142f. and 144–148 from V. R. Burkhardt, *Chinese Creeds and Customs*, vol. II, 1953–58.

University of Notre Dame, Center for Pastoral and Social Ministry, for permission to utilize and quote from pp. 36–60 from Laurence G.

Thompson, "The Scrutable Chinese Religion," in J. D. Whitehead, Yu-ming Shaw, and N. J. Girardot, eds., *China and Christianity; Historical and Future Encounters*, 1979.

Mrs. Arthur Waley and the University of London, School of Oriental and African Studies, for permission to reprint from pp. 15f. from Arthur Waley, "Notes on Chinese Alchemy," *Bulletin of the School of Oriental and African Studies*, vol. VI, pt. 1, 1930.

Table of Chinese Religious History

Ruling Dynasties	*Major Religious Events and Characteristics*

I. Formation of Native Traditions

Hsia (?–? 1751 BCE) (not yet confirmed by archaeology)

Shang (?1751–?1111) (last centuries also called Yin)

Oracle bones used for divination; ancestor worship already dominant; worship of spirits of natural phenomena

Chou (?1123–221) 722–481, "Springs and Autumns" (period covered by *Ch'un Ch'iu*) 403–221, "Warring States" (feudal system destroyed)

Feudal polity, *Scripture of Song Lyrics* (*Shih Ching*), *Scripture of Archaic Historical Documents* (*Shu Ching*), *Scripture of Change* (*Yi Ching*); Master K'ung ("Confucius") (551–479); *Springs and Autumns* (*Ch'un Ch'iu*) and commentaries; The Old Master (Lao Tzû) and *Scripture of the Tao and Its Individuating Power* (*Tao Tê Ching*). Formative Age of Philosophy: Master Mo (Mo Tzû) (c. 480–390), Master Mêng ("Mencius") (c. 390–305), Master Chuang (Chuang Tzû) (c. 365–290), Master Hsün (Hsün Tzû) (c. 340–245), et at.; *Analects* (*Lun Yü*), *The Central and Universal Moral Law* (*Chung Yung*), *The Highest Form of Learning* (*Ta Hsüeh*), *Li* texts, *Scripture of Filiality* (*Hsiao Ching*)

Ch'in (221–206) (First Emperor unifies China)

First Emperor establishes totalitarian dictatorship, attempts thought control by book burning; rise of "religious Taoism" (although not yet so called)

Ruling Dynasties	*Major Religious Events and Characteristics*

II. Introduction, Assimilation, and Dominance of Buddhism

Former Han (206 BCE–9 CE)	Imperial polity finally established; first great expansionist empire; Literati Tradition becomes State orthodoxy; scholars concentrate on texts of Canon of the
Later Han (23 CE–220)	Literati; State university founded to teach this canon; great age of credulity and superstition begins; early varieties of religious Taosim flourish; Buddhism enters China and Buddhist missionary work begins
Three Kingdoms (220–265) (China partitioned)	Rise of so-called Neo-Taoist philosophy
Tsin (265–420)	Taoism and Buddhism eclipse Literati Tradition; Kô Hung (*Pao P'u Tzû—The Master Who Holds in His Arms the Uncarved Block*) (253–333?)
China partitioned between Southern (Chinese) and Northern (non-Chinese) Dynasties (420–589)	Buddhism flourishes
Sui (589–618) (China united under Chinese rule)	
T'ang (618–907)	China is world's greatest civilization; Buddhism reaches zenith of its influence, and then its temporal prosperity is destroyed by State (845); first stirrings of renascence of Literati Tradition

III. Renaissance of Native Tradition: Dominance of New Literati Philosophy

Five Dynasties (907–960) (brief period of disunion)	
(Northern) Sung (960–1127)	Chinese high culture attains its peak; New Literati Schools of the Principle and Mind ("Neo-Confucianism") reassert ancient native tradition against Buddhism
Second partition of China, between Southern Sung (Chinese) and Kin (non-Chinese) (1127–1280)	Cultural brilliance continues despite political weakness; Chu Hsi (1130–1200) is great synthesizer of the new School of the Principle and commentator on Literati Classics, whose interpretation of the canon was "orthodox" until twentieth century

Ruling Dynasties	Major Religious Events and Characteristics
Yüan (1280–1368) (all of China under Mongol rule)	Europe gets its first glamorous impression of Cathay from book of Marco Polo (in China 1275–1292)
Ming (1368–1644) (last Chinese dynasty)	New Literati School of the Principle at first dominant, but School of the Mind as formulated in the teachings of Wang Yang-ming (1472–1529) comes to the fore in mid Ming; unbroken contact with Europe begins: Matteo Ricci, S.J. reaches Peking (1600), followed by hundreds of Catholic missionaries
Ch'ing (1644–1911) (all of China under Manchu rule)	School of the Principle orthodoxy straitjackets Chinese thought; "Rites Controversy"; Catholic missions decline and missionary work proscribed; Protestant missions begin (1800); China invaded by Western world (nineteenth and twentieth centuries) and then by Japan (late nineteenth to mid-twentieth centuries)

IV. Disruption of Tradition by Western Impact

Republic of China (confined since 1949 to Taiwan, i.e., Formosa) (1912 to date); People's Republic of China (Communist-controlled mainland) (1949 to date)	Collapse of imperial polity; disruption of tradition

---

Data on dynasties much simplified. Dates for Hsia and Shang follow Tso-pin Tung, *Chung-kuo Nien-li Chien-p'u* (Taipei: Yee Wen Publishing Co., 1960); dates of Chou philosophers follow Mu Ch'ien, *Hsien-Ch'in Chu-tzu Chi-nien* (Hong Kong: University of Hong Kong Press, rev. ed., 1956), vol. II, final chart.

YIN (late SHANG) "Feudal" polity	CHOU Feudal polity disintegrates; great states emerge	CH'IN/HAN Unification under imperial polity

Year, BCE

1500 1250 1000 750 500 250 0

Ancestor cult spreads among all classes.

Ancestral cult in royal family ?and nobility. Zoomorphic sacrificial bronze vessels.

Great clans develop mythical/legendary genealogies.

?Totemism. Elaborate burial sacrifices among elite, including human sacrifices. *Shang ti* (Supreme Ruler in Heaven) Nature gods. Astronomical knowledge advanced. Conceptualization of time in endless sequence ("stems and branches" system).

Human sacrifice largely abandoned.

Shang ti largely replaced by reference to *t'ien* (Heaven) among philosophers.

Basic cosmological and meta-physical concepts develop: *tao, yin-yang*, five elemental operational qualities (*wu-hsing*), *ch'i* (vital breath).

State cult develops in accordance with supposedly ancient practices codified in *Li* texts.

Shu Ching
Shih Ching
Yi Ching (divination sections)

Master K'ung establishes moral qualifications of *chün-tzŭ*, or literatus/gentleman. Tzŭ Ssŭ, Mêng Tzŭ, and Hsün Tzŭ shape Literati doctrines.

Doctrines of Literati School become State orthodoxy.

but

?Lao Tzŭ—*Tao Tê Ching*
Chuang Tzŭ
(basic texts of Taoism)

Age-old magical practices merge with new cult of immortality (the goal to become *hsien*).

"Taoist" pantheon develops. "Taoist" cults. "Taoist" communities. "Taoist" rebellions. Faith healing most important.

Time Line of Chinese Religious History

Tales about immortal transcendents, living mainly on offshore islands.

Alchemy (attempt to concoct elixir [*wai-tan*]).

Yogic practices.

Internal gods (body is a microcosm).

Buddhism enters China.

Texts translated over several centuries, introducing Indian schools. Sangha and monachism, magical powers of monks, sūtras, images.

Folk religion (the exact nature of folk belief and practice undocumented, but it was certainly spiritistic and magical) takes on Taoist ·······

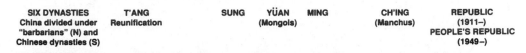

| SIX DYNASTIES
China divided under
"barbarians" (N) and
Chinese dynasties (S) | T'ANG
Reunification | SUNG | YÜAN
(Mongois) | MING | CH'ING
(Manchus) | REPUBLIC
(1911–)
PEOPLE'S REPUBLIC
(1949–) |

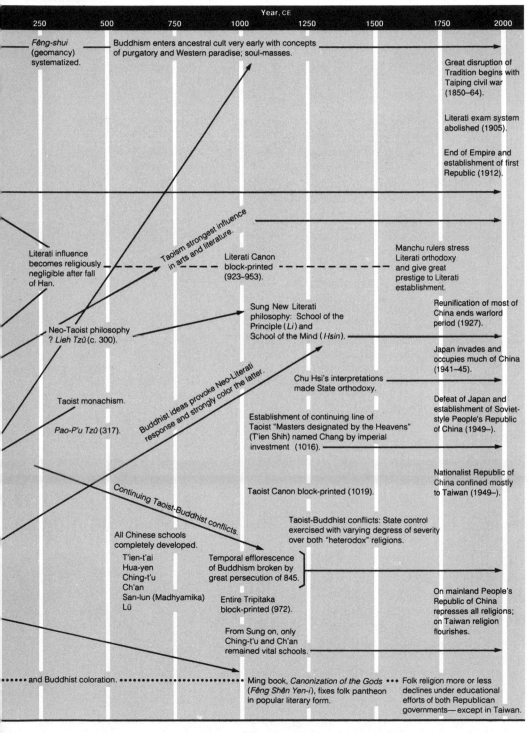

Year, CE

| 250 | 500 | 750 | 1000 | 1250 | 1500 | 1750 | 2000 |

Fêng-shui (geomancy) systematized.

Buddhism enters ancestral cult very early with concepts of purgatory and Western paradise; soul-masses.

Great disruption of Tradition begins with Taiping civil war (1850–64).

Literati exam system abolished (1905).

End of Empire and establishment of first Republic (1912).

Taoism strongest influence in arts and literature.

Literati influence becomes religiously negligible after fall of Han.

Literati Canon block-printed (923–953).

Manchu rulers stress Literati orthodoxy and give great prestige to Literati establishment.

Sung New Literati philosophy: School of the Principle (*Li*) and School of the Mind (*Hsin*).

Reunification of most of China ends warlord period (1927).

Neo-Taoist philosophy ? *Lieh Tzŭ* (c. 300).

Japan invades and occupies much of China (1941–45).

Buddhist ideas provoke Neo-Literati response and strongly color the latter.

Chu Hsi's interpretations made State orthodoxy.

Taoist monachism.

Defeat of Japan and establishment of Soviet-style People's Republic of China (1949–).

Pao-P'u Tzŭ (317).

Establishment of continuing line of Taoist "Masters designated by the Heavens" (T'ien Shih) named Chang by imperial investment (1016).

Nationalist Republic of China confined mostly to Taiwan (1949–).

Taoist Canon block-printed (1019).

Continuing Taoist-Buddhist conflicts.

Taoist-Buddhist conflicts: State control exercised with varying degress of severity over both "heterodox" religions.

All Chinese schools completely developed.

T'ien-t'ai
Hua-yen
Ching-t'u
Ch'an
San-lun (Madhyamika)
Lü

Temporal efflorescence of Buddhism broken by great persecution of 845.

On mainland People's Republic of China represses all religions; on Taiwan religion flourishes.

Entire Tripitaka block-printed (972).

From Sung on, only Ching-t'u and Ch'an remained vital schools.

•••••• and Buddhist coloration. •••••••••••••••••••••••••••• Ming book, *Canonization of the Gods* (*Fêng Shên Yen-i*), fixes folk pantheon in popular literary form.

••• Folk religion more or less declines under educational efforts of both Republican governments— except in Taiwan.

Introduction

The reader, even before opening the book to this page, may have felt some curiosity about the title. Why Chinese "religion" rather than Chinese "religions"? Surely more than one religion has been important in this most ancient of living civilizations? The slightest acquaintance with Asian history will have introduced one to terms like *Confucianism* (which we shall call the Literati Tradition), *Taoism, Buddhism.* However little one may know about these terms, it is at least clear that they refer to distinctive forms of philosophical-religious thought and practice.

It is indeed the purpose of this book to give life to such terms and in the doing to make apparent the rich variety of religious expression in China. And yet an even more pervasive theme in our exposition is what we may call the *Chineseness* of all these varieties of religious expression. Through the long ages of her history, China has been exposed to many religions, including Judaism, Islam, and the several forms of Christianity, as well as more exotic types such as Manichaeism and Zoroastrianism. All these remained what they were when they came to China: foreign. The only religion of non-Chinese origin that succeeded in naturalizing itself in China was Buddhism.

Our use of the word *religion* in the singular is intended, then, to convey our interpretation that the character of religious expression in China is above all a *manifestation of the Chinese culture.* To attempt to understand religion in China as several systems of doctrine is to read Western experience into a quite different set of circumstances. In the past almost every member of Western society belonged to some religious sect, each sect being distinguished from others by its insistence upon certain doctrinal propositions. In China laypeople did not usually belong to an institutionalized sect, nor did their religious life have anything to do with signing articles of faith. Except in the case of the professional religious living apart in monasteries, religion in China was so woven into the broad fabric of family and social life that there was not even a special word for it until modern times, when one was coined to match the Western term.

Most significant of all, in the West the development of religion was closely bound up with the lively history of ideas. Because of the central place of doctrine in religion, it necessarily shared in the questionings, the changing insights, the disputations, and the actual warfare of the Western world of ideas. Philosophers, theologians, and scientists endlessly pondered and argued and revised the hypotheses upon which sectarian tenets were based. But in China not only did doctrinally founded churches not exist, but the worldview and the ethic did not undergo such restless revisions. Even the impact of Buddhism, which began at about the time of the common era, failed to change materially the fundamental Chinese outlook. Instead, after a thousand years Buddhism itself was largely accommodated to these ingrained views.

Because of these facts, we have thought that the most meaningful introduction to Chinese religion is one that stresses, first, the worldview that finds expression in religion and, second, the functioning of religious expression in Chinese society. The worldview and the society here pictured are those generally characteristic of China during the past two thousand years. In a final chapter we have given a brief description of the changes being wrought in this great tradition by the circumstances of the most recent century. Such changes are certainly far reaching, but we are as yet too close to the processes to be able to predict the outcome, not to mention the uncertain fate of Soviet Communism, which has collapsed throughout much of the world in which it was dominant. Although the People's Republic of China as such has not collapsed, it has changed radically, and its future is in much doubt. In any case, the developments of the contemporary period can be understood only in their relationship to the traditional religion; and that traditional religion, far from having passed from the scene, is still very lively.

CHAPTER 1

The Early Chinese Worldview

NATURE

The Naturalistic Universe

The universe of the ancient Chinese was naturalistic in the sense that it was characterized by the regularity that Western philosophy has called "law"—*but it lacked the Western assumption of an outside "lawgiver."*[1] Three features of this regularity were conspicuous to the ancients: first, the cyclical processes, such as night following day followed by night, or the rotation of the seasons; second, the process of growth and decline, exemplified by the waxing and waning of the moon; third, the bipolarity of nature. The latter meant not simply that everything had its opposite but that opposites were necessary and complementary to each other. These opposites tended to merge into each other and even to become each the opposite of its former self. The ground or fundamental stuff of the universe was seen to be homogeneous, and all particular phenomena were individualized through these processes. The bipolarity of nature was no doubt the latest principle to be grasped, being by far the most sophisticated.

In fact, once this third principle was recognized, it could be seen to account for the other two, which were merely its operational aspects. As a principle, it was one of the most fruitful and useful ever devised by the mind of man for making sense out of the infinite multitude of diverse facts in the universe. Today, described as positive and negative electrical charges, it is the basis of "matter" according to science (we are not suggesting that the ancient Chinese knew about electricity); in traditional China, expressed through the concepts of *yin** and *yang*, bipolarity constituted the specific characteristic of Chinese metaphysics. Once this principle had suggested itself, perhaps as early as 1000–500 BCE,[2] the Chinese were able to develop a perfectly coherent theory of the cosmos. Nature

---

*Boldfaced terms are defined in the glossary.

was seen to operate through the interplay of light and darkness, heat and cold, male and female, and so forth. The *yang* (as represented by the first of each pair) and *yin* (the second of each pair) were not in absolute and permanent opposition to each other. They might best be described as definable phases in a ceaseless flow of change:

> When the sun goes the moon comes; when the moon goes the sun comes. The sun and moon give way to each other and their brightness is produced. When the cold goes the heat comes; when the heat goes the cold comes. The cold and heat give way to each other and the round of the year is completed. That which goes wanes, and that which comes waxes. The waning and waxing affect each other and benefits are produced. (*Scripture of Change,* "Appended Commentary," Part II; *Yi Ching, Hsi Tz'û, hsia*)

It is significant that this bipolar worldview did not, in its ancient, classical formulation, have anything to do with a struggle between basic principles of good and evil. *Yin* and *yang* were equally essential forces in the ceaseless dynamic of an impersonal universe.

In the material world produced through this process, there was an infinite variety of phenomena, and the Chinese by late Chou times (fifth to third centuries BCE)* had, like other ancient peoples, overcome this confusion by classifying all things into what seemed to be irreducible elements. As a consequence of the principle of constant transformation embodied in the *yin-yang* theory, the Chinese concept of the primary elements focused on the fundamental *qualities* observed in things. These qualities were not static but were ceaselessly interacting, transforming, and replacing each other. The Chinese word *hsing,* which has customarily been translated as "element," is actually a verb meaning "to walk, to go, to act." There were five *hsing,* given in the *Hung Fan* chapter of *Shu Ching* (see Appendix 1) as water, fire, wood, metal, and earth (their order and mutual reactions differ in other texts). Thinking of *hsing* as verbal will help us to keep in mind their active nature (water overcoming fire, fire burning wood, and so forth), while thinking of *hsing* as adjectival will help us to understand their elemental nature (that is, all things may be categorized as either "watery," that is, liquid; "fiery," that is, gaseous; and so forth). So as to emphasize both of these aspects of the Chinese term, we will throughout this book refer to the *hsing* as *the five elemental operative qualities.* Their ever-changing character is also indicated by the rendering *the five phases.*

The Supreme Ruler in Heaven

Although the universe thus functions through the workings of "law without a lawgiver," there is at the same time a personalized power of conspicuous importance in the thinking of the ancient Chinese. At the dawn of their history, twelve centuries before the common era, the writing on oracle bones (see pp. 1–32) and ritual bronze vessels, as well as the somewhat later texts preserved in *Shu Ching* and *Shih Ching* (see Appendix 1), speak

*For dates of the dynasties into which Chinese history is conventionally divided, see Table of Chinese Religious History preceding the Introduction.

frequently of a Supreme Ruler in Heaven called *ti,* or *shang ti. Ti* is written with a graph that later becomes a title of the Chinese emperor, while *shang ti* means the superior *ti,* or the *Ti*-on-High. These appellations have often been rendered by translators as "God." *T'ien* is a word that has the simple meaning of sky and the more pregnant meaning of heaven. In its latter significance it is happily rendered in English with the capital letter, for of course we commonly substitute *Heaven* for *God* in such expressions as "Heaven help me!" or "Heaven only knows!" It is *t'ien* that eventually becomes the customary term for the Supreme Ruler, and this shows very well the impersonal character the latter often came to assume in the Chinese mind by the last two or three centuries of the Chou dynasty. *Ti* lost its connotation of the Highest and became an appellation not only of the earthly emperor but of deities subordinate to Heaven.

Nevertheless, *shang ti* was retained as the name, or part of the name, of the Supreme Ruler in Heaven in the worship performed by the emperor in postfeudal (that is, after Chou) times. The question as to the correct connotation of these Chinese terms remains open despite several centuries of discussions and investigations by Western scholars. Our view is that the Supreme Ruler in Heaven, although the highest deity, is not equivalent to the God of Western religion or philosophy. Like the Old Testament Jehovah, *shang ti* or *t'ien* is pictured in the ancient texts as being concerned with the actions of man and as the source of the "mandate" from which the ruling dynasty receives its legitimacy. From *shang ti* or *t'ien* come blessings and punishments. But there is no hint that he is the Creator of the universe or the Cause of its functioning. Like Jehovah, the Chinese Supreme Ruler is a tribal god, and indeed one plausible interpretation is that the term *ti* or *shang ti* actually means the High Ancestor of the ruling house. It is only later, when the depersonalized *t'ien* becomes the Highest in a trinity of Heaven, Earth, and Man, that we might ascribe a God-like power to the Supreme Ruler. And yet even this Heaven of later times is not the Ultimate or the Absolute. For that we must explore another term, the famous *tao.*

Tao

This is such an important word in Chinese thought that translators have often felt it best to leave it in transliterated form. Key terms in any great tradition are inevitably distorted or even falsified by translation, and they can be grasped in something like their true significance only by seeing their operation in many contexts. In studying Buddhism, for example, such words as *nirvāṇa* and *śūnyatā* are rightly considered as technical terms and customarily left untranslated. This may well be the best way to treat *tao.*

For our purposes it will be sufficient to explain that there are two general applications of the term *tao* in Chinese thought. The first is fortunately easy to appreciate because it is a metaphor that we also use: From the commonplace meaning of a road, path, or way, the analogy is drawn of a Way, or *the* Way. In this usage *tao* refers to truth—ethical, religious, or other—and in terms of conduct it means the normative standard:

> The Master said, "The *tao* is not far from man. If what one takes to be the *tao* is far from man, it cannot be considered [the true] *tao*." (*The Central and Universal Moral Law* XIII.1; *Chung Yung*)

This passage from *Chung Yung* (see Appendix 1) is rendered into English by Ku Hung-ming,* a scholar with an excellent command of English, in such a way as to bring out fully this sense of *tao*:

> Confucius remarked: "The actual moral law is not something away from the actuality of human life. When men take up something away from the actuality of human life as the moral law, that is not the moral law."[3]

One other example, from *Analects* (see Appendix 1), will suffice:

> The Master said, "Shên, my *tao* is unified by a single [principle]. . . ." When the Master went out, the [other] disciples asked, "What did he mean?" Tsêng Tzû replied, "The *tao* of our Master is only *chung* and *shu*." (*Analects* IV.15; *Lun Yü*) (Shên was the personal name of the disciple Tsêng Tzû. *Chung* is usually translated as loyalty or conscientiousness and *shu* as reciprocity.)

The second sense of *tao* is more specifically pertinent to understanding the Chinese worldview. It is this sense that has been made most famous by the often-translated text *Tao Tê Ching*, traditionally attributed to the Old Master (Lao Tzû, sixth century BCE), a somewhat older contemporary of Master K'ung. But although *tao* was such a central concept to the Old Master and his school that it gave its name to that school, it is by no means the exclusive property of the Taoists. *Tao* in the sense we are discussing is, from one point of view, that regularity of operation in the universe that has earlier been noted. But it is more: It is the reality behind or within appearances, the ultimate metaphysical truth. Like the God of some Western philosophers or the Void (*śūnyatā*) of Mahāyāna Buddhism, it is that about which nothing can be predicated but because of which all particular phenomena have their being. The opening lines of *Tao Tê Ching* struggle to put this essentially inexpressible concept into words:

> The [human] way can be discussed
>   But not the Eternal Way;
> Names can be defined
>   But not the Eternal Name.
> As undefined, It is the beginning of Heaven-and-Earth;
> As defined, It is the Mother of the ten thousand things-and-beings.
> Therefore, because It is eternally desireless
>   We perceive Its wonder;
> Because It eternally possesses desire
>   We perceive Its subtle workings.
> These two—[desire and desirelessness]—emanate together
>   But are differently named,
> And both are called mysterious—
> Mystery of mysteries, the Gateway of all mysteries. (*The Old Master* 1;
>   *Lao Tzû*)

---

*Note that Chinese always give surname first; the given name follows, either a single word or a double name hyphenated.

Without going any further into various metaphysical interpretations of *tao*, we summarize by saying that *tao* might be likened to the laws of nature or, better, to nature itself. And whether taken as Being or as Nonbeing, or as the Principle in all particular things, it is in any case never conceived as Deity.

Supernatural Beings

There is thus perhaps no real Deity with the capital letter to be equated with the God of Western religion. We have seen that Heaven eventually becomes the term customarily used for the Supreme Ruler, but we now know that behind or beyond Heaven there are the workings of *yin* and *yang*, which have their source in the *tao*. Such would be the metaphysical view of sophisticated minds. It is probable that a few of these minds were in all ages able to content themselves with such an abstract theory, but certainly most, even of these educated elite, shared to some extent the belief in supernatural powers prevailing among the great masses of the people. Not the *tao*, and not the one, omnipotent God of Western monotheism, but a countless host of greater and lesser deities accounted in the popular mind for what went on in this world.

There is nothing distinctively Chinese in the way whereby the forces of nature were personified or the heavenly bodies were believed to exercise a direct influence in human affairs, or the way in which otherwise inexplicable occurrences of disease and other misfortunes were attributed to malignant spirits. The deification of human beings characteristic of both family and popular religions is somewhat more exceptional, although not unique. These matters will be taken up in later chapters. Here we wish only to underline the point that in the Chinese worldview there was *an unseen but completely real dimension to the world: that of the spiritual beings.* This was the dimension in which the deified ancestors dwelt, and it was the dimension inhabited by the malevolent ghosts of those whose sacrifices had been discontinued or who had otherwise been wronged in their earthly term. The malevolent ghosts sought revenge on mortals, and much of the popular religion was concerned with protection against their attacks. Charms, exorcism, communication through mediums, sounding of gongs and firecrackers, placing of spirit-walls to prevent entry of evil spirits through a doorway, offerings to placate them, the burning of incense, prayers, fasting—the long catalog of such practices gives ample evidence of the reality of dangers to people from the spiritual dimension.

A Gestalt Cosmology

The total worldview of the popular religion may thus not unreasonably be called *animistic.** Although in popular view the most important spiritual beings were of human origin, there was no lack of other spirits such as those of animals, plants, and nonorganic objects, including stones and

---

*I am well aware that this term is considered passé by modern scholars. I would replace it with a more suitable term if one could be found, but thus far I have not been able to find one.

stars, rivers and mountains. And although the educated intelligentsia would certainly not hold the more naive and crude notions of the peasant populace, they did share the same general outlook, at least to the extent that they never set humans and nature apart.

To modern people in the West, it must require a great effort of the imagination to empathize with the traditional Chinese feeling. We are so accustomed to seeing the physical world as something "out there," as an environment (often hostile to us), or as a purely material object for our exploitation, that we can scarcely comprehend the Chinese sense of the wholeness of the universe, in which man is a part and only a part.* This intimate feeling of being at home in nature is shown in many ways in the traditional Chinese culture: in the philosophical writings, particularly the wonderful flights of Master Chuang (365–290 BCE), as a perennial theme of poetry through the ages, and visually in those landscape paintings that place man in perspective as a tiny observer of the vast universe—an observer who is seeking to absorb himself therein.

In an integrated universe, it will occur to humans to seek out the signs writ large in nature whereby they may confirm that human actions are in accord or discordant with the *tao* of this universe. In the *Shu Ching* we may read how these signs were interpreted by the Chou people:

> The several kinds of evidence are rain, sunshine, heat, cold, wind, and their seasonableness. When all five of these come in due amount and order, the vegetation thrives luxuriantly. When one of them is too much it is bad, and when one is too little it is [likewise] bad. What we call the auspicious evidences are solemnity, to which seasonable rain is the correlate; good order, to which seasonable sunshine is the correlate; wisdom, to which seasonable heat is the correlate; good planning, to which seasonable cold is the correlate; saintliness, to which seasonable wind is the correlate. What we call the inauspicious evidences are violence, to which constant rain is the correlate; arrogance, to which constant sunshine is the correlate; dissipation, to which constant heat is the correlate; rashness, to which constant cold is the correlate; stupidity, to which constant wind is the correlate.
>
> . . .
>
> What the king examines is the year; what the ministers and warrior aristocrats examine is the month; what the chiefs and local rulers examine is the day. When the seasonableness of year, month, and day is unchanging, the hundred kinds of grain thereby ripen, the administration of government is thereby enlightened, talents among the common people are thereby revealed, families are thereby peaceful and healthy. . . . (*Scripture of Archaic Historical Documents*, "The Great Plan"; *Shu Ching, Hung Fan*)

In another section of the same text, we find a clear illustration of the application of this theory. The Regent, uncle of the young king, is accused of having plotted to usurp the throne. Heaven responds to this calumniation by sending down its testimony in the form of natural disasters:

---

*In our own time, it is interesting to see this traditional view of Westerners being modified by the ecological exigencies now so conspicuous.

In the autumn, when the abundant crop had not yet been harvested, Heaven sent down great storms of thunder, rain, and wind. The grain was beaten down and large trees were uprooted. . . . The King and Great Officers put on their ceremonial headdresses to open the document [that had been placed] in the metal-strapped depository. And then they found the statement in which the Duke of Chou [that is, the Regent] had offered himself as tribute [to the ancestors] in lieu of the Martial King. . . . The King [i.e., the Martial King's son] held the document and wept, saying, . . . In times past the Duke labored on behalf of the royal house, but I, the minor child, did not understand it. Now Heaven acts to overawe us in order to show forth the virtue of the Duke of Chou. We, the Little Child (another deprecatory term used by kings) will go in person to meet him. . . . When the King went out to the suburb Heaven sent down [gentle] rain and turned away the winds, and the grain then revived. The two lords [i.e., King and Duke of Chou] commanded the people of the country to raise up all the big trees that had been uprooted and replant them. The harvest was then abundant. (*Scripture of Archaic Historical Documents,* "The Metal-Strapped Depository"; *Shu Ching, Chin Têng*)

Such a belief in the interactions of people (particularly represented in the person of the Son of Heaven, as the king was titled) and the rest of nature continued to be a basic aspect of the Chinese worldview up to modern times. The reading of omens and portents was a pronounced feature of the Chinese religion.

It is surely this "gestalt cosmology" that gives to the worldview of the native Chinese tradition its specific character. Lacking the premise of a God "out there" who created and controls the universe and requires human worship, the typical Western form of religion did not develop. Lacking the theory that human souls are particularizations of the universal Brahman, the typical Indian form of religion likewise did not develop. The Chinese religion, based on the premises we have outlined, developed on its highest level a mysticism perhaps not essentially different from the mysticisms of other religions but nevertheless felt to be identification with the *tao,* or nature itself, and not with God, beyond or outside of nature. The Chinese religion, while giving to Heaven power to punish people's misbehavior, defined this misbehavior as actions inimical to the harmonious workings of the universe. The Chinese religion conspicuously lacked the central concept of the ever-brooding presence of Almighty God continuously attending to the sins and virtues of every individual, swift to save or damn, requiring submission, belief, faith, and adoration.

MAN*

Theory of the Soul

In view of the central place of ancestor worship in Chinese culture (which we shall examine in detail later on), one might suppose that a systematic

---

*It is perhaps wise to point out that we here, and in many other places, use "man" in the universal sense of humankind.

rationale would have been developed to clarify the nature of the soul. The Western mind has always felt the necessity for logical "proofs" of such things, and the Western religion emphasizes doctrine. The Chinese mind, however, did not feel this compulsion to formulate speculative systems, and Chinese ideas concerning the soul must be gleaned from here and there, never having received any thoroughgoing formal treatment.

Although we have no way of knowing the age in which the Chinese began to formulate their specific notions concerning the human soul, it is obvious from the fact that ancestor worship was already a fully developed cult at the dawn of history that survival beyond death was the accepted belief. For literary evidences concerning this belief, we have to rely on the same books we have already cited, as well as others that made their appearance in late Chou times. From these sources we discover that ideas about the soul and its survival emerge from the general cosmological views already outlined.

In this way of thinking, the human being, like every other thing in the universe, is a product of the operations of *yin* and *yang*—most obviously, in fact, since new life is produced through the union of male and female. This reduces the status of human souls to something less exalted than that assumed in India or the West. Human beings are not the special creations of God, much less are they God Himself. In the works of the Taoist philosophers, most picturesquely in the book of Master Chuang (365–290 BCE), the Chinese naturalism is expressed in its most extreme form:

> Master Lai suddenly fell ill. Panting and gasping, he was at the point of death. His wife and children gathered around and wept over him. Master Li, who had gone to inquire about his condition, drove them away so they would not startle [the dying man] during the process of change. Leaning against the door he said, How great is the [Power] that Makes and Transforms! What will you become next? Where will you be sent? Will you become a rat's liver? Will you become the arm of an insect?
>
> . . .
>
> Master Lai replied, A son has only to be ordered by his parents to go east or west, south or north, and he obeys. The Yin and Yang are no less to a man than his parents. As they have brought me near to death, not to obey would be to resist them. How could I blame them for it (i.e., for bringing about my death)? Now the Great Clod* has carried me in my bodily form, favored me with life, given me ease in old age, and will put an end to me in death. Therefore, what has made my life good will [likewise] make my death good. When a master smith is casting his metal, were it to leap up saying, I must become a Mo-yeh (the name of a famous sword of antiquity), the master smith would certainly regard it as a metal of evil omen. When now, having once succeeded [in acquiring] human form, were I to say, Only as a human, only as a man, the Making and Transforming [Power] would certainly regard me as a person of ill omen! Let us take all Heaven-and-Earth as a great furnace, and the Making and

---

*For this figure of speech see H. G. Creel's essay "The Great Clod," in *Wen-lin,* ed. Chow Tse-tsung (Madison: University of Wisconsin Press, 1968), pp. 257–268; later reprinted in the collection of Creel's essays entitled *What Is Taoism?* (Chicago: University of Chicago Press, 1970), pp. 25–36.

Transforming [Power] as the master smith—then where could I go that would not be all right? Calmly I lay me down, and when I am given form I shall awake. (*Master Chuang*, scroll 6, "The Great Master"; *Chuang Tzû*, "*Ta Tsung Shih*")

In this view it may be said that there is really no room at all for the soul. *Tao,* functioning through the operations of *yin* and *yang,* produces both grosser material manifestations and subtler spiritual manifestations. A human being is a combination of these, and upon death the former would return to Earth (which is *yin*) while the latter would ascend to the bright, ethereal region of Heaven (which is *yang*). Although there seems to be a dualism in the human constitution, it thus differs from the dualism of body and soul that has plagued the Western philosophers. Perhaps the human constitution in this Chinese concept could be likened to a mixture in a test tube. During life it is kept in stable solution by vigorous activity, but with the cessation of that activity due to death, it separates out, the coarser components settling to the bottom, leaving the pure liquid above.

But all this is too abstract to satisfy the common need for a more comforting theory, a theory certainly required for ancestor worship. In China, as elsewhere, the vulgar notion of the soul would be that of a pale shadow of the living person, usually invisible, but capable of horrifying people occasionally by appearing before them as a grotesque caricature of the mortal form. Such ghostly apparitions have been a staple of Chinese stories from early Chou times to the present. However, there was a distinction made between such sinister apparitions and the benevolent souls of properly cared-for ancestors. In the popular way of speaking, the former were called *kuei,* meaning demons, devils, and ghosts, while the latter were referred to as *shên,* meaning kindly spirits.

The material or *yin* component of the soul (called *p'o*) was that which would turn into a *kuei* if not placated by suitable burial and sacrifices. As for the burial, it was thought that this portion of the soul would reside in the grave as a natural habitat, both it and Earth being *yin.* If the deceased were properly interred and sacrificed to, the *p'o* soul would rest peacefully, while the spiritual or *yang* soul (called *hun*) would send down blessings to the surviving family members. This power of the *hun* soul derived from its nature as *shên,* which not only was a generic term for kindly spirits but also was used in reference to all deities.

Thus the rites of burial and sacrifice were sanctioned both by fear of the dead becoming a vengeful demon and by hope that the dead would become a benevolent god. Such a fear and such a hope underlie all of Chinese religion.

But we have not yet completed the Chinese theory of the soul. What has been sketched to this point is the native theory deriving from the remote past. At the beginning of the common era, the Indian religion of Buddhism had reached China, and within a couple of centuries enough of its texts had been translated into Chinese that new, imported notions of the afterlife began to influence Chinese concepts. These notions ultimately became inextricably entangled with the older Chinese ideas, particularly in the popular mind.

Although one of the Buddha's fundamental teachings was nonexistence of self—that is, of a "soul" in any permanent sense—common sense seemed to demand some sort of continuing agent to carry out the process of karmic "justice." ***Karma,*** universally accepted in Indian religions including Buddhism, was originally an impersonal physical "law," comparable to the laws of action and reaction, or the conservation of energy. As popularly interpreted, however, it became a sort of merit and demerit system according to which the condition of one's future existence was determined by one's past actions. One reaped in the next life what one had sown in this. Furthermore, before being cast up by the wheel of life-death-rebirth into that next existence, one had to expiate in purgatory all of one's evil deeds. It is interesting that the most important social function of Buddhist monks in China was the priestly one of saying "soul masses" to alleviate as much as possible the sufferings of the soul in purgatory.

The chief value of these popular Buddhist notions was that they furnished incentive to do good and shun evil, while at the same time providing an explanation for the puzzling question of why virtue was so often unrewarded and vice so frequently profitable—the answer in this case being that the books were always balanced although the figures had been written in the unknown ledger of a past existence. *Karma* required the soul as its agent—at least in minds unequipped to understand the higher Mahāyāna philosophy of Emptiness (*śūnyatā*)—and so (by about 300 CE) this soul had become an integral part of Chinese Buddhism.*

During later centuries, when Buddhism had spread all over China and was the strongest religious force in the land (its influence increased until the mid-ninth century and was only seriously weakened by the rise of the new **Literati** philosophy in the Sung dynasty), these ideas about *karma*, rebirth, and purgatory were adopted into the folk religion. The end result was a purgatorial system organized along Literati bureaucratic lines, with a well-organized program of karmic bookkeeping, trial in courts exactly like those of the magistrates in the Chinese empire, and punishment in various hells where the tortures meted out fitted the crimes of the guilty souls. Those rare souls with an excess of good deeds over bad were able to pass directly into new births in favorable circumstances without undergoing these torments or were able to find eternal bliss in the Paradise of the West.

There were thus two theories of the soul, the first based on the *yin/kuei* and *yang/shên* concept of the native tradition and the second based on the imported Indian belief in karmic process. The first is perhaps more closely bound up with the family religion and its ancestor worship, but the influence of the second is also very strong, especially in the funeral rites, which are a vital part of the ancestral cult.

Man to Man

The Chinese worldview was focused to a considerable extent on the relations of man to man. Chinese philosophical discourse throughout the ages concerns itself with the nature of human nature and the ethical impera-

---

*Chinese Buddhism is discussed in Chapter 8. For more detailed treatment of Buddhism, see Richard H. Robinson and Willard L. Johnson, *The Buddhist Religion*, 3d ed. (Belmont, CA: Wadsworth, 1982).

tives of family and social life. This is not to deny various issues of great importance in the religious outlook of Chinese intellectuals. From the latter Han (first century of the common era) on, the influence of Taoism and Buddhism was every bit as strong as that of the Literati tradition, and we by no means want to contribute to the perpetuation of the myth of a "Confucian China."* But whatever personal religious views one might hold, all Chinese shared general and specific concepts about the social order and individual conduct, derived from those Literati texts to which we have so often alluded.

As we shall see in Chapter 3, the religion of the family was the universal religious institution of China, and the ethical views of the Literati tradition were essentially a rationalization and extension of the familial virtues. The principles of this familial morality were derived from natural relationships rather than abstract theory. By the early Chou dynasty the *Shu Ching* refers to "the five classes," meaning fathers, mothers, eldest brothers, younger brothers, and sons, and to the obligations of each "class." In *Mêng Tzû* (see Appendix 1) there is a somewhat different but similarly homely classification attributed by the philosopher Master Mêng (c. 390–305 BCE) to the times of the legendary sage-emperor Shun:

> Between father and son there is affection; between prince and minister there is integrity; between husband and wife there is a proper distance; between senior and junior there is proper precedence; between friend and friend there is faithfulness. (*Master Mêng* IIIA.4.8; *Mêng Tzû, T'eng Wên Kung, shang*)

And in the Literati codes, *Records of Rituals* of the Literati Tradition (see Appendix 1), compiled in early Han (second century BCE), yet a third form of the same domestic ethic is expressed:

> The father is merciful, the son filial; the elder brother is good, the younger brother submissive; the husband is upright, the wife complaisant; the adult is kind, the child obedient. (*Records of Rituals*, "Evolution of Rituals"; *Li Chi, Li Yün*)

This age-old familial morality, preached by Master K'ung and his principal followers and eventually enshrined in the Canon of the Literati, came to permeate all of Chinese society. To the vast majority of the Chinese, who followed conventional careers, these precepts were the moral norm; to the minority who were different, it was this tradition from which they differed. Even Buddhist and Taoist monks and nuns, living apart from society, were still guided in their conduct largely by this family style of morality advocated by the Literati Tradition.

Above the level of the code of familial relationships was the body of ethical teachings meant for the "superior men," the small minority who received a literary education and who were thereby destined to govern the nation and to guide its cultural development. This higher tradition was

---

*By this is meant the notion, still quite widely entertained by the modern "descendants" of the Literati and hence by Western students, that everything of importance in the traditional Chinese civilization was "Confucian" in derivation and character.

directly inspired by the life and words of Master K'ung (551–479 BCE). The Master exemplified the ideals by which all educated men should guide their conduct. He was a man to whom truth, honor, and the furtherance of just government meant everything. He stood for the good ways of the ancient sages. He sought all his life for a prince who would use him by putting his principles into practice; but when a ruler found expediency more profitable than principle, Master K'ung left his service. Before Master K'ung, in China as in old Europe, a "gentleman" was a man of noble blood; after Master K'ung, a gentleman was a man who possessed the *character* a gentleman should possess, regardless of his blood. This emphasis upon character, upon moral excellence, was the great contribution of Master K'ung to Chinese society.

The gentleman was to cultivate his own character, and, equally important, he was, like his Master, to put this highly cultivated character at the service of the State whenever this was feasible. The educated—those who mastered the Literati Canon—served as officials, governing the untutored masses; this government was in theory one of moral example rather than coercion. Master K'ung had said, "The Gentleman is like the wind; his inferiors are like grass. When the wind blows the grass must bend" (*Analects* XII.19). The full implication of this remarkable conception of government as moral example is seen in a passage near the beginning of the canonical *Ta Hsüeh* (*The Highest Form of Learning;* see Appendix 1):

> The men of old who wished to make their bright virtue shine throughout the world first put in order their own states. In order to put in order their own states they first regulated their own families; in order to regulate their own families they first disciplined their own selves. In order to discipline their own selves they first rectified their own minds (or, hearts); in order to rectify their minds they first resolved sincerely upon their goals; in order to resolve sincerely upon their goals they first broadened their understanding of things to the utmost. The broadening of understanding to the utmost was accomplished by studying the nature of things.
>
> When they studied the nature of things then their understanding became complete; when their understanding was complete then they resolved sincerely upon their goals; when they were sincerely resolved upon their goals then their minds (or, hearts) were rectified. When their minds were rectified then they were able to discipline themselves; when they could discipline themselves then they could regulate their families; when they could regulate their families then they could put in order their own states; when their own states were in order then they could bring peace to the world.
>
> From the Son of Heaven (i.e., the emperor) down to the common people there is a single [principle]: discipline of the self is fundamental.

Thus, aside from their family religion, the educated elite in China had as their primary religious obligation the perfection of themselves to serve as moral paragons. The self-discipline of the Literati was therefore quite different from the asceticism and yogic concentration of Buddhist practice, or the breath control, dietary, alchemical, and other techniques of religious Taoism (see Chapter 6).

Moral perfection was summed up in the term *rên* (often romanized as *jên*), whose graph eloquently expresses its basic requirement: It is formed from the elements "man" and "two." From this composition of the word, translators have derived such renderings as "man-to-manness" and "human-heartedness," attempting to improve on older definitions such as "benevolence" or "goodness." There is actually no doubt that in common usage *rên* came to be no more than goodness or even just charity, but to Master K'ung it stood for such an exalted ideal that he had never known a person to whom the word could truly apply.

Aside from *rên*, the virtues stressed in the teachings of Master K'ung and his school are down-to-earth and easy to understand, or at least we can approximate them with the names of virtues familiar to Western morality: righteousness, loyalty, trustworthiness, modesty, frugality, in-corruptibility, courtesy, learning, and the like. If they seem like moral platitudes, it is because they were practical ideals in the education of gentlemen destined to run the empire. The important thing to understand is that it was this *concentration on character building* that engaged the minds of the men who governed China and created her high culture. It was this that engaged them, rather than other forms of the religious quest.

Finally we should note that in this naturalistic view of man there is no original sin, no inherent depravity from which man can be lifted only by a savior. There was, to be sure, a running debate throughout the history of Chinese philosophy about whether human nature is good, bad, or morally neutral. But even those philosophers who proposed the second of these alternatives did not conceive of "badness" as a sort of taint, ineradicable except by divine grace. The majority view in the Literati Tradition was that given its authoritative expression by Master Mêng, who argued that human nature was inherently good. His greatest opponent was Master Hsün (c. 340–245 BCE), but Hsün Tzû merely insisted that men were inherently *inclined* toward evil and selfishness, and he believed that they would become good through education. The Literati Tradition subsequently blended these two views: The goodness of human nature was generally accepted in theory, while education was given the place of supreme importance in practice. In any case, there was no question of sinfulness and salvation in the Western sense.

CHAPTER 2

Prescientific Theory and Religious Practice

It is not within the scope of this book to deal with complex questions of the origins of religion according to psychological and anthropological theories. However, we consider that the strangeness of the traditional religious life of the Chinese masses to the student in contemporary Western society requires at least a few remarks concerning its milieu.

In Chapter 1 we became acquainted with the worldview of the early Chinese native tradition. This worldview was mainly that of the elite educated class, as it was formulated in the texts of the Literati Canon and by several of the great philosophers of the later Chou dynasty. When we consider the outlook of the Chinese people as a whole, we find a rather different worldview. It is not unrelated to the more sophisticated view of the intelligentsia, but it is more an animistic than a naturalistic one. In this popular worldview the ancient tradition native to China was markedly influenced by Taoism and the Buddhism imported from India, as we have already noted in our discussion of the theory of the soul. By way of background to the popular animism with its Buddho-Taoist admixture, we shall make a few observations regarding man's life in the prescientific world.

REGULARITY AND CAPRICE IN THE PRESCIENTIFIC WORLD

It is not easy for the Westerner living in a highly industrialized, scientifically progressive, technologically advanced civilization to visualize even how his or her grandfather lived only fifty years ago. Such is the accelerating rate of scientific-technological progress that now there are greater changes between decades than formerly there were between centuries. But the first requirement for understanding the popular religion of China is the ability to enter into the spirit of a people whose lives and thoughts are as foreign to us today as those of our own medieval forebears. Like these, the great masses of the Chinese population were peasants, illiterate, or only semi-literate, unimaginably provincial in their experience, dwelling in tiny villages or small towns in the midst of their fields, largely out of contact with the high culture of the elite class, uncared for by the remote imperial government but always subject to taxation, corvée (forced labor), and military conscription. Their masters were the landowner, the county magistrate, the local bandit chief. Living at all times on the very margin of subsistence, they had so few earthly possessions that we can scarcely conceive of such poverty.

For all their ignorance and confinement, these peasants were wise in the ways of the seasons, skilled in the management of water, and unsurpassed in their mastery of tillage. And though they read no books, they were thoroughly imbued with the Literati ethic, which at least after the beginning of the common era, became widely disseminated through proverbs and moral axioms, the tales of storytellers and the rustic stage, and the ancestral cult. In fact, the gulf between the peasant masses and the philosophers was not nearly so great as that between a laborer and an academic philosopher today. Chinese philosophy for the most part stayed in touch with the simple realities of life and nature rather than flying to the stratosphere of abstract speculation. Such concepts as *yin, yang,* and *tao,* the five operational qualities, the "gestalt cosmology" (see Chapter 1), and so forth, were not only comprehensible in their elementary form to the untutored peasant mind but must actually have derived originally from the "nature wisdom" of the peasant.

We have emphasized that an important part of this worldview was the consciousness of *regularity in change.* But this comforting, sensemaking regularity was far from perfect. The capriciousness of nature was also notorious, and to no one more than the peasant. On the one hand, so dependable were the seasonal changes that in north China the solar year could be divided into twenty-four periods of fifteen days each,[1] and the specific natural phenomena peculiar to each period would usually, in fact, occur exactly as charted in the calendar. On the other hand, all too often the seasonable rain would fail to arrive, or the frost would come too early. Despite the peasant's mastery of the techniques of agriculture, despite his indefatigable toil and his incredibly patient care, now and then he would be overwhelmed by some sudden catastrophe such as flood, drought, or plagues of insects.

Life itself was precarious in a way we can hardly realize. Death of the mother in childbirth was common, and death of infants was even more frequent. As recently as the 1920s, a study of rural areas in central China revealed that "one-half of those born in China die before they are twenty-eight years of age."[2] No vaccinations or inoculations immunized people from such prevalent diseases as smallpox and typhoid. No antibacterial medications prevented infections from reaching lethal potency. No surgery removed the swollen appendix. No measures of hygiene and sanitation were understood that could have forestalled the frequent, widespread epidemics of cholera, malaria, or plague. The terror of disease lay not only in its customarily fatal outcome but perhaps even more in the unpredictability with which it struck. It is the same terror with which we today think about cancer. Yet today we are confident, because of the past record of science, that the cause and cure for cancer and every other dread disease will be found, but in China there was no such history of progress on which to base such a hope.

Conditions of this sort produce as a natural psychological defense an attitude of resignation to the inevitable. This resignation, often described as "fatalism," was frequently noted by earlier Western observers, who were accustomed to reproach the Chinese for such a pessimistic and spiritless attitude. These observers forgot that only a few lifetimes ago their own ancestors required an equal amount of fatalism (expressed as resignation to the will of God) to bear up in a world of unpredictable disasters beyond human control. It is only the power acquired through science that has enabled people to become optimistic and actually successful in many of their encounters with the afflictions of nature. Modern man turns to science, confident that by choosing the correct application of scientific method, any problem can be solved.

Prescientific man could have no such confidence because prescientific methods had no history of increasing success. These methods resembled what we call science in that they were attempts to make sense out of the infinite multitude of facts in the universe and that on the theoretical bases thus constructed systems of practical application were erected. In China as in Europe these prescientific efforts could not attain the authority we today attribute to science, because in fact their *results* were undependable. No matter how logically coherent the prescientific theories might have been, when practically applied there were simply too many contradictory results. In other words, these systems were what we today call pseudosciences—although they were not of course "pseudo" to the people of their time. There was unquestionably a certain amount of empirical truth in these pseudosciences that kept alive their credibility; and to people who lived before scientific method had been perfected, they were one important means by which to cope with the environment. The Chinese pseudosciences were in a general way the counterparts of those familiar to us in Western history. Although they had their special Chinese features, the Western terms are indicative of their nature: astrology, chronomancy, physiognomy, and so on. Chinese medical theory was likewise pseudoscientific, dominated by the *yin* and *yang* functions of the five elemental operative qualities—the latter an interesting comparison with the four Aristotelian "humors" of premodern Western medicine.

The pseudosciences were an outgrowth of the naturalistic worldview on the one hand and the animistic view on the other. The regularity in change of the first view furnished a basis for hypotheses of order in nature, while the conception of the world and all things in it as alive conditioned the particular nature of these hypotheses. In the Chinese popular religion the ordered aspect of nature faded somewhat into the background, so to speak, and the animistic aspect was more prominent. This is not surprising since the function of religion was to give support to people in coping with the problems resulting from the unpredictable and capricious aspects of the world, rather than to provide an intellectually satisfying cosmology. The simplest way to account for disorders was to picture them as the willful activities of beings. These beings were in the ingenuous mind very much like human beings, except that they dwelt in the unseen spiritual dimension and had superhuman powers.

In fact, the whole animistic system was but an extension of the ideas we have already examined in our section on the theory of the soul. The gods, even those who had the most efficacious power, were essentially the same as the *yang* soul—called *hun* and titled *shên* (deity), as we recall—of human ancestors. The demons or malignant beings were essentially the same as the *yin* soul—called *p'o* and titled *kuei* (ghost or devil)—which issued from an inauspiciously sited or neglected grave to wreak vengeance on mortals. The ancestral religion, as we shall see in Chapter 3, stressed those acts that would obtain blessings from the *yang* soul and appease the *yin* soul of one's ancestors. Just so, in the wider contexts of the community or the whole nation, the animistic religion functioned to secure the blessings of the deities and appease or render harmless the demons.[3] Thus, man played his part in maintaining that order of nature of whose fundamental processes he was conscious, and thus he had at least some hope that he could by his actions improve his fate.

The pseudosciences, then, were attempts to read the meanings of certain sets of signs that human ingenuity had detected and arranged into logical sequences. When such meanings are directly related to present and future happenings in people's lives, then pseudoscience becomes a form of *divination*. This term is also used to refer to another technique that seeks to bring man into communication with the spiritual beings in the invisible dimension.

DIVINATION

There are two major motivations in divination. The first is the desire to understand the operations of the natural and supernatural forces in the environment so that one's own actions may be in accord with them, thus producing favorable results. The second is the filial responsibility to keep in touch with deceased family members so that one may do whatever mortals can do to help them in the nether world. The first may be seen as a logical procedure in light of the native worldview; the second results from acceptance of the Buddhist notions about the fate of the soul.

The particular techniques of divination practiced in China have been as varied as those found in other cultures. But whatever method was employed, there was no hard and fast line between consulting the deities and reading the invisible ink in the book of natural principles. The rationalistic wing of the intellectuals might scoff at crude notions of ghosts and gods and hold to entirely naturalistic conceptions; and yet many of their ideas were, from the vantage point of science, no more valid than the very superstitions they derided. In this respect there is a close correspondence with premodern Europe, whose learned men likewise seem to us to have been almost comically deluded about the real workings of the universe. There is even a correspondence in the scholasticism of the medieval Chinese philosophers with their colleagues in medieval Europe. The Literati philosophers of the School of the Principle (*li*), whose Thomas Aquinas was Chu Hsi of the twelfth century, spun elaborate webs of metaphysical and cosmological theory and even emphasized that one should search out the Principle in things; but, after all, their searching was entirely speculative and lacked experimental and mathematical basis.*

There is still a further parallel between these Chinese thinkers and the premodern Europeans: The latter could not find the road to true science because they were prisoners of tradition—their reverence for Aristotle, Galen, the Bible, and other ancient authorities constituted a mental block. In exactly the same way, the Chinese were victims of their reverence for ancient authorities. Although Buddhism had introduced various types of idealistic thought, the native naturalism prevailed. The most influential source of this naturalistic theory was the *Scripture of Change*, the *Yi* (or *I*) *Ching*.

The *Yi Ching*

The *Yi* is one of the core works of the Literati Canon (see Appendix 1), but it is no more the exclusive property of the Literati than the concept of *tao* is the special possession of the Taoists. It is no doubt one of the most influential books ever written, no small part of its continuing, universal appeal being that it is so ambiguous and suggestive that every reader is challenged to find its true significance. Unfortunately, it will not be possible here to convey any adequate idea of its contents, which would involve us in lengthy technical discussions. We must be satisfied to indicate in a general way its place in the protoscientific worldview of the Chinese.

The *Yi Ching* evolves from eight trigrams consisting of all the possible combinations of broken and unbroken lines, placed one atop another:

The eight trigrams are further developed into sixty-four hexagrams by the simple method of putting one trigram on another and carrying out the same procedure to combine broken and unbroken lines in all possible combinations.

The unbroken line stands for *yang*, the broken line for *yin*. The diagrams are symbols as wholes, and each line is also a symbol. There grew up about each diagram a text to explicate its significance, line by line and as a whole. It seems certain that the original work was a diviner's text. By casting lots the diviner determined whether the first line would be *yin* or *yang*; he then built up the diagram from bottom to top, casting lots for each line.

The oracular judgments on the diagrams are no doubt the heart of the *Yi Ching*, but at various unknown times during the Chou dynasty, other sections were added to give us the present text. Tradition attributes these additions to ancient sages, including Master K'ung himself. It is these com-

---

*The new Literati movement of Sung and Ming times (usually called "Neo-Confucianism") is discussed in Chapter 7.

mentaries that have lifted the work from its original position as a fortune-telling manual to the status of a profound revelation about the principles of the cosmos. Unfortunately, as we have remarked, this philosophizing is so far from lucid that many of the most intelligent minds in Chinese history have failed to explain it satisfactorily. Nevertheless, the symbolism of the diagrams became in the Chinese world the main system of conceptualization of the universe. In the prescientific attempt to formulate universal principles and grasp the operational modes of nature, the diagrams played a part comparable to that of mathematics in modern science. The diagrams were dynamic, in the sense that the arrangement of lines changed as one took different readings, and *it was this changing that interested the Chinese mind*—hence the title *Scripture of Change,* or *Yi Ching,* indicative of the Chinese view that the cosmos was a functioning organism rather than a static object. Because the concern of Chinese scholars was predominantly with moral, social, and political problems, and not with the physical world as such, the content of the commentaries was bent to humanistic purposes. Nevertheless, it supplied the humanistic philosophers with what seemed a sound metaphysical rationale.

Now the interesting thing, the thing we must grasp in order to appreciate the functional part played by the *Yi Ching* in Chinese religion, is that there was a subtle, vital shift in the attitude with which the diagrams were regarded. Originally they had been symbols—visual representations of what happened in given circumstances. But eventually they came to be invested with *operational power.* They no longer simply stood for specific changes, they actually brought about these changes. It was this belief that gave the *Yi Ching* its dominance in the Chinese worldview and molded many of the elaborate, pseudoscientific theories. The diagrams were key components in the complex system of correlations that underlay all this pseudoscience and that involved the five elemental operative qualities and many numerical constructs.[4]

Divination could be performed for any situation to relate it to any other situation by virtue of the fact that the diagrams were thus related to all the primary factors in the scheme of things. These primary factors included not only the elemental operative quality dominant in the particular situation but also the color, musical note, flavor, position of various heavenly bodies, compass point, season, and so forth.

Fêng-shui — to go with the flow of the Tao

As far as religion is concerned, the most influential pseudoscience was that of "winds and water," the literal translation of *fêng-shui.* This is usually called "geomancy" in Western writings, but we prefer the transliterated term because the Chinese pseudoscience does not correspond very well with any Western lore. *Fêng-shui* constitutes a system of divination for determining the auspicious siting of human dwellings—for the living or for the dead. The rationale is that which we have already considered, namely, that people may help improve their own fate by determining the workings of nature and then bringing their own actions into accord with them. The theories of *fêng-shui* purport to explain what the pertinent natural processes are, and the practices of *fêng-shui* are designed to effect the desired results. Since we already know the basic premise that the spirits of the dead are very influential in the world of the living, it is unnecessary to explain why the siting of graves should be a crucial matter or why the homes of the living should be located in the most favorable situations.

We shall not be surprised to learn that the fundamental thing is to place the grave or home properly with regard to the functioning of *yin* and *yang*.* The former is represented in the technical vocabulary of *fêng-shui* as the white tiger, and the latter is called the azure dragon—which, in fact, stand for the cardinal points of west and east. Eitel has summed up the basic theory as follows:

> The azure dragon must always be to the left, the white tiger to the right of any place supposed to contain a luck-bringing site. This therefore is the first business of the geomancer on looking out for a propitious site, to find a true dragon, and its complement the white tiger, both being discernible by certain elevations of the ground. Dragon and tiger are constantly compared with the lower and upper portion of a man's arm: in the bend of the arm the favourable site must be looked for. In other words, in the angle formed by dragon and tiger, in the very point where the two (magnetic) currents which they individually represent cross each other, there may the luck-bringing site, the place for a tomb or dwelling, be found. I say it *may* be found there, because, besides the conjunction of dragon and tiger, there must be there also a tranquil harmony of all the heavenly and terrestrial elements which influence that particular spot, and which is to be determined by observing the compass and its indication of the numerical proportions, and by examining the direction of the water courses.[5]

The topographical characteristics of the earth are in themselves manifestations of the *yin* and *yang* forces that can be seen more obviously in meteorological phenomena, and that as wind, rain, clouds, clear-sky heat, and so forth are quite fittingly designated as "breaths" (*ch'i*). But in the Chinese view the earth is no different from the heavens in pulsating with the breaths of the two primal forces:

> Wherever there is nature's breath pulsating, there will be visible on earth some elevation of the ground. Where nature's breath is running through the crust of the earth, the veins and arteries, so to speak, will be traceable. But nature's breath contains a two-fold element, a male and female, positive and negative . . . breath. . . . Where there is a true dragon, there will be also a tiger, and the two will be traceable in the outlines of mountains or hills running in a tortuous and curved course. Moreover, there will be discernible the dragon's trunk and limbs, nay, even the very veins and arteries of his body, running off from the dragon's heart in the form of ridges or chains of hills. As a rule, therefore, there will be an accumulation of vital breath near the dragon's waist, whilst near the extremities of his body the energy of nature's breath is likely to be exhausted. . . . But even near the dragon's heart, the breath of nature, unless well kept together by surrounding hills and mountains, will be scattered. When the frontage of any spot, though enjoying an abundance of vital breath, is broad and open on all sides, admitting the wind from all four quarters,

---

*Even whole cities were located and laid out in accordance with the principles of *fêng-shui*.

there the breath will be of no advantage, for the wind scatters it before it can do any good. Again, suppose there is a piece of ground with plenty of vital breath, and flanked by hills, which tend to retain the breath, yet the water courses near the place run off in straight and rapid course, there also the breath is scattered and wasted before it can serve any beneficial purposes. Only in places where the breath of nature is well kept together, being shut in to the right and left and having a drainage carrying off the water in a winding tortuous course, there are the best indications of permanent supply of vital breath being found there. Building a tomb or house in such a place will ensure prosperity, wealth and honour.[6]

From these remarks it will be understood why the entranceways to temples usually have at least slightly U-shaped walls and why the tombs of southern China are surrounded by horseshoe-shaped walls. For what nature has failed to provide, man may artificially correct.

Such artificial improvements of a situation are equally necessary to prevent the malign effects either of the topography itself or of malicious spiritual beings:

Now, all these evil influences, whether they be caused by straight lines of hills or water courses or by rocks and boulders, can be fended off or counteracted. The best means to keep off and absorb such noxious exhalations is to plant trees at the back of your abode and keep a tank or pond with a constant supply of fresh water in front of your house. This is the reason why in South China every village, every hamlet, every isolated house has a little grove of bamboos or trees behind and a pond in front. A pagoda, however, or a wooded hill, answers the same purpose. . . . Another device to keep off malign influences is to place opposite your house gate a shield or octagonal board with the emblems of the male and female principles, or the eight diagrams painted thereon, and to give the pathway leading up to your front door a curved, or tortuous direction. Lions carved in stone or dragons of burnt clay also answer the same purpose, and may be placed either in front of a building or on top of the roof; but by far the best and effective [sic] means is to engage a geomancer, to do what he says, and to pay him well.[7]

Why should the *yin* and *yang* be personified as they are in *fêng-shui*? The answer to this question illustrates very well the correlative thinking of the Chinese pseudosciences. The system of correlations associates east with spring and west with autumn, as is quite appropriate in view of the symbolism of rising and setting sun. Spring, which brings all things to birth, is naturally *yang*; autumn, portending the death of all things as seen most clearly in vegetation, is naturally *yin*. This correlation is but one of many that the *fêng-shui* expert would make and for which he used his elaborate compass.[8]

In the center of this compass is the needle, which, like so many things Chinese, is viewed in reverse to our way of thinking—that is, it is seen as pointing south, rather than north. Surrounding the pit with its needle is a series of concentric circles, numbering from eighteen to twenty-four or even more, according to the completeness of the instrument. These circles contain the markings for all the various factors that must be considered in determining whether there is "a tranquil harmony of all the heavenly and terrestrial elements which influence that particular spot." Such factors include the eight trigrams, the cyclical signs called "celestial stems" (*t'ien-kan*) and "terrestrial branches" (*ti-chih*),[9] planets, stars, constellations, various arrangements of the five elemental operative qualities, and others.

With so many factors to be correlated in addition to the visually determined aspects of the terrain, it is no wonder that often "the doctors differed." It was this wide leeway for interpretation afforded by all these calculations that kept alive the credibility of *fêng-shui*.[10] If, despite the careful choosing of a spot for tomb or home, bad luck still visited the family, the obvious explanation was that the practitioner first consulted had not analyzed all the factors correctly—an explanation that the next expert would be sure to underline as he rectified the findings of his colleague.[11]

The Almanac

The principles given scriptural authority in the *Yi Ching*, and embodied in *fêng-shui*, have been operative in all the pseudosciences. But one did not have to consult a specialist in order to know the trend of natural forces during the course of the year. In every home there would be found the almanac, which combined calendrical and cabalistic (occult) information in exactly the same manner as the almanacs frequently found in American homes only a few generations ago. Publication of the calendar was from the most ancient times a distinctive prerogative of the government; in fact, it was one of the symbols of the regime's legitimacy. It was issued in various versions, the contents of the cheapest being limited to the most essential information, and the contents of the most elaborate being quite encyclopedic, forming a sort of popular manual for the household. For example, the almanac for 1952, issued in Hong Kong and designated by the combination of the "celestial stem" called *rên* and the "terrestrial branch" called *ch'ên*, contains the following items, among many others:

> High and low tides of Kwangtung province; Taoist charms; the story of the encounter of Master K'ung with a precocious child; a list of the names of the "3,000" disciples of Master K'ung; the place-origins of Chinese surnames; a treatise on the analysis of dreams; fortune-telling methods (using physiognomy, palmistry, coins); the stories of the Twenty-four Paragons of Filiality; methods for cultivating longevity; the *Thousand-character Essay* (a sixth-century piece); the *Household Maxims* of the philosopher Chu Hsi; etc., etc.

All this material is copiously illustrated with wood-block cuts, and some of the printing is in two colors, red and black. But the essential information is that concerning divination, as based on the astrological implications of the stems and branches, the five planets with their associated operational qualities, and the gods of certain stars. A "basic almanac" will give guidance about actions that may be undertaken on each day of the year; a fuller version such as the one here described will devote many separate sections to all the various aspects of divination, including the ruling natural forces, the connection of these with the forces ruling the life of a person born at any particular time, and the general and specific characteristics of every day and even every hour of each day.

For example, the following advice is given in one divinatory section of the Hong Kong almanac under discussion. On the twelfth day, denoted by the cyclical signs *hsin* and *ssû*, of the fifth month (that is, June 4, 1952)—a day under the influence of the operational quality of metal and hence its associated planet, Venus—one should avoid mixing soya sauce, making liquor, or going on a journey. It is suitable, however, for getting together with friends, for taking up one's official duties, for marrying a wife or marrying out one's daughter, for making clothes, for moving, for treating an illness, for setting up the posts or raising the ridgepole of a house. . . .

If it seems that such mechanical or arbitrary divination could hardly command real belief, one need only consider that similar material is commonly found in bookshops and published in the newspapers of America today and recall that many well-known personages in contemporary Western society are rumored not to take any important action without consulting their horoscope, in order to see the authority of this age-old, universal system lingering still in our scientific milieu. One can understand how much more pervasive and persuasive its influence would have been in the premodern age. The almanac thus shows us the eclectic character of Chinese popular religion, with its blend of naturalistic and supernaturalistic features.

Spirit Mediums

From the most ancient times, the Chinese religion has used mediums for communicating with the spiritual realm. The medium is not like the gypsy woman with her crystal ball; he (or she) is rather the Chinese version of the shaman, who by certain techniques puts himself into a trance, during which he is possessed by the spirit. The spirit may be that of any of the innumerable beings, eminent or humble, who inhabit the unseen dimension, and the medium speaks as the mouthpiece of this being. The spirit may be the chief deity of a temple who will give instructions to his followers, or it may be the soul of a person whose kinsfolk want to contact him as he is undergoing the purgatorial interlude. The medium may be a professional, usually a young person having special gifts marking him for this career; or mediumship may be a temporary ability conferred on a layperson. The professional may be the star attraction of a temple, drawing to it crowds of people to seek the advice and help of the god, or he may have only a small private circle of clients. The medium may work matter of factly without any props at all; or as the popular performer in a big temple, he may require special costumes, a sedan chair in which to be carried in procession with his god's image, weapons for inflicting self-torture and expelling demons, musical stimulation, various attendants, an interpreter, and so forth. Sometimes the spirit speaks through the planchette, a technique analogous to the automatic writing of the West. Often the medium is given the power to speak in tongues, the most convincing demonstration of true possession by the spirit being the ability to speak a dialect that in his normal state he does not even understand.

The medium, in the capacity of spokesperson or representative of the deity, is naturally able to bless people by the power of the deity's spirit or to exorcise demons. The deity will give his power to an amulet, through the medium, who may cut his tongue and smear the charm with a bit of the blood. The medium of a temple may serve as medical adviser, psychologist, and business counselor to his clients as he relays to them the guidance of his familiar spirit. Some of the topics on which temple mediums in Singapore were consulted by Chinese clients, according to a field study undertaken in 1950–1951, included the following, in order of frequency: "miscellaneous illness," "bad luck," possession by evil spirits, erring spouses, childbirth, investment advice, news of relatives in distant parts, the choice of auspicious dates, gambling advice, wayward children, accidents, advice concerning partnerships, insanity, protection in courts, and communication with the dead.[12]

The final item on this list is also a familiar service of mediums in the Western world. In China the communication may be for the purpose of comforting the dead or of receiving information and advice from them. An eyewitness account of a séance held for both of these purposes, a commonplace event in Hong Kong, is given by Burkhardt:

> Two sisters, employed as wash-amahs (laundry-women) in different houses in Hong Kong, wished to get in touch with the spirit of their deceased mother, who is buried in a village near Kukong, up the North River from Canton. The journey is expensive and tedious, and letters are few and far between. . . . A third sister is working in Singapore, but fails to answer letters. The idea was that a talk with the mother would clear up questions of the family welfare and solve the mystery of the sister's silence.
>
> The Colony has no lack of mediums, and the most unexpected women appear to be gifted in this way. A few are professionals, but the vast majority are amateurs who have no fixed fees, and give their services for "lucky money" a percentage of which is always returned. . . . The medium's only properties consist of a cigarette tin filled with rice and covered with a scrap of red paper, which acts as an incense burner. Having lit her three sticks, she clasps her hands above her head, intones a short prayer, and then seats herself in front of the improvised altar. Her clients sit alongside her on the sofa, and provide her with the data consisting of the name of the departed with whom communication is desired and the exact location of the grave.
>
> The medium closes her eyes, and joins her open hands with the finger tips touching and thumbs separate. This forms the "Eight directions," in one of which every spirit in the universe is to be found. The first communication was startling, for the spirit replied that the mother was not available, as her father-in-law wished to speak with his grand-children instead. Being of the senior generation he naturally had precedence, and no objection could be raised to his monopolising the conversation. He first identified himself by giving an account of the family, which children had died, and how the others were employed. These details are always expected to ensure that the right spirit is at the other end of the line. Having established his identity, the grandfather declared that the family had decayed since his days and, that though not actually in want, his descendants were none of them prosperous. . . . He attributed the reduced circumstances of his descendants to the fact that a house had been built in front of the family mansion which had broken its luck. . . .*

---

*That is, blocking off the benign emanations deriving from a site with good *fĕng-shui.*

As to the correspondence with the girl in Singapore the old man stated that her letters were being stolen, and that they should write by registered post with receipt to sender. . . . On the termination of the conversation the old man was of course asked if he were in need of anything. He replied that he was well off for clothing, but could find a use for $500, and gave minute directions as to how it was to be sent. The mode of communication was through the "Third daughter-in-law" and "Fifth Princess" through whom the medium carries out all her transactions with the Spirit world. . . .

In sending these remittances it is usual to remember other dead members of the family at the same time, lest their spirits should feel resentment at being neglected. In this case the mother, with whom communication was first sought, would certainly be propitiated by a packet. Gifts are also included in the despatch on behalf of other living members of the family, who have not had the opportunity of hearing the request of the deceased. . . .

Of course the old gentleman's modest demand for a remittance of $500 was not taken at its face value and, when the time for despatch arrived, packets of notes on the Bank of Hell, and quantities of white paper stamped with a golden square were purchased from the purveyor of underworld commodities. . . .

A lucky day, fifteenth after the conversation with the grandfather, was chosen for mailing the packet, and at noon the consigner presented herself with her parcels at the medium's hut . . . [which] consists of two rooms and a lean-to kitchen, scrupulously clean throughout. The bamboo table altar was backed by a watercolour of her Patron Saint, "The Third Daughter-in-Law." . . .

The money to be despatched is placed on the altar accompanied by a quantity of cheap blank paper slips with rough holes punched in two rows lengthways. These represent the insurance, and are intended to distract malignant spirits who infest the route from interference with the packets. . . . The priestess, after lighting three sticks of incense, places herself on the right of the altar and the client takes up her position on the left. After committing the packages to the safe keeping of the saint, with a few short prayers to beseech her good offices, the money is enclosed in the preaddressed envelopes. The officiant offers them one by one, igniting a corner of the envelope from the candles on the altar. They are then handed to the consigner who moves to the front of the altar and waves the blazing mass three times up and down, before carrying it to the door to be consumed in a brazier.

The whole ceremony only occupies about ten minutes and the participants have the same confidence in this mode of despatch as they have in the services of the General Post Office.[13]

MAN AGAINST DEMONS

The deities, or spiritual beings whom we have designated by the general term *shên,* represent the benignant influences constantly working on humankind from the unseen, but entirely real, spiritual dimension of the world. Since that dimension is in effect but a continuation of the visible world, evil must exist in it as well as good. We know already that the *shên* are the spiritual essences of the *yang* souls and that the *kuei,* or demons, are the spiritual essences of the *yin* souls. We also know that although the *yin-yang* theory originally had no moral connotation and was only a way of conceptualizing the workings of the universe, in the popular way of thinking these terms when applied to souls took on the connotations of good and evil. The *shên* are honored, flattered, and asked for blessings; the *kuei* are feared, guarded against, and propitiated.

Although the Chinese perhaps invented nothing new in the realm of demonology, they certainly developed the subject as extensively as any people on earth. Their *kuei* are of every conceivable variety and inhabit every environment. Animals, plants, insects, mountains, forests, and waters all harbor specters. They are at work in illness and suicide; they operate as vampires and vultures.

The broadest generalization covering the activities of malignant spirits is that it is they who are responsible for any untoward happening, any sort of trouble that cannot readily be explained by a more obvious cause. From nightmare to madness, from strange noises to ghostly apparitions, from melancholia to death by smallpox, from losses at gambling to the ruination of a once-flourishing family, from tripping to drowning—the catalog of devils' mischief is endless. Everyone was exposed to danger throughout every day of his or her life, although certain circumstances were especially favorable to the evil designs of these spirits. Women in childbirth and helpless infants were obviously vulnerable, as could be seen in their high mortality rate.

But it is especially significant that in the last analysis the depredations of malignant spirits were not a principle of evil working for its own ends but were actually the functioning of *karma*. The *kuei* were after all maleficent because they had been wronged, either through improper burial or neglect or in their mortal term. Their vengeful natures might cause them to harm those who were apparently innocent, but if one could know all the facts, one would find the karmic process working in the long run with perfect justice. Plenty of cases in which the work of evil spirits was quite apparently retributive justice were known to everyone. Some of these involved persons who had been driven to suicide by merciless creditors, mothers-in-law, or officials and who, in return, drove their persecutors to confession, to ruin, to punishment by the law, or even to suicide on their own part.

Defense and Propitiation

Even though *karma* theoretically would work its way, of course nobody—innocent or guilty—would passively submit to the attacks of its agents in the form of evil spirits. Precautions against attack took many forms, a few of which have already been mentioned in our discussion of *fêng-shui*. Charms and amulets were universally employed, placed in the home and worn on the person.[14] Guardian figures were painted on the gates, and walls were placed across the entranceways beyond, in both temples and homes, to keep out evil spirits. Small children, particularly the all-important males, would be called by derogatory names by their parents in order to fool the demons into thinking that they were of so little value that there was no point in attacking them. The spiritual power of a *shên* was a potent antidote to the baleful influence of the *kuei,* and there were many household gods that served this purpose.

Just as the common man stood in awe of the Literati officials, so the common run of specters would not dare to bother these powerful personages, and those things that gave them this power—notably the books and other furnishings of the scholar's study—were in themselves talismans against the evil ones. In China, as elsewhere, the surest safeguard against the malicious power of demons was the purity of a moral life bolstered by deep learning and true faith in religion. The power of the Literati derived in actuality from their knowledge of books, and this "knowledge," like the Western knowledge of the Bible, was above all knowledge of the true Way. Needless to say, the more strictly religious character of the Buddhist and Taoist priests gave them in the popular mind much power against the devils. The Taoists especially were professionally qualified as demon fighters and would be employed to write charms, to drive evil spirits out of the home with incantations and sword waving, and to exorcise the demons who possessed people's bodies and souls.*

The *yin* spirits might also be propitiated and not simply warded off. It was recognized that many of them were more to be pitied than censured, particularly those who were categorized as "hungry ghosts"; that is, those whose plight was simply that they had no sacrifices from their descendants. One of the most widely observed festivals in the yearly religious calendar was that which took place on the fifteenth day (full moon) of the seventh month, called the *"kuei* festival," or, as it has been largely taken over by Buddhism, the *Yü-lan hui,* often described in English as All Souls' Day. During the entire seventh month the gates of Hades were open so that the hungry ghosts might roam about; they returned to their gloomy abode on the last day of the month, which is the birthday of their special savior, the Chinese Bodhisattva Ti-tsang. The *kuei* festival was marked by many observances intended to comfort the neglected spirits and to ensure that their resentment would not bring misfortune to the living. Services were held in all Buddhist temples and many private homes. Offerings were set out, incense was burned, families tended to the tidying up of their own tombs, and "spirit money" and many other paper items for the use of the spirits were sent across in conflagrations. In many places paper boats with paper crews were set afire and sent out on lakes, rivers, or the seas. Nor were the bereaved spirits neglected in the official religion, for every local seat of government was furnished with a special altar dedicated to them.†

Exorcism

Exorcism means the driving out of *kuei.* Its success is dependent on the triumph of *yang* over *yin,* and many individual features of exorcist rituals

---

*These magical functions of the clergy may be traced back to the specialists in esoterica (*fang-shih*) of late Chou times (see reference to *fa-shih,* occult specialists, in Chapter 6).

†We have written in the past tense, but it is to be noted that in this, as in so many other features of the popular religion, the beliefs and practices of the past linger on today wherever they have not been prevented by government measures against "superstitions."

will be recognized as deriving their efficacy from their *yang* nature. In the following description, taken from Burkhardt, we have set the obvious *yang* symbols in italics.

> A special altar is arranged on which are burning *candles* and *incense sticks*. In many countries *peach wood* is believed to possess mystic qualities . . . so the exorcist is provided with a sword of that material, or the demon-dispelling weapon formed by welding copper cash *coins* into a tapering line. This was also hung above the bed of a person suffering from nightmares. The priest places it upon the altar and prepares a scroll on which *talismanic inscriptions* are penned. The officiant reverently burns the charm and mingles the ashes with a cup of *pure water* from the spring. With the *sword* in his right hand, and the cup in his left he prays for power. "*Gods* of Heaven and Earth, invest me with the healing seal that I may purge this dwelling of all evil lurking therein!" Having received his mandate, he invokes the demons. "As quick as lightning, begone." He then picks up a sprig of *willow* which he dips in the cup, and sprinkles first the east, then west, north and south corners of the house. To re-enforce the spell he fills his mouth with the water, and spurts it against the east wall with the *invocation* "Slay the azure spirits of the east, spawn of unlucky stars, or let them be expelled to a distant country." The red demons of the south, the white in the west, and the yellow in the centre, are similarly banished to the accompaniment of *gongs* and *crackers* whose efficacy is commensurate with the riot of sound they create. When the pandemonium is at its height, the exorcist raises his voice to be heard above the din and screams: "Evil spirits of the East get you back to the East, of the South return thither. Let all demons seek their proper quarters and vanish forthwith." The officiant then makes his way, sword in hand, to the door and goes through the exercises to preclude all chances to return.
>
> Exorcists are not tied down to a set form of ritual, and vary their methods to suit their clientele. Sometimes the doorposts are sprinkled with the *blood* and feathers of a freshly killed *cock,* and a single demon may be disposed of by fixing a padlock round his neck.[15]

The most dramatic scene in the entire picture of man's warfare with the malignant spirits is the attempt to cast out devils that have taken over a human being. Demon possession is a very ancient and universal phenomenon, on which the last word has not yet been said. Whatever scientific explanation may be offered, such possession has seemed an undeniable fact to countless witnesses up to the present day. Here is an eyewitness account from the autobiographical book by Peter Goullart published in 1961:

> We arrived at a medium-sized stone courtyard, half-way up the hill, situated in front of a temple. There was a small group of onlookers standing in corners in the shadow of the wall, among them a distracted couple who . . . were the energumen's parents. The energumen (one possessed) himself, a rather emaciated man of about twenty-five . . . lay on an iron bedstead on a rush mat. He was very pale and there was a wild, roving look in his fevered eyes. The [Taoist] priest . . . was attired in full ritual robes and stood before a portable altar on which was an incense burner, the small image of a god, a vase with holy water, a ritual sword and other articles and a book from which he was reading. Two

monks were assisting him, whilst four muscular men watched the prostrate demoniac.

The abbot was reading the scriptures in a monotonous, droning voice, repeating *mantras* [spells] over and over again with a great deal of concentration. Then he stopped and, taking an elongated ivory tablet, the symbol of wisdom and authority, he held it ceremonially in both hands in front of his chest and approached the bed slowly. There was a visible transformation on the energumen's face. His eyes were filled with malice as he watched the priest's measured advance with a sly cunning and hatred. Suddenly he gave a bestial whoop and jumped up in his bed, the four attendants rushing to hold him.

"No! No! You cannot drive us out. We were two against one. Our power is greater than yours." The sentences poured out of the energumen's distorted mouth in a strange, shrill voice, which sounded mechanical, inhuman—as if pronounced by a parrot. The priest looked at the victim intensely, gathering all his inner strength; beads of perspiration appeared on his thin face.

"Come out! Come out! I command you to come out!" He was repeating in a strong metallic voice with great force. "I am using the power of the One compared to whom you are nothing. In His name I command you to come out." Immobile, he continued to focus his powers on the energumen's face. The man was struggling in the bed with incredible strength against the four men who held him. Animal growls and howls issued from time to time from his mouth which became square, his teeth gleaming like the fangs of a dog. . . . I had the impression that a pack of wild animals was fighting inside his body. . . . Terrible threats poured out of the contorted mouth, now fringed in white foam, and interspersed with such incredible obscenities that women had to plug their ears with their fingers. . . .

Again the abbot cried his command to the unseen adversaries to leave the prostrate man. There was a burst of horrible laughter from the victim's throat and suddenly with a mighty heave of his supernaturally strengthened arms he threw off the men who held him and jumped at the priest's throat like a mad bloodhound. But he was over-powered again. This time they bound him with ropes and fastened the ends to the bedposts. . . . The abbot, still immobile, continued his conjurations in a metallic voice, his eyes never leaving the body. With unutterable horror, we saw that it began to swell visibly. On and on the dreadful process continued until he became a grotesque balloon of a man.

"Leave him! Leave him!" cried the monk concentrating still harder. . . . Convulsion shook the monstrous, swollen body. . . . It seemed that all the apertures of the body were opened by the unseen powers hiding in it and streams of malodorous excreta and effluvia flowed on to the ground in incredible profusion. . . . For an hour this continued and then the energumen, resuming his normal size, seemed to come to rest, with his eyes watching the unmoved priest who was still reading. . . .

The priest stopped reading; with sweat pouring down his face, he backed down to the altar, laid down the tablet and took up the ritual sword. Threateningly and commandingly he stood again over the energumen.

"The struggle is useless!" he cried. "Leave him! Leave him in the name of the Supreme Power who never meant you to steal this man's body!" Another scene of horror evolved itself before our dazed eyes. The man on the bed became rigid and his muscles seemed to contract turning him into a figure of stone. Slowly, very slowly, the iron bedstead, as if impelled by an enormous weight, caved in, its middle touching the ground. The attendants seized the inert man by his feet and arms. The weight was such that none of them could lift him up and they asked for assistance from the onlookers. Seven men could hardly lift him for he was heavy as a cast-iron statue. Suddenly he became light again and they put him on a wooden bed which had been brought in. A long time passed with the abbot reading and commanding interminably. At last he sprinkled the inert man with holy water and advanced to him again with a sword. His concentration was so deep that he did not seem to see anybody. He was utterly exhausted and swayed slightly. Two novices came up to support him.

"I have won!" he cried triumphantly in a strange voice. "Get out! Get out!" The energumen stirred and fell into dreadful convulsions. His eyes rolled up and only the whites were visible. His breathing was stertorous and he clawed his body until he was covered with blood. Foam was issuing from his mouth and a loud gurgling sound. . . .

"Damn you! Damn you!" came a wild scream from the foaming lips. "We are going but you shall pay for it with your life." There was a terrific struggle on the bed, the poor man twisting and rolling like a mortally-wounded snake and his colour changing all the time. Suddenly he fell flat on his back and was still. His eyes opened. His gaze was normal and he saw his parents who now came forward.

"My parents!" he cried weakly. "Where am I?" He was very feeble and they carried him out in a specially ordered sedan chair. The abbot himself was in a terrible state of prostration and was half-carried and half-dragged away by his novices.[16]

Mr. Goullart was prepared to believe the statement of his Taoist hosts that these exorcist priests sacrificed years of their mortal lives as the price for every victory of this kind, their vital forces drained and spent. Whatever explanation we can think of for the phenomenon of demon possession itself, and whether this account is somewhat embellished by the author's imagination, the ritual of exorcism is dramatically illustrated.

CHAPTER 3

The Family:
Kindred and Ancestors

The central importance of the family is no doubt a specific distinguishing characteristic of Chinese society, and the function of the ancestral cult is certainly a specific distinguishing characteristic of the Chinese family. The family is, of course, important in Western religion, with its sacrament of marriage, its commandment to honor the parents, and its duty to raise the children in the true faith. But the religious character of the Chinese family goes far beyond these aspects. This character, developing out of the so-called ancestor worship, makes religion in China more a family matter than an individual choice. *Family religion is basic; individual and communal religion are secondary.* For this reason we shall give prior consideration to this familial cult.

CENTRAL IMPORTANCE OF THE
ANCESTRAL CULT IN CHINESE CULTURE

Ancestor worship is not restricted to the Chinese, but whereas it has usually been considered a feature of primitive cultures, in China it has been the very warp of a high culture throughout millennia. There is evidence of the centrality of the family cult as far back as the Shang or Yin dynasty before 1000 BCE. Such findings include tombs with a rich content of artifacts, the foundations of royal palaces, and much else. History, meaning the evidence given by written documents, starts with this material, in the form of inscribed bronze ritual vessels and **oracle bones.** It is these oracle bones that show us most clearly how the religious system of the most ancient age was based on ancestor worship.

The oracle bones were instruments of divination. The diviner smoothed off the surface of tortoiseshell or cattle scapula and bored into this surface a series of concave depressions. He then scratched onto the reverse surface a question the king wished to put to the supernatural powers. Touching a red-hot poker to the cavity beside the inscribed question, the diviner produced cracks in the bone, which he then interpreted as the response. The answer was noted down, and confirmation that the answer had been correct was often added later by way of maintaining the credibility of the oracle.

These bones with their writing have been of the utmost value to historians in revealing some facets of the ancient culture. But the question that particularly concerns us is the identity of the "supernatural powers" to whom the questions were addressed. In the words of Tung Tso-pin, a leading authority on the subject, "The one hundred thousand pieces of oracle bones and shells contain little but the questions the reverential Yin kings put to their ancestors and the answers in the form of cracks. . . ."[1] Tung concluded, after more than thirty years of study of these bones and shells and all the other archaeological evidence, that despite their other religious beliefs "it was still ancestor-worship that held the most important position in the religious life of the Yin people. 'To serve the dead as if they were living'—we can say that the piety of the Yin people did reach that degree."[2] And again, "almost all the elaborate religious rituals of the Yin dynasty were meant for the ancestors."[3]

Thus, we see that the basic importance of ancestor worship in Chinese religion, on which all modern observers have agreed, has been characteristic since the most remote past. But ancestor worship is not merely the ritual observances of individuals. It is rather the root from which grows the trunk of the lineage tree with its many family branches. In order to grasp the meaning of ancestor worship, we shall need to understand the lineage and family system to which it has given rise.

THE LINEAGE AND ITS FAMILIES
AS A RELIGIOUS CORPORATION

The Chinese word we have rendered as lineage is **tsu**. *Tsu* refers to the male descendants of a common ancestor, bearing the same surname, and including their wives and children.* Because in the course of several generations this will become a very large group, the *tsu* will naturally separate into sublineages and their constituent families who may live in the same vicinity or spread apart, according to circumstances.

Since the *tsu* is patrilineal, the families of wives are excluded. A woman marries into her husband's lineage, and her relationship with her father's lineage becomes minimal. Since ancient times the countryside of China has been dotted with villages, with a market town or city here and there.

---

*We ignore the complexities of the subject and give the simplest possible definition. One should be aware, however, that historically many changes have taken place in the family system and that there are innumerable local variations on the system and its religious components.

Many of these villages, even today, are in fact lineage villages whose families live in separate compounds but close together. Brides for the village's boys are obtained from neighboring villages, or perhaps from one particular village, while the girls are in turn sent to those villages in marriage. The term for the woman's lineage is *outside-tsu*, or *outside relatives*.

The marked difference between the Chinese and Western systems is thus the vital role of the lineage in the former. Whereas in the West the nuclear families typically split off from the patrilineal stem, which was therefore biologically but not socially senior, in China the families typically remained attached to their lineage and thus organically parts of a larger functioning whole. The lineage with its families might be either more or less cohesive, depending on various economic and social factors. But in any case the reality of the lineage corporation was effectively symbolized by the religious cult of the common ancestors—particularly the founding ancestor.

The origins of this corporation are lost in antiquity, but in the ritual codes written several centuries before the beginning of the common era, we have the detailed outline of its structure and functioning. This structure places each individual in a specified position with regard to all others according to generation and collateral distance. These relative positions are not only indicated by kinship terms but are strikingly exemplified in the degrees of mourning. The closer the relationship, the more the ceremonial grief required. Thus, for example, a man wore the coarsest sackcloth for the longest time (nominally three years, but actually somewhat over two) in mourning for his parents, as did a wife for her husband and her husband's parents; a less primitive dress would be worn for only nine months for such relatives as a married aunt, a first cousin, or (by a wife) for her husband's grandparents.

The elaborate mourning rites and the wearing of mourning garments for long periods of time served to renew the lineage ties, especially when life expectancy was short and deaths in an average *tsu* were frequent. Furthermore, the ultimate reunion of the kinsmen in the ancestral temple served to confirm lineage solidarity. The ancestral temple was the home of the tablets inhabited by the spirits of all the lineage's deceased members. Here the souls of the ancestors were visibly personified in the rows of wooden tablets standing in order according to their respective generations and relationships on shelves under the tablet of the High Ancestor of the lineage. Periodically all available members of the lineage would assemble in the temple to celebrate their communal sacrifices to their forebears. Genealogical records, kept sometimes for many centuries, as well as "family instructions" written by leading personalities, were additional instruments for maintaining the in-group feeling of the lineage.[4] Finally, the Chinese State reinforced the institution of the *tsu* and its constituent families by leaving in the hands of its elders all governmental authority, except that unavoidably the responsibility of the State, and by backing up with criminal law (*fa*) the family lineage prescriptions for proper conduct (*li*). It is to these *li* that we now turn for further understanding of the religious character of the Chinese family.

RELIGIOUS AND ETHICAL FUNCTIONS OF *LI*

The word *li* is of broad connotation, extending from the most weighty religious ceremonies to the trivialities of daily etiquette. It means ritually proper deportment in all social circumstances. The graph with which it is written is composed of two parts, a significs indicating communication with the supernatural and an additional element that is originally a pictograph of a sacrificial vessel containing some object. There could hardly be a more explicit indication of the religious basis for proper social behavior. We know little of the *li* of the Shang or Yin age, but from the succeeding Chou dynasty we have voluminous records. In the earlier centuries of the period, the aristocratic rulers of the feudal states were apparently governed by an elaborate code resembling the chivalric codes of the European knights. At every court there were officials whose expert knowledge of the code was essential to the rulers. Master K'ung himself (551–479 BCE) was an authority on *li*, and the school that developed to spread his teachings laid great stress on this subject.

The *li* were not originally of universal application, for in the society of Chou China there was a sharp distinction between nobility and commoners. Just as in feudal Europe, the former supposedly behaved in accordance with the unwritten principles of noblesse oblige, but the latter were subject to harsh punishments. In the Chinese phrase, the *li* did not extend to the commoners, and punishments did not extend to the nobles. But as the feudal system disintegrated during the latter half of Chou and gave way to what was in effect a system of rival, independent states, the political conditions produced a social mobility unfavorable to the survival of an aristocratic caste. By the Han dynasty, in the second century BCE, when the polity was finally established in its imperial form, we may say there was a general extension of both *li* and *fa:* Much of the former became accepted throughout the Chinese society, while the abolition of the hereditary nobility meant the applicability of the criminal law to all persons with little distinction. (In later times the new aristocracy of the Literati held a privileged position in law, but they could at any time be reduced to commoner status for due cause.)

In "The Canon of the Literati" in Appendix 1 will be found a brief description of the works dealing specifically with *li*. Like the Torah of Judaism, these writings on the one hand represent the compilers' understanding of the ways of the ancients, and on the other have served as the living law for all subsequent generations.[5] If to modern eyes much of this material is incredibly hairsplitting, we must remember that it is our age that is exceptional in its freedom of thought and behavior. In any case, there was a sound rationale in the background of these codes:

> They are the rules of propriety [*li*] that furnish the means of determining (the observances towards) relatives, as near and remote; of settling points which may cause suspicion or doubt; of distinguishing where there should be agreement, and where difference; and of making clear what is right and what is wrong. . . . To cultivate one's person and fulfil one's words is called good conduct. When the conduct is (thus) ordered, and

the words are accordant with the (right) course, we have the substance of the rules of propriety. . . .

The parrot can speak, and yet is nothing more than a bird; the ape can speak, and yet is nothing more than a beast. Here now is a man who observes no rules of propriety; is not his heart that of a beast?. . . Therefore, when the sages arose, they framed the rules of propriety in order to teach men, and cause them, by their possession of them, to make a distinction between themselves and brutes.[6]

The profound influence of *li* as seen by the codifiers is clearly set forth in the following:

In the right government of a state, the Rules of Propriety serve the same purpose as the steelyard in determining what is light and what is heavy; or as the carpenter's line in determining what is crooked and what is straight. . . . When a superior man (conducts the government of his state) with a discriminating attention to these rules, he cannot be imposed on by traitors and imposters.

Hence he who has an exalted idea of the rules, and guides his conduct by them, is called by us a mannerly gentleman, and he who has no such exalted idea, and does not guide his conduct by the rules, is called by us one of the unmannerly people. These rules (set forth) the way of reverence and courtesy; and therefore when the services in the ancestral temple are performed according to them, there is reverence; when they are observed in the court, the noble and the mean have their proper positions; when the family is regulated by them, there is affection between father and son, and harmony among brothers; and when they are honoured in the country districts and villages, there is the proper order between old and young.[7]

The functional purpose of the *li* so well expressed in these passages is fully borne out in the numberless rules actually found in the code: that is, in functional terms they serve primarily to demarcate the senior from the junior, the superior from the inferior. Whether it was the social system in the large, or the small but complete system of the *tsu* and its families, the underlying principle was hierarchical. This was so whether the *li* dealt with the religious or the secular aspect:

The son of Heaven [the king] sacrifices (or presents oblations) to Heaven and Earth; to the (spirits presiding over the) four quarters; to (the spirits of) the hills and rivers; and offers the five sacrifices of the house—all in the course of the year. The feudal princes present oblations, each to (the spirit presiding over) his own quarter; to (the spirits of) its hills and rivers; and offer the five sacrifices of the house—all in the course of the year. Great officers present the oblations of the five sacrifices of the house—all in the course of the year. (Other) officers present oblations to their ancestors.[8]

On a less exalted plane:

He who pares a melon for the son of Heaven should divide it into four parts and then into eight, and cover them with a napkin of fine linen. For the ruler of a state, he should divide it into four parts, and cover them with a coarse napkin. To a great officer he should (present the four parts) uncovered. An inferior officer should receive it (simply) with the stalk cut away. A common man will deal with it with his teeth.[9]

Although the feudal order, in which such rules were the most effective means of reiterating rank, disappeared after Chou times, the spirit and even much of the substance of the codes continued in effect. Anyone with experience of social life among the Chinese today will recognize the following pattern of courtesy:

> Whenever (a host has received and) is entering with a guest, at every door he should give place to him. When the guest arrives at the innermost door (or that leading to the feast-room) the host will ask to be allowed to enter first and arrange the mats. Having done this, he will come out to receive the guest, who will refuse firmly (to enter first). The host having made a low bow to him, they will enter (together). When they have entered the door, the host moves to the right, and the guest to the left, the former going to the steps on the east, and the latter to those on the west. If the guest be of the lower rank, he goes to the steps of the host (as if to follow him up them). The host firmly declines this, and he returns to the other steps on the west. They then offer to each other the precedence in going up, but the host commences first, followed (immediately) by the other. They bring their feet together on every step, thus ascending by successive paces. He who ascends by the steps on the east should move his right foot first, and the other at the western steps his left foot.[10]

Recognizing that the *li* served as the means of emphasizing status in the society, we may ask why such a system should have been developed in the first place, and once developed, why it was successful—that is, accepted by the society for ages. As in every society, the whole code of behavior rested on an ideal. The ideal in China was called *hsiao*, which is commonly rendered as "filial piety." As with other fundamental concepts of a culture, simple translation cannot fill out the rich range of meanings in this term, and we must study it in some detail.

HSIAO: THE MOTIVATING IDEAL

The written symbol for *hsiao* (filiality) is as clear in its significance as is the graph for *li:* It consists of the graph for old, supported by the graph for son placed underneath. There could be no simpler nor yet more adequate summary of the ideal of *hsiao*. In amplification we may adduce a few of the countless statements on the subject to be found in the pages of the Literati Canon.

From the sayings of Master K'ung: In reply to a question about what *hsiao* is, "The Master said, 'While [the parents] are living, serve them with *li*; when they die, bury them with *li*; sacrifice to them with *li'* " (*Analects* II.5.3). From the sayings of Master Mêng, the authority second only to Master K'ung: "Master Mêng said, 'Which is the greatest duty? Duty to parents is the greatest. . . . Among our many duties, the duty of serving the parents is fundamental . . . .' " (*Master Mêng* IV A.19.1.2).

From the *Hsiao Ching* (see Appendix 1), a work that puts into the mouth
of Master K'ung a systematic discussion of the subject, a famous passage:

37

*The Family:
Kindred and
Ancestors*

> The Master said, "Filiality is the root of virtue, and that from which civi-
> lization derives. . . . The body, the hair and skin are received from our
> parents, and we dare not injure them: this is the beginning of filiality.
> [We should] establish ourselves in the practice of the true Way, making a
> name for ourselves for future generations, and thereby bringing glory to
> our parents: this is the end of filiality. Filiality begins with the serving of
> our parents, continues with the serving of our prince, and is completed
> with the establishing of our own character." (*Scripture of Filiality* I; *Hsiao
> Ching*)

Again, from the same work:

> The Master said, "In serving his parents the filial son is as reverent as
> possible to them while they are living. In taking care of them he does so
> with all possible joy; when they are sick he is extremely anxious about
> them; when he buries them he is stricken with grief; when he sacrifices to
> them he does so with the utmost solemnity. These five [duties] being dis-
> charged in full measure, then he has been able [truly] to serve his par-
> ents." (*Scripture of Filiality* X)

And still again: "There are three thousand [offenses] meriting the five
punishments, but there is no crime greater than unfiliality" (*Scripture of
Filiality* XI). Lest this be thought to be merely a rhetorical statement, we
mention the fact that unfilial conduct was a serious crime under the law. It
was a right of parents to put an unfilial child to death, or at least to de-
nounce him or her to the authorities for punishment prescribed in the
criminal statutes. Cursing one's parents was a capital offense. We may understand the full implications of *hsiao* by noting what sorts of behavior
were indictable:

> The grounds for such an accusation were the prosecution or cursing of
> one's grandparents or parents; not living with grandparents or parents
> and separating one's property from theirs; failure to support one's
> grandparents or parents; marrying, entertaining, or ceasing to observe
> mourning before the end of the required mourning period; concealing a
> parent's death; and falsely announcing a grandparent's or parent's
> death. . . . However, if a parent prosecuted a child as unfilial on other
> grounds, the authorities would not reject the case for this reason.[11]

Hsiao is thus the basis of the family's government, the cardinal virtue of
the good person, and the most powerful force operating to maintain the
orderliness of society required by the State. Now let us see what *hsiao*
meant in practice.

Marriage is in all cultures rationalized as an institution for the production and nurturing of children. But whereas we tend to think of this in
terms of the future of humanity—or at least the future of our own line—
the Chinese tended to think of it as the most important requirement *for the
support of the older generation and the generations that had already passed away.*
The duty of Chinese children was theoretically to devote themselves without reservation to the welfare of their parents. The duty of a son's wife

was to share in this complete devotion to her husband's parents. The personal feelings of the son and his wife were hardly taken into account. The codes of *li* contained explicit instructions:

> [Sons and sons' wives] should go to their parents and parents-in-law [on the first crowing of the cock]. On getting to where they are, with bated breath and gentle voice, they should ask if their clothes are (too) warm or (too) cold, whether they are ill or pained, or uncomfortable in any part; and if so, they should proceed reverently to stroke and scratch the place. They should in the same way, going before or following after, help and support their parents in quitting or entering (the apartment). In bringing in the basin for them to wash, the younger will carry the stand and the elder the water; they will beg to be allowed to pour out the water, and when the washing is concluded, they will hand the towel. They will ask whether they want anything, and then respectfully bring it. All this they will do with an appearance of pleasure to make their parents feel at ease. . . .
>
> While the parents are both alive, at their regular meals, morning and evening, the (oldest) son and his wife will encourage them to eat everything, and what is left after all, they will themselves eat. . . .
>
> No daughter-in-law, without being told to go to her own apartment, should venture to withdraw from that (of her parents-in-law). Whatever she is about to do, she should ask leave from them. A son and his wife should have no private goods, nor animals, nor vessels; they should not presume to borrow from, or give anything to, another person. If any one give the wife an article of food or dress, a piece of cloth or silk, a handkerchief for her girdle, an iris or orchid, she should receive and offer it to her parents-in-law. If they accept it, she will be glad as if she were receiving it afresh. If they return it to her, she should decline it, and if they do not allow her to do so, she will take it as if it were a second gift, and lay it by to wait till they may want it.[12]

Thus, the son and his wife were required to live with his parents, owed absolute obedience to them, and had no independent property rights. Chinese literature is full of edifying stories about filial sons and daughters and daughters-in-law who were reputed actually to have sacrificed everything for the comfort and well-being of their parents, according to such ideals.

Marriage, far from being primarily a union of man and woman to satisfy their personal desires, was primarily a family matter, as is shown in the fact that the bride was chosen by the son's parents and usually would never have been seen by him before the wedding. Everything about the betrothal and wedding, including the religious sanctions, was calculated to reinforce the subordination of the young couple to the bridegroom's family—especially his parents. For example, the expensive presents given to the bride's family emphasized that she was in fact being purchased by the boy's parents for their son. The matching of horoscopes and the traditional belief that marriages were "made in heaven" lent an air of inevitability to decisions that actually were made on hardheaded business or "political" grounds by parents and go-betweens (the latter essential in this, as in many other social relations). Formal worship of the bridegroom's an-

cestors brought the bride under the supernatural authority of his forebears
and reminded her that her membership in her natal lineage was termi-
nated. She was now a probationer, so to speak, among the kinsmen of her
husband—and both of them were economically dependent on his parents.
Only by earning the respect, or at least the tolerance, of the parents, could
the new wife really gain security in her role; thus filial conduct toward her
in-laws was literally a matter of life and death. The children of this union
were likewise regarded as essential to completion of the couple's filial responsibilities, as is indicated by a saying of Master Mêng that became
proverbial: "There are three ways in which one may be unfilial, of which
the worst is to have no heir" (*Master Mêng* IV A.26.1).

Not to have an heir was a heinous offense against *hsiao* because without
such an heir the ancestral sacrifices would be discontinued. In the event
that the wife should not, in fact, produce a son, an acceptable substitute
would be found either by making the son of a concubine the heir or by
adopting a son from some close branch of the *tsu*. Where there was more
than one son, the eldest was charged with the responsibilities of the ancestral cult. In feudal times the aristocracy followed the rule of primogeni-
ture, and so firmly did the special position of the eldest son become settled
in the Chinese society of ancient times that even the disappearance of the
feudal system and the establishment of a more equalized inheritance law
did not radically change it.

Destined as he was to replace his father as head of the family and to be
invested with the solemn duties of principal sacrificiant to the ancestors,
the eldest son was from childhood set above his younger brothers. They
owed him, in fact, almost the same obedience and respect that they owed
the father himself, since the latter's authority would eventually pass to
him. The same principle, when applied more broadly to the *tsu*, gave the
eldest son of the direct line the same sort of status among all the males of
his generation:

> Eldest [male] cousins in the legitimate line of descent and their brothers
> should do reverent service to the son, who is the representative chief of
> the family and his wife. Though they may be richer and higher in official
> rank than he, they should not presume to enter his house with (the
> demonstrations of) their wealth and dignity. . . .
>
> A wealthy cousin should prepare two victims, and present the bet-
> ter of them to his chief. He and his wife should together, after self-
> purification, reverently assist at his sacrifice in the ancestral temple.
> When the business of that is over, they may venture to offer their own
> private sacrifice.[13]

We are now in a position to appreciate why the rites of mourning and
the sacrifices to the ancestors are the fundamental manifestation of the
Chinese religion, embodying as they do the sacred character of the lineage
and its families as a kinship corporation. The great principle of *hsiao*, which
should govern the lives of all its members, was expressed in formal modes
of behavior systemized as *li*, and the culminating acts of *li* were those of
ancestor worship.

THE THEORY OF ANCESTOR WORSHIP

Meaning of the Term

Let us recognize at the outset that the expression *ancestor worship* is much disputed in its connotations and hence unsatisfactory. The word *worship* should not mislead us into supposing that there is a generally accepted interpretation of the real purport of these *li* comprising the ritual services to the ancestors. As early as the seventeenth century, this question arose among the Catholic missionaries, who had to decide whether or not their converts would be allowed to continue the practices concerned. The question took this form: Are these rites truly religious, or are they less than that, something like respectful memorials?

It was far from being an academic question. Indeed it took on the proportions of a major doctrinal dispute, known in history as the "Rites Controversy," involving popes and Chinese emperors and leading eventually to the downfall of the Jesuit position in China and expulsion of all missionaries from Chinese soil. The problem was never resolved, and to this day there is no agreement on the interpretation of the rites—which suggests that the question may have been wrongly put in the first place. It is, in fact, a question that could only have arisen in the Western mind, which is accustomed to placing the family, the individual, and religion into separate categories. In addition to this inappropriate categorizing, there is the difficulty that Western definitions of *religion* itself are conflicting and disputed. We propose therefore to avoid dealing with such a question at all, and it is to be understood that we use the term *ancestor worship* as a matter of convenience.

The first point to understand about ancestor worship is that it is confined to the kinship group. As Master K'ung said, "Sacrifice to spirits which are not those of one's own dead is [mere] flattery" (*Analects* I.24.1). Ancestor worship thereby played an indispensable role in reinforcing the cohesion of family and lineage. It should also be pointed out that this kinship group strength was achieved at the price of divisive effects in Chinese society as a whole. The ancestral cult was the one universal religious institution, but by ensuring the exclusiveness of each *tsu*, it fastened on the nation a system of closely knit in-group units, each of which claimed the major share of each individual's loyalties and efforts at the expense of a larger social consciousness.

There were certain underlying assumptions in the ancestral cult. Obviously such a cult assumed continuance of personality in some form after death of the physical body. It further assumed the possibility of continued contact between dead and living family members. Finally, in the light of the family system and its hierarchical structure, it was assumed that original relationships remained in full force despite the death of a senior. In fact, because of the mysteriousness of their postmortem condition, the deceased seniors were conceived to possess even more spiritual power than they had possessed in life. The love and fear of the son for the father were perhaps increased by the latter's continuing presence in spiritual, rather than physical, form.

The ancestors were thus in a sense deified. *This conception of deification of the ancestors ultimately colored all of the Chinese religion, which may be seen as an extension of this idea.*

Status of the Ancestors

In order to understand the status of the ancestors, we may turn to the earliest literary records, dating from the first centuries of the Chou dynasty. In *Shu Ching (Scripture of Archaic Historical Documents)* and *Shih Ching (Scripture of Song Lyrics)*, the ancestors of the ruling house are pictured as dwelling "on high" in some sort of close association with, and subordinate capacity to, the Supreme Ruler in Heaven. Their power over their descendants seems to derive from this position; that is, they are able to intercede with *shang ti* or *t'ien* to send down blessings or calamities:

> It is not that our former kings will not assist us, their descendants. It is just that Your Majesty is dissolute and cruel, and is thereby bringing about his own ruin. Therefore Heaven rejects us. (*Scripture of Archaic Historical Documents,* "The Earl of the West Slays [the Prince of] Li"; *Shu Ching, Hsi Pai K'an Li*)
>
> . . .
>
> The recorder then [wrote] the prayer on wooden strips. It said, Your first grandson So-and-So has met with a severe illness. If you three Kings are in fact obligated [to present] a royal son to Heaven, let T'an be substituted for the person of So-and-So.* (*Scripture of Archaic Historical Documents,* "The Metal-Strapped Depository"; *Shu Ching, Chin T'êng*)

Many sections of *Shu Ching* have been aptly described as political propaganda, in which the Chou rulers are attempting to persuade the descendants of their former overlords, the Shang or Yin kings, that they should acquiesce in the new regime. A couple of passages from such sections will illustrate the assumption that the spiritual world is but another dimension of the temporal world, the two being in intimate association:

> In ancient times our former kings mutually shared [both] ease and toil with your grandfathers and fathers. . . . Now when we are offering the Great Sacrifice to our former kings, your ancestors follow in their train to share and enjoy them. (*Scripture of Archaic Historical Documents, P'an Kêng*)
>
> . . .
>
> In ancient times our former rulers labored for your grandfathers and fathers. . . . If in your hearts (or, minds) you plan to kill us, our former rulers will soothe your grandfathers and fathers, and your grandfathers and fathers will certainly abandon you and not save you from death. (*Scripture of Archaic Historical Documents,* "The Metal-Strapped Depository")

---

*"First grandson" means the reigning sovereign; his name is tabu, hence he is referred to obliquely as So-and-So. The "three Kings" are the three generations of ancestors of the ruling sovereign, who are of course in "Heaven"; T'an is the personal name of the reigning sovereign's brother, the Duke of Chou, who thus offers himself in sacrifice if this will satisfy Heaven. This is the case referred to in a previous quotation from *Shu Ching* (see p. 7).

Mutual Dependence of Dead and Living

From those most ancient times the assumption was that living and dead
were dependent on each other, the latter for sacrifices and the former for
blessings. *Shih Ching* presents vivid pictures of the transaction between
the two parties, which took place in the ancestral temple:

> Where the weeds grew thick
> We cleared away the brambles.
> Why has this been done since ancient times?
> [To clear the ground] for glutinous and panicled millet
> [So that] our glutinous millet will flourish,
> Our panicled millet be abundant.
> When the barns are full,
> And the stacks of grain innumerable,
> We shall use it to make liquor and viands
> For offerings, for sacrifices.
> [The Personator of the ancestors] is seated and invited to partake,
> And thereby bring down great blessings.
> . . .
> All is in order, all maintain strict decorum;
> The oxen and sheep are pure.
> We proceed with the seasonal sacrifice,
> Flaying the victims, boiling them,
> Arranging them [in the vessels], placing these [on the stands].
> The one who says the prayers makes offerings inside the temple gate.
> The sacrifices are very splendid.
> The august forefathers—
> Their spirits enjoy the offerings,
> Their filial descendants shall receive good fortune.
> They will reward them with many blessings,
> With limitless myriads of years of life.
> . . .
> We are exhausted,
> Having performed every ritual without error.
> The skillful offerer of prayers makes announcement,
> Going to the filial grandsons:
> "Your filial sacrifices are fragrant,
> And the spirits [of the ancestors] have enjoyed drinking and eating.
> They will confer upon you a hundred blessings.
> As you ask, so shall you receive.
> [Your rituals] have been in order and on time,
> Properly and carefully conducted.
> [The ancestors] will forever bless you to the utmost,
> Myriads and tens of myriads of times." (*Scripture of Song Lyrics*, "The
> Thick Weeds"; *Mao Shih* 209, *Ch'u Tz'û*)

The relationship of mutual dependence, with its expectation of tangible blessings in exchange for filial nourishment, may be said to describe
the common attitude of Chinese to the present. A proper ceremonial funeral, burial in a grave auspiciously located according to the principles
of *fêng-shui* (see Chapter 2), the spirit-tablet reverently set up and regularly given homage, and the more formal sacrifices on special occasions—

for these demonstrations of the continuing love and remembrance of their descendants, the ancestors would send down to them the sorts of things any parents would wish for their children: good luck, health, happiness, official position, wealth, sons, love of virtue, long life, and a peaceful death.

Significance of the Rites in the Eyes of the Literati

Although such an ingenuous view was held by the great masses of simple people—and we need to keep in mind that in all ages the Chinese populace has consisted largely of illiterate, or semi-literate, peasants—there was a more sophisticated interpretation. The educated elite tended toward a less literal, or more cautious, or even completely rationalistic, belief:

> He sacrificed as if [the deceased] were present; he sacrificed [to the spirits] as if those spirits were present. (*Analects* III.12.1)

The problem in this passage is the sense in which "as if" is to be taken. It might mean "as if—although in fact they are not"; or it might mean "as if—assuming that they actually are present even though unseen."

> The Master did not discuss strange phenomena, feats of strength, disorders, or spirits. (*Analects* VII.20)

Although we are told here that Master K'ung did not discuss spirits, we are not told *why* this was so, and the answer to this question is not necessarily that he did not believe in them.

> Chi Lu asked about serving the souls of the dead. The Master said, "Not being able [adequately] to serve [living] men, how can we serve the souls of the dead?" [The disciple then said,] "I venture to ask about death." [The Master] said, "Not yet knowing [?what we ought to know] about life, how can we know about death?" (*Analects* XI.11)

This famous utterance has usually been taken to indicate a *disinterest* in the supernatural, an interpretation that is surely borne out in the rest of the *Analects*. The Master of this record is concerned with human beings and not with the realm of the spiritual. On the other hand, to jump from this to the conclusion (as so many have done) that Master K'ung was "agnostic" is just as certainly wrong. The same work gives us many statements of the Master referring to Heaven, to the power of Heaven, and even to Heaven's protection and sponsorship of Master K'ung himself. He was regarded by later generations as the final authority on *li*, and the *Analects* furnishes proof that he took the ancestral rites very seriously.

The explicit rationalizing of the rites of the ancestral cult was the work especially of the philosopher Master Hsün (c. 340–245 BCE), whose interpretations found their way into *Li Chi*. According to his view:

> Within the sacrificiant there is an accumulation of thought about, and affectionate longing for, [the deceased]. Upon him come, all untimely, feelings of calamity, and gaspings for breath. Thus, while others are

happy and harmonious, to the loyal subject and the filial son* there come feelings of calamity. Those feelings which come upon him are deeply moving and, if they find no release, the accumulation of thoughts makes him feel frustrated and inadequate, and he is conscious that ritual has been deficient and incomplete.

. . .

Therefore the Former Kings devised for this situation [sacrificial] texts expressing to the utmost veneration for the venerable and love for the parent. Hence I say the accumulation of thoughts about, and affectionate longing for, [the deceased] is the utmost degree of loyalty and faithfulness, of love and respect, and the full bloom of ritual and culture.

. . .

Were it not for the Saints (i.e., those Former Kings) there could be no understanding of this. The Saints clearly understood them (i.e., the meaning and purposes of the sacrifices); military aristocrats and nobles carry them out serenely; officials consider they must be observed; while among the hundred surnames (i.e., the aristocratic families) they have become customary. To the noble man (i.e., the ideal man of Master K'ung's philosophy) they are a human way, while among the hundred surnames they are thought to be serving the souls of the dead. (*Master Hsün, "On Ritual"; Hsün Tzû, Li Lun*)

It is easy to see how it was possible for those who wished to understand ancestor worship as merely "reverence" and not "worship" to find firm ground for their interpretation in the authority of Literati texts themselves. But if we reconsider the last sentence in the paragraph quoted, we note that the philosopher expresses a clear and significant distinction: "To the noble man they are a *human* way, while among the hundred surnames they are thought to be *serving the souls of the dead.*" How few, after all, are the noble men, and how greatly are they outnumbered by the "hundred surnames,"† especially in a premodern, peasant society. An adequate description of Chinese religion must include not only the outlook of the small percentage of superior men, but also the more naive beliefs of the ordinary folk.

THE PRACTICES OF ANCESTOR WORSHIP

From the formal point of view, ancestor worship may be divided into (1) the funeral rites, (2) the mourning observances, and (3) the continuing sacrifices to the *manes* (spirit of the deceased). From the functional point of view, these practices serve to express the grief of the survivors in accepted or ceremonial manner; to help the spirit of the dead in its progress through purgatory; to give peace to the *p'o* (*yin*) soul in the grave and forestall its becoming a malevolent ghost; to obtain the blessings of the *hun* (*yang*, hence *shên*) soul for the family; to give the family and lineage a continuing

---

*Throughout this passage the author has in mind sacrifices offered by a subject to his lord, as well as those offered by a son to his parents.

†This expression came to mean the "common people" after the feudal age, when commoners acquired surnames.

sense of wholeness; and, of course, to demonstrate the love and remembrance—whether real or affected—in which the family continues to hold its deceased members.

Although there are innumerable local variations in the practices involved, they are still only variations on the same themes. Here, as in every aspect of Chinese culture, there is an essential unity despite superficial diversities. Every province, county, and even smaller unit in China will have its voluminous accounts of the local customs prevailing from ancient times, while the reports of foreign observers in various parts of China are likewise rich in details; but after all, the underlying theories are the same, based on the *li* texts of the Literati Canon or the Buddhist notions discussed in Chapter 2.

Funeral Rites

It would be desirable to describe in detail the funeral rites and to set forth their rich symbolism in all its complexity. Nothing would better convey the significance of the family religion in Chinese culture upon which we have insisted. Far from being an isolated event in the lives of the family members, a harrowing experience best gotten over as quickly as is decently possible so that the family life may get back to normal, the funeral and the subsequent mourning are protracted, momentous, and integrally a part of the normal flow of that family life. Properly performed, they assure the comfort and well-being of the deceased in his spiritual existence and, consequently, the good fortune of his descendants. The funeral rites are, in fact, the binding force that holds together the family and the clan as a religious corporation through the generations.

Unfortunately, the space available to us does not permit even an outline of these rites, so we must be content to summarize their most essential features.[14] This summary is based on accounts of the actual practices of the present day in one Chinese province, the island of Formosa, which the Chinese call Taiwan. Keeping in mind the introductory remarks made above, we may say that these Taiwanese practices are representative, mutatis mutandis, of what is done in other parts of China.

Longevity is one of the blessings most devoutly hoped for by the Chinese, and longevity is the standard euphemism used in the funeral when referring to death. For example, the graveclothes are called "longevity clothes." One begins to prepare oneself for death by getting ready such garments when one reaches the age of about fifty. A stout coffin and even a tomb, favorably sited according to *fêng-shui* theory, are also a comfort to an old person, who is thus assured of the well-being of his or her soul.

One who is dying is placed upon boards supported on trestles and covered with a mat, in the main room of the home. The icons of the deities enshrined at the altar in this room are now covered to avoid contamination by the evil influences—something that is indeed guarded against at every step of the rites.

When life has departed, the corpse is washed and garbed in the graveclothes. In this, as in everything else connected with the funeral, the "filial son"—that is, the eldest son (with his wife)—plays the leading role. Now he seats himself outside the house wearing a "coolie hat" with a bamboo

Burning of paper replicas of things thought to be needed by the deceased. In the foreground, note family members in mourning garb, and musicians.

fillet into which are inserted two small red candles. His seat is a bamboo stool set upon a winnowing basket. He holds his arms outstretched with a piece of hemp rope across his shoulders, and the graveclothes are put on him, inside out. He is fed with "longevity noodles." The graveclothes are then transferred from the filial son to the corpse. It is worth noting that the graveclothes themselves are in the style of the Han dynasty (206 BCE–221 CE), an example of the profound conservatism of this family religion.

All the family let their hair go unkempt, don sackcloth, and keep up a ritual wailing during specified times. The outside family arrives to condole and takes part in the ceremonies. The mourning garments and the announcement cards are white, the color of death. What is not white is red, the color of life, and hence good fortune. Thus these two colors symbolize the two themes of fear-propitiation and hope-supplication, which run through the funeral rites and indeed through all Chinese religion, as has been pointed out.

The *hun*, or *yang* soul, upon which rest the hopes of the survivors and to which they address their supplications, is to reside permanently in a wooden spirit-tablet on the altar in the home. Even before the soul is formally installed in this tablet, it must be given a temporary resting place, which is called the "soul-silk." That is actually a paper object about a foot high and three inches wide, in the shape of a blunt sword, on which are written the tabu name of the deceased and certain other particulars. It is placed before the corpse to receive the prayers of the family, is later carried in the elaborate funeral procession, and is finally borne home from the grave by the eldest grandson. Once back in the main room of the home, it is placed upon a small table that serves as a temporary altar. There also is placed an incense brazier that holds a bit of earth from the grave. Incense is kept burning continuously, and the soul-silk receives the solicitous service of the filial son and other family members, as well as Buddhist and Taoist priests. Eventually, after the time has arrived to install the permanent spirit-tablet, the soul-silk is carefully disposed of by burning. Now the spirit-tablet is placed upon the altar beside the other ancestral tablets, while a pinch of the ashes from the brazier that stood before the soul-silk is put into the braziers of these other tablets. This is the final act of the funeral rites and is appropriately called "joining the braziers," symbolizing, of course, the unity of all the ancestors and hence of the family and lineage.

Every act of the funeral rites is performed in accordance with the prescriptions set forth in the ancient codes of *li*. But there is one conspicuous addition of later times: the participation of Buddhist and Taoist priests. The greater the financial means of the family, the more of these professional priests will be engaged and the more frequently they will hold their services. Following the death, these services continue for seven weeks, which is a Buddhist innovation, and priests must be called in as often as possible. They perform on certain instruments, chant *sūtras*, and pray for quick passage of the soul through purgatory (the so-called soul-masses). Some of these services last from noon to midnight, while others may begin one morning and go on until the third morning.

The funeral of poor people may be concluded within one to three days, but the wealthier the family, the longer will the burial be delayed. During

Buddhist monks acting as priests in funeral services. Note the special hat of the presiding priest. Writing on the cloth drape says, "Bring all beings to enlightenment."

this period of delay, the coffin remains in the main room, where it is constantly oiled to make it more waterproof and airtight while its inmate receives ritual sacrifice and wailing. In many cases the burial of the coffin does not mark the end of the affair. It is followed within some years by what is called the "lucky burial." This involves exhuming the bones, washing, drying, and sunning them, and then storing them in a "gold* peck-measure"—that is, an earthenware jar about three feet high and one foot in diameter. Following an indefinite period of storage, the jar and its contents are finally buried in a spot selected as especially auspicious by a *fêng-shui* augur.

Mourning

In our discussion of the lineage and its families as a religious corporation, we pointed out that relationships were clearly exemplified by the degrees of mourning. This in itself is sufficient to show how much more important, how much more formalized, mourning was in China than in the West. Entirely aside from the normal human manifestations of grief, these ceremonial mourning practices served to reaffirm the family's internal cohesion and its status structure and to demonstrate its virtue to the outside society. Far from being an individualistic expression of feeling, the mourning was regulated by detailed instructions set forth in the *li* scriptures, sanctioned by public opinion, and enforced if necessary by the law.

Five degrees of mourning were established. We will illustrate the mourning practices by a brief quotation from *Yi Li* (*Ceremonial and Ritual;* see Appendix 1) on the prescriptions for the deepest mourning:

> THE THREE YEARS' UNTRIMMED MOURNING
>
> This mourning dress consists of an untrimmed sackcloth coat and skirt, fillets of the female nettle hemp, a staff, a twisted girdle, a hat whose hatstring is of cord, and rush shoes.
>
> The principal mourner lives in a booth built of branches leant against the house. He sleeps on straw and pillows his head on a clod.
>
> He wails day and night, with no set times.
>
> For food he sups on congee, made twice a day, morning and evening, with one handful of grain.
>
> He does not put off the head or waist fillet when he sleeps.
>
> After the sacrifices of repose, he cuts a hole in the side of the booth and fits lintel and door-posts to it. He lays a mat over the straw, and sleeps on this. For food he eats coarse rice, and has water for his drinking. He wails once in the morning and once at night only.
>
> When he assumes the raw-silk hat, at the end of the first year of mourning, he lodges in a structure called the "outer sleeping apartment," and eats for the first time vegetables and fruit, partaking also of his ordinary food. No definite times are then prescribed for his wailing.[15]

Such mourning was observed for the father, for the Son of Heaven by the feudal lords of Chou times, by a father for his heir, and by an adopted heir for certain family members.

---

*The "gold" refers to the color of the skeletal bones, indicating that the deceased, when reburied, will bring blessings to the descendants.

There are many passages in the canonical texts in which the mourning practices are rationalized. We cite only one, showing the attitude of Master K'ung himself toward the three-year mourning:

> Tsai Wô asked about the three-year mourning, [his opinion being that] one year was already long enough. "If the noble men do not for three years carry on the practices of *li*, then *li* will certainly be harmed by this; if for three years they do not perform music, then music will certainly be lost. [In the space of a year] the old crops of grain are already no more, and the new grain has come up. . . . After one year [the mourning] might be ended."
>
> The Master said, "To eat fine rice, and to wear brocaded silk—would you feel comfortable doing [these thing after one year]?"
>
> [Tsai Wô] said, "I would."
>
> The Master said, "If you would feel comfortable, then do them. But the noble man, while in mourning, cannot relish the taste of his food, cannot enjoy the sound of music, cannot feel comfortable in his place— therefore he does not do [these things]. Now if you would feel comfortable, then do them."
>
> When Tsai Wô had left the Master said, "Yü (Tsai Wô's personal name) is really heartless. Only after a child is three years old does it leave its parents' arms; and [thus it is that] the three-year mourning is observed everywhere under Heaven. Didn't Yü [himself] have the three-year love of his parents?" (*Analects* XVII.21)

As we have said, these as well as other of the *li* passed from the monopoly of the nobility into widespread observance among the people as a whole following the end of the feudal age (about 200 BCE). Nevertheless, there were great discrepancies among the classes with regard to the strictness and elaborateness of their conformity to the ideal. The complete abandonment of one's daily duties prescribed for the eldest son was hardly practicable for a peasant family struggling to survive from year to year. Sumptuary laws also provided gradations in the required and allowed observances according to social class.

Nevertheless, among those able to follow them, the *li* were in force. The elite scholar class, as the avowed upholders of the Literati principles, were especially the conservators of these practices. A minister of state engaged in work of great importance to the government must yet retire from office upon the death of his parent and observe the three-year mourning. Neglect of this filial duty would not only be considered disgraceful but would be punished by law. Of all the *li*, however, the mourning rites have suffered most curtailment with the changing conditions of contemporary times. Modern life simply does not allow extended withdrawal from society by survivors, least of all the new head of a family.

Continuing Sacrifices to the *Manes*

Sacrifices are an aspect of Chinese religion most easily traced to the remote past. The burial of a king or other great personage was accompanied in Shang or Yin times by many sacrifices, whose remains have in recent decades been uncovered by archaeologists. The great royal tombs at Anyang in Honan province, the last capital of that dynasty, contained both animal and human sacrifices, in addition to the bronze vessels and oracle bones already mentioned. The quantities of other goods accompanying the deceased to the grave indicate that the Shang kings were thought to require in their spiritual existence the same sorts of things they had needed during their mortal span. This theory took hold and was expanded to the populace as a whole, and in post-Han times was combined with the imported Buddhist notions we have already discussed.

The blending of the native and Buddhist theories means that sacrifices are in part a special function of the professional priests and in part the responsibility of the family and lineage heads. There is no need for any special consecration of the latter to such a function; their sacrifices to the ancestors are, after all, simply a continuation of the filial duties required of the son during the parents' lifetime. On the other hand, the effectiveness of these sacrifices marking such vital occasions as the mortuary rites would be substantially increased by the mysterious spiritual power commonly attributed to those who have been ordained in any religion.

The ancestors dwelt in three specific places: within the home, within the family or lineage cemetery, and within the lineage temple. As we know, the *yang* soul resided in the spirit-tablet enshrined on the altar. Its presence in the company of the icons of other gods worshiped by the family further emphasized the deified status of the ancestor. Before the ancestral tablets, as before the other gods, were set the sacrificial implements— candles, incense, flowers, wine, and food. Not only was the head of the household supposed to see to it that these sacrificial offerings were renewed constantly, but whenever any event of importance occurred in the family, he was to announce the particulars to the spirits in the tablets. Thus the continued presence of the ancestors was made tangible to the family in their daily lives.

In the cemeteries owned by lineages able to afford them, the tombs of the ancestors would theoretically be arranged in a manner that would indicate their positions within the kinship system. On several occasions during the year, as specified in the calendar of religious festivals, the family would visit the cemetery, see that the tombs were in good condition, and offer sacrifices and prayers. The cemetery and the grave were thus an intimate part of the family's sphere of interest and activity, rather than objects of dread designed to segregate the dead from the living. The old people in the family not only received the special respect of the young but would often, as we have seen, be comforted by the acquisition during their lifetimes of graveclothes and coffins. A son who would provide such things in advance, for the peace of mind of his parents, was especially filial. This extended even to preparation of the tomb while the parent was still in good health. Among the peasant masses the expense of a cemetery was of course prohibitive; hence the graves of the ancestors were often scattered here and there on untillable patches of land lying amidst the fields*—a circumstance which, however, emphasized even more the closeness of past and present generations.

The factor of expense also limited possession of a lineage temple to the economically prosperous. Those who had the means would purchase land,

---

*Whenever possible, of course, even the poor tried to obtain burial space with good *fêng-shui*—perhaps in foothills that were not cultivated.

Renovating and sacrificing at tomb of ancestor on ch'ing ming *(see
Chapter 10).*

erect a temple, and appoint lineage members as caretakers. At the periodi-
cal gatherings in this temple there would be accomplished the formal sacrifices to the ancestors, the communal feasting that renewed the kinship
ties, the setting in order of genealogical records, and the settling of any
business concerning the whole lineage by conference of its chiefs. The central fact of such gatherings is, of course, that everything was said and done
in the presence of the ancestors, who not only sanctioned the decisions of
the family and lineage heads but who also shared in the pleasure of their
descendants as they enjoyed themselves and felt the reality of their attachment with the group.

Keeping Their Glory and Their Teachings Alive

Finally, in such strong lineages, aside from the spirit-tablets, the tombs,
the ancestral temple, and all the religious rites associated with them, the
memory of the ancestors was kept alive though the frequent recalling of
their names and deeds. Genealogical accounts were maintained, often for
many generations, and the young were taught reverence for their forebears. Some lineages treasured documents from the distant past in which
eminent ancestors had laid down precepts for their descendants. Ameri-
cans who are proud to be able to trace their ancestry back to colonial days
may be astounded by the pedigrees recorded in the Chinese lineage books:

> Our family tree owes its existence to a sprout of a royal family planted in
> consequence of a feud somewhere in the lower Yellow River Valley some
> three thousand years ago. . . . My first ancestor in the Chiang line was

made the first feudal lord to rule over that land toward the end of the twelfth century B.C. . . .

From our first ancestor down to the present day all the names in the direct line have been recorded in our genealogy. How authentic they are I cannot tell, for their lives were so obscure that verification is not easy.[16]

. . .

On the New Year's Eve of my twelfth year . . . my father called me into his study and sent me to ask my grandfather whether I might be shown the family clan book. . . .

It was a memorable evening. All the lanterns in the hall were lit and my father, after changing his dress and burning incense at the ancestral shrine, climbed up a ladder and took down very respectfully the wooden case in which the clan books were kept. There were thirty or forty volumes. . . .

Father . . . raised his voice and made a gesture of respect when the first name appeared. "This," he said, "so far as the records show, was our first ancestor." He did not speak the name, "Hsu," because it is not customary in China for a person to address or speak of an elder by name; he called him "Yuan-ching Kung." Yuan-ching was another name of our first ancestor, and Kung a respectful term used in referring to elders. . . . "Yuan-ching Kung lived," continued Father, "at the end of the first century B.C. and was appointed by the Emperor Ai government-inspector and Governor of Yen Chou." . . . The rule he made for his family is printed in large characters in the clan book. It consists of only four words: "Benevolence," "Righteousness," "Sincerity," and "Endurance." He commanded that each member of the family should be trained in these four qualities.[17]

The most eminent family in China is that of Master K'ung himself. The ancestral home in Ch'üfu, Shantung province, has been preserved through the centuries as a shrine. The seventy-seventh lineal descendant, Mr. K'ung Tê-ch'êng, presently lives in Taiwan as a refugee from Communism. He holds the title of Duke, the only hereditary patent of nobility still extant (it was conferred in 1233). Appropriately enough, Mr. K'ung has several honorary positions of importance in connection with the preservation of the traditional Chinese culture and is in great demand throughout East Asia as a lecturer on Literati Tradition.

The connection of all this with the ancestral cult is evident. The careful maintenance of the genealogies* and the indoctrination of the children with the glorious traditions of their forebears help to keep the religious sentiment alive, and they reinforce the lineage and family solidarity in the most vivid way. This may serve as a touchstone for the vitality of the ancestral religion on which the whole structure of Chinese society and culture has been raised.

---

*It is hardly necessary to point out that, although genealogies may contain a considerable element of fiction, this is immaterial as far as their validity and function for the family and lineage members are concerned.

CHAPTER 4

The Community:
Gods and Temples

The ancestral cult is basic to Chinese religion because it is the one universal institution and because it molded Chinese society into its traditional form. And yet despite this form, in which the interests, responsibilities, and loyalties tended to be focused inward to the family and lineage rather than outward to the public realm, there did exist, in fact, important extrakinship social groups, such as the local community, the nation, and the occupational guilds. The family therefore did not claim the individual one hundred percent. Furthermore, in China as elsewhere, there were many individuals whose needs drove them to seek satisfaction outside the kinship and secular institutions. Such persons would join a private religious club, become lay devotees of Buddhism or Taoism, or actually take the tonsure and become monks or nuns. The religious expressions of the individual will be discussed in Chapters 6–9; here we shall consider the religious life of the community as it has been manifested in the popular cults.

The popular religion with its deities, as it is described below, dates from around the end of the Han dynasty, about 200 CE. The character of popular religion in earlier ages is obscure. But in general, the difference between the two stages is the admixture of Buddhism and institutionalized Taoism that began in the latter half of the Han period.

THE GODS

General Characteristics

Regardless of the origin or significance of the deities, they are nearly all humanized by the popular religion. That is to say, they have acquired biographies that tell of their human lives—lives marked by omens, precocious superhuman powers, and signs, of course. Thus they are not merely anthropomorphic, but they were actually human in their earlier term, just like the ancestor gods. This is not to say that all deities were historical persons. Many were originally merely personifications of natural phenomena such as wind, rain, rivers, mountains, and stars, while many were legendary figures. Still others have been fabricated out of whole cloth and may be called fictitious, such as certain characters in a novel of the Ming dynasty (1368–1644) called *The Canonization of the Gods*. Some are survivals of antique nature worship; some are Taoist masters who attained immortality and the ability to work big magic; some are Indian Buddhist importations or Chinese Buddhist creations; some are famous statesmen or generals or just and merciful magistrates; and some are men or women of the people who manifested strange, miraculous powers. There are deities whose popularity has endured for centuries all over the country, and there are many more who gained only local fame, passing into oblivion after a short time.

The popular trio of stellar gods of longevity (left); official position, implying wealth and honors (center); and blessings, especially sons (right). These are often found on the central ridge of the temple's roof, but they are found as decorative themes in other contexts as well. Shou (longevity) is probably the most omnipresent motif in all Chinese arts and crafts. The figure is of an old man with a white beard who is still in ruddy good health; his forehead and belly bulge with the vital breath (ch'i) indicating attainment of Taoist immortal transcendency; he holds the calabash, representing the crucible of the Taoist elixir (and much else), in one hand and the peach, symbolizing immortality, in the other.

The Western observer, accustomed to serious theological explanations for deity, might find this seemingly casual and unsystematic pantheon bemusing. The polytheism of Chinese religion is such a stumbling block to understanding that we will briefly deal with it here:

> To those who do not come from this tradition of a single jealous God, the diffusion of divine power is logical and obvious. The manifestations of power are infinite and various; nothing would seem more natural than to attribute their causes to many diversified deities. In this world, which is necessarily the model for the supramundane dimension, one approaches different persons for different sorts of results. According to such a view, the power that causes the river to flow is a different power than the one that governs disease, just as the function of the farmer differs from that of the metalsmith.
>
> This being so, we can comprehend why deity in China is anthropomorphized and why it is multiple. We can go beyond the sort of superficial depiction of "idolatry" that assumes not only gross ignorance, but a sort of baseness of character in Chinese worship. Objectification of divine power in statues of mud or bronze or wood representing many differently named deities is not a naive belief in the divinity of inanimate objects, but a visual representation of the accessibility of superhuman aid—the aid requested being within the province of power of a particular deity.[1]

The gods are alive because they have manifested themselves through their works. Their spiritual power, called *ling* in Chinese, is the evidence of their existence. This is why, to borrow an apt phrase from Maspero, "people become gods every day in China."[2] Any claim or attribution of *ling* that gains a certain public currency may result in deification of a person. Rumors having spread and credibility having been established through confirmation that the spirit responds to prayers, a temple will be put up through public subscription. From then on the growth or decline of the cult is a matter of the god's efficacy. This means that the death of the gods is also commonplace. When public confidence in the power of a deity has waned, he will be neglected and eventually forgotten.

This continuing process of obsolescence is responsible for the fact that although there are innumerable gods whose names and biographies may be found in the extensive hagiological literature of Taoism and Buddhism and on the rolls of the State religion, in the actual religious life of the people at any one time or place there is a fairly limited number of gods. The interest of the local community in their gods is a matter of their usefulness and hardly extends to historical information about them—except, of course, insofar as that information as popularly known fixes their particular area of spiritual power, their specific sort of *ling*.

It is this specialization in power, rather than origins or titles, that identifies the deities as individuals. They are not personifications of abstract virtues or passions or activities like Greek gods but rather are more like human officials who have the power to grant or withhold favors within the limits of their own jurisdiction. Many of them are indeed designated as officials in the spiritual hierarchy, counterparts to the bureaucrats in the old imperial tables of organization. Such deities may be known as individuals by name, but more often they are simply known by the titles of their offices. The vast spiritual bureaucracy is well organized on paper, but

again the people know little and care less about the systematic formaliza-
tions in the books.

A Sampler of the Gods from Taiwan Province

To illustrate some of the generalities expressed thus far, we shall in this
section describe the major deities of the popular religion in present-day
Taiwan.[3] According to a religious census published in 1960, there were in
Taiwan, for a population of about 10 million, well over four thousand temples of all sorts.* Enthroned as chief deities in these temples were eighty-
six different gods. Although this seems to be a large pantheon, a relatively
small number of deities commanded by far the greatest share of popularity. There were nine with over one hundred temples each; these we may
call the major deities. Another nineteen had at least twenty temples apiece.
The other fifty-eight gods in Taiwan are of only minor importance in the
popular religion.

The deities are not necessarily individuals. They also include groups
and "multiples." An example of a group would be the "Kings of the Three-
Mountains Country" (see p. 60). By "multiples" is meant deities identified
by title or office rather than as individuals. The local earth gods would be
examples of this type. Of the nine major deities, six are individuals, two
are multiple, and one is a group.

1. *Wang-yeh.* "Royal Lords." Tutelary gods of immigrants from Fukien
   province, across the Taiwan Strait, whose descendants comprise
   four-fifths of the local population (by "local population" we mean
   to except those "mainlanders" who fled to Taiwan when the mainland fell to the Communists after World War II). These gods illustrate the vagueness about biographical facts mentioned above: One
   opinion is that they are the souls of loyal ministers of the Han and
   T'ang dynasties, but another opinion holds that they are the souls
   of 360 scholar-officials of the late Ming dynasty. Several may be enshrined in a single temple. They both bring and prevent pestilence.

2. *Kuan-yin Fo-tsu.* "Goddess of Mercy." No doubt the most popular
   deity in all of China; every foreign account of Chinese culture men-
   tions her. Originally *Kuan-yin,* or Kuan Shih Yin, was a bodhisattva
   called, in Indian Buddhist texts, Avalokiteśvara, one of the two assistants (or avatars) of the Buddha Amitābha. The Buddhist origin
   is indicated in the title *Fo-tsu,* meaning literally "Buddha-ancestor"
   and also is used to indicate the Patriarchs of Buddhist sects. Although still one of the major figures found in purely Buddhist temples, *Kuan-yin* was long ago taken to the hearts of the masses and
   transformed into a compassionate mother figure. In the popular religion she is the embodiment of loving kindness, giver of male children to childless wives, and source of help in time of need.

---

*A more up-to-date figure is well over five thousand temples for a population near-
ing 17 million, in 1977. This sufficiently indicates the remarkable efflorescence of religion in Taiwan during less than twenty years.

3. *T'ien-shang Shêng-mu.* "Holy Mother in Heaven." Despite this title, she is in no way similar to the Holy Mary of Catholicism. She provides a classic example of the process by which "people become gods every day in China." The beginnings of the cult are obscure, but the generally accepted story is that she was born in the year the Sung dynasty was founded (960 CE) on the island of Meichou just off the coast of Fukien province. Her birth was attended by auspicious portents. She was an exceptionally pious girl, and at the age of thirteen she met a Taoist master who presented her with certain charms and other secret lore. When she was sixteen she manifested her magical power by saving the lives of her father and elder brother, whose boat had capsized. Other tales of her supernatural intervention were told by grateful recipients of her mercies. When she died, still a young girl, a temple was erected in her community, seeking to attract her continuing favors.

    As decades and then centuries passed, stories of miracles wrought by the goddess accumulated up and down the southeastern seaboard, and she became a familiar guardian spirit, particularly among seafarers. By the mid-twelfth century the imperial court itself had learned of her reputation for spiritual power and gave her official recognition as a deity of national importance. This meant that the State incorporated her worship in the schedule of sacrifices to be performed by the bureaucracy throughout the land.

    The cult continued to grow until the goddess became one of the major deities of southeastern China and the most important deity of sailors, fishermen, and all who must hazard their lives upon the waters. She received high titles by imperial decree; for example, in 1409 she was called *t'ien fei,* "Imperial Concubine of Heaven," who "protects the country and shelters the people, looks after [those who call on her] with mysterious *ling,* and saves universally by her great kindness." This imposing title was elevated by the K'ang Hsi Emperor in 1683 to *t'ien hou,* "Consort of Heaven." To the people, she is more familiarly known as *Ma-tsu,* a Fukienese word for grandma.

4. *Fu-teh Chêng-shên.* "True God of Blessings and Virtue." The local earth god (***t'u-ti***) found everywhere in China, this "multiple" deity is most numerous because every tiny residential area, even every home, has its own god. Because of his prominence in the Chinese religion, every work on the subject has discussed the *t'u-ti.* His temples are commonly small and unimpressive; he may even have to make do without a shrine. But the humbleness of his shrines is rather an indication of his closeness to the people than of any contempt for him. It is the earth god who is, in fact, most intimately involved in their lives:

    > They are the gods of their district, so they protect, care for, and control the locality. The people have come to appeal to them for everything which affects their lives. All births and deaths are

reported to them. In cases of danger to the community, they are taken from their little temple, and placed where they may see all that is happening. In this way they are thought to better understand the conditions, and be more ready in their assistance. They are thought especially to protect their worshipers against mildew, locusts, and caterpillars, or to permit the crops of the one neglecting them to be destroyed. As the people believe a faithful heart will gain their favor, and bring a rich harvest, they are continually found in worship before their shrines. . . .

In addition to the Earth Gods of the locality, there are little *t'u-ti* of the home. These little images are found in nearly every household. They usually are kept on the floor under the altar board; thus they are as close to the Earth as possible. They are supposed to control the particular spot on which the building rests, and thus be a protection to the house and its inmates.[4]

5. *Shih-chia Fo.* Śākyamuni Buddha. Although he occupies a position of central importance in purely Buddhist establishments, he has not usually been so popular in the community religion. His current prominence in Taiwan is a phenomenon of post–World War II years.

Local earth god receiving sacrifices by representatives of every family within his area of jurisdiction. This is a sacrifice of the winter solstice, 1971, in the small town of Shui-li, Taiwan.

6. *Hsüan-t'ien Shang-ti.* "Emperor-on-High of the Dark Quarter." Also
commonly known as *Pei-chi Yu-shêng Chên-chün*, "Protecting Holy
True Lord of the North Pole [Star]," he is the sole survivor in the
living religion of the spirits who in high antiquity ruled the four
quarters of the universe. In more recent centuries his function has
become generalized as a protector, as in the case of many warrior-
type figures in the popular pantheon, and this function is reflected
in the title by which he is best known as a national deity throughout China: *Chên-wu Ta-ti*, "Truly Martial Great Emperor."

He is reported in the official histories to have appeared to Emperor Hui Tsung (reigned 1101–1126) of the Sung dynasty, an accomplished painter, and the likeness sketched by the emperor is the
prototype of his modern image:

> Usually an armed squire is placed behind him, carrying his black
> banner; the god himself is set on the back of the tortoise encircled
> by the serpent, and floating on the waters, as is fitting, since he is
> the ruler of the North, and water is the element corresponding to
> the northern quarter.
>
> This tortoise and this serpent upon which he rests are interpret-
> ed in totally different ways by the various Chinese authors: To
> some they are two celestial officers placed under his orders;
> according to others, they are, on the contrary, enemy demons
> whom he has conquered, and whom he is treading under his feet.
> In point of fact, the wreathed serpent and tortoise are the god him-
> self in his first shape, more ancient than the present anthropomor-
> phic personage. They are met with from the time of the Han
> dynasty as the symbol of the Northern region of the world in the
> funeral chambers of the second century, where they face the Red
> Bird, the symbol of the South, and are opposed to the White Tiger
> (the West) and the Green Dragon (the East).[5]

7. *Kuan Shêng-ti-chün.* "Holy Emperor-Lord Kuan." The warrior-
protector par excellence; Western authors generally call him *Kuan
Ti*, "Emperor Kuan." He will serve as a good example of the historical personage deified. In the romantically pictured epoch of the
Three Kingdoms (220–265 CE), Kuan Yü (to use his mortal name)
was one of a famous trio of generals. His character and exploits
were popularized in the great work of historical fiction entitled *The
Romance of the Three Kingdoms*, written during the fourteenth century. The extraordinary success of this novel was not confined to
those sufficiently literate to read it but was spread among the entire
populace through the medium of the storytellers and the stage. It is
quite accurate to say that it not only supplanted the official records
of the period in the Chinese mind but gave every rustic an astonish-
ing familiarity with the pseudohistory of Kuan Yü and his compan-
ions and foes. Through the centuries his cult as a martial hero,
protecting against evil spirits, has become ever more popular. In
addition to his basic protective function, he is also a patron saint of
literature and of commerce.

8. *Pao-shêng Ta-ti.* "Great Emperor Who Preserves Life." Here is a
   deity who, although of major importance in Taiwan, does not seem
   to be known nationally. He is a specialist in healing the sick, a role
   that is also played by several other gods. In his mortal life he was a
   doctor of Ch'üanchou prefecture in Fukien province, and his devotees in Taiwan are descendants of Ch'üanchou immigrants. His
   mortal name was Wu Pên, which accounts for another appellation
   by which he is commonly known, *Wu Chên-rên,* "Wu, the True
   Man"—*chên-rên* being a technical term in Taoism for those who
   have perfected themselves in the arts of immortality. He is said to
   have cured an empress of the Sung dynasty, as well as a tiger
   whose throat was obstructed by the bones of a woman he had
   eaten. The grateful tiger became a guardian spirit in Wu Pên's temples after the latter had been deified. It will again illustrate the in-
   difference to historical fact to mention that *Pao-shêng Ta-ti* is also
   said by some Taiwanese to be the soul of an entirely different man,
   likewise a physician, but alive during the T'ang dynasty, half a millennium earlier than the time of Wu Pên.

9. *San-shan-kuo Wang.* "Kings of the Three-Mountains Country." The
   country to which the title refers is the homeland of Hakka immigrants, in Kuangtung province. The Hakka are a distinctive minority group of Chinese who make up about one-fifth of the local
   Taiwanese population. These tutelary deities were brought by the
   Hakka during the seventeenth and eighteenth centuries. The kings
   are a group of spirits of three mountains that are said to have assisted the imperial troops in putting down an insurrection in the region during the T'ang dynasty. In gratitude for their help, they
   were canonized by imperial decree. This may serve as a good example of animism in the folk religion extended further into the religion of the State.

TEMPLES AND THEIR FUNCTIONING

The deities are housed in temples that may be called palaces. That is to
say, they are the official residences of their exalted inhabitants, rather than
gathering places for a congregation. Temples vary from unpretentious to
grand, from one-room structures no bigger than a dog kennel to complexes
of halls arranged row on row and separated by spacious courtyards. Despite a thousand variations, they share a similarity in appearance because
all Chinese buildings, sacred or secular, derive from the same architectural principles. The temple is therefore just a more or less elaborately or-
namented version of the Chinese "basic building":

1. It is in a compound surrounded by a wall.
2. The main entrance is in the south face of the wall. Since hoary antiquity, all Chinese buildings wherever possible have been oriented
   along a north-south axis; the master—emperor, household head, or

god—sits in the north facing south. The entranceway is a triple gate of which each doorway is closed by heavy double wooden leaves. The whole of this entranceway is recessed within the wall and covered by a truncated version of a building roof. It is raised above ground level, and one enters by ascending several stone steps. The doors are painted with the guardian figures of warrior-generals who stand in protective stances to keep out evil spirits.

3. Stepping through the gate one finds oneself in the gatehouse. From here one looks into a square of buildings with a courtyard in the middle. The buildings running longitudinally on the east and west are subsidiary, used for the daily living purposes of the temple's caretakers or perhaps for housing subordinate deities in the side chapels. The main hall (or halls, if there are several) runs transversely and is commonly divided into a large room in the center flanked by side rooms on east and west. The center room may be distinguished by a double roof, and its entranceway is similar to the main gate.

4. All of the buildings are raised off the ground on platforms of pounded earth faced with stone and are entered by ascending stone steps.

5. The buildings are essentially wooden frames, whose most important features are the rows of sturdy round pillars defining the size and outline of the structure and the unique system of beams and brackets that supports the roof. The walls, whether external or internal, play no structural role but are in effect screens. The outside walls are commonly brick, and the inside walls may be brick or wood and may or may not reach the ceiling (since there may or may not be a ceiling).*

6. The most striking part of the temple is the roof, that unmistakably "Chinese" feature. Instead of simply sitting on the walls like the typical Western roof, it looks to be, as it structurally is, independent of the building itself; therefore, one has the impression that it is light and free despite its relatively massive proportions. The eaves extend well out beyond the walls, forming a sort of canopy over the building. In northern China the curve of the eaves is moderate and the ends are short, giving a rather sober effect. On southern temples, however, the eaves soar outward and upward in great arcs, with long-stretching tips. Along the ridge and the eaves are ornamental pottery figures of mythical birds and beasts and legendary humans. Again, these are more numerous and exuberant in execution in the southern style. Finally, whenever financial resources permit, the roof will be covered with special colored tiles.

---

*The description in this paragraph will have to be modified, at least for Taiwan, in reference to the construction of temples since the 1950s. Now concrete with reinforcing steel rods is used for temples as well as secular buildings, and the unique beauty of the traditional wood construction is no longer found.

7. The colorfulness of the roof is matched by the walls, posts, and interior decoration of the building. The Chinese preference is for strong colors—red, blue, green, gold, white, black. The posts are bright Chinese red, and the doors likewise. Down the pillars and across horizontal plaques here and there are pious mottoes and quotations from the sacred books inscribed in gold. The ceiling, if there is one, is also for ornamental purposes, serving as a gorgeously painted canopy over all or part of the room. Otherwise the complex structure of the rugged beams with their specifically Chinese bracketing system is left exposed.

8. If the compound contains more than one hall, the first one will likely be used to house lesser deities, and the principal deity will be enthroned in a rear hall. His dignities are again a matter of the financial resources available. At the very least, the icon will be the size of a doll, seated on a table, with the altar before him bearing the customary sacrificial utensils. At the other extreme, the deity will be represented by an image life-size or larger, not only painted and gilded but garbed in beautifully embroidered robes and fitted with a glittering crown. He will sit on a throne within an elaborately carved wooden shrine, covered by a resplendent baldachin (or canopy). On his left (the place of honor in China) and right hands will stand smaller figures as his attendants. If he is a god of high rank, these attendants may themselves be important deities.

A major temple, Taipei, Taiwan. Note the elaborately decorated roofs and pillars.

The most important object in a Chinese temple is the incense brazier, from which the smoke goes upward into the numinous realm carrying the petitions of worshipers. This is a particularly ornate example, with dragon handles, tiger feet, and other symbolic decoration. Antique graphs give the name: Precious Hall Reaching to the Clouds (Ling Hsiao Pao Tien). In small graphs just above is the name of the large temple complex: Palace of Guidance (Chih Nan Kung), a famous Taoist center of "dream divination" in the Taipei suburb of Mucha.

9. If the temple is of any size, there will be deities other than the principal god enthroned there. These may be ranged along the sides of the main hall or may be housed in separate chapels. In the popular religion, a temple is apt to have quite a mixed company of the gods, including those from the Buddhist and Taoist pantheons as well as the particular deities favored by the local community.

The smallest temples, as we have mentioned, are no more than tiny shrines. Such temples, housing the local earth god or other spirits that may be humble in rank but very close to the daily lives of the people, are found everywhere, in the busy streets of a town and out in the fields of the countryside. Their occupants must often be contented with a plain brick altar and no ornamentation whatever; in fact, the deity himself may be represented by no more than a tablet or even just a rude inscription.

Temples are so conspicuous everywhere in China that one is at a loss to account for the claim of so many foreign writers that the Chinese are an irreligious people. Even aside from the ubiquitous small shrines just described, every village and every small subsection of a town or city will have its community temples, generally the largest and most ostentatious structures in the neighborhood. Such a temple functions not only as a religious center for the community but often as a schoolroom, meeting place for community business, playground for youngsters, and threshing floor at harvest time. The construction of temples was a major expense to the local people, and the fact that the people would give so much of their meager income is in itself impressive proof of their sincere belief in the efficacy of the deities.

Community temples would be under the overall management of a local committee and might or might not have the permanent services of a resident priest. The priest might belong to the Taoist order whose vocation was noncelibate and whose function was the practice of magic and exorcism.* Or they might be served by lower-level religious "technicians," such as mediums or shamans.

The doors of a temple stand open at all times. Individuals may come at any time to bring their personal problems to the god. One lights several sticks of incense and places them in the brazier on the altar, bows or prostrates oneself before the altar, burns mock paper money, and offers sacrificial edibles. The god is asked for help on a wide variety of matters (see Chapter 2). Very often he is consulted about the advisability of taking some course of action. This is done by several divinatory techniques, of which a common one is to throw on the floor two pieces of wood shaped like the halves of a fat banana that has been sliced lengthwise. The positive or negative response of the god is indicated by the manner in which the pieces land on their flat or rounded sides. The altar is provided with a vase containing many long, narrow bamboo slips, each numbered. The supplicant shakes the vase until one slip protrudes above the rest. Taking this slip to the attendant, the latter gives the inquirer a printed oracle from the set numbered in accordance with the bamboo slips. In many temples there is also a fortune-teller who is frequently consulted for the reading of horoscopes and who serves as amanuensis (secretary) for the illiterate.

Besides these commonplace, everyday functions, there are certain times when the temple is thronged with people and abustle with activity. One biographical fact about the god will be known to all—his birthday. This is the festival of the god, marked by ceremonies, processions, feasting, and theatricals. We quote from the eyewitness account of an experienced observer:

> On August 2, 1930, at the town of Li-t'o, west of Yachow [in Szechwan province], the writer witnessed a *T'u-tsu-hui,* or a festival on the birthday of the god of earth, or the Lord of Earth. There was a procession along the city streets, which were literally packed with sightseers and worshipers. Along the way there were many offerings of pork and beans,

---

*See Chapter 6.

and much lighting of candles and incense and burning of spirit money. Many who participated in the parade had their faces painted with odd streaks of gold, and black and white paint, and wore caps on which mottoes were written. People of both sexes and of all ages marched in the parade, some of them carrying small sticks of decorated wood. It is believed that the festival causes the crops to prosper, heals diseases, and wards off calamities.

In the parade were two pavilions in which were hats, shoes, candles, and many dresses and gowns. Then came a large, red-faced god, with a fan in his hand, carried in a pavilion or large sedan chair on the shoulders of coolies. Three bombs, or short guns, were occasionally set off to announce the coming of the god, and a band played typical Chinese music. Following the god were scores of common people, each carrying a wooden placard. As the god passed by, he was loudly hailed by the spectators, some of whom carried in their arms infants whom they wished the god to bless and protect. Following those who carried the placards were musicians with gongs, timbrels, and horns. Next came Ch'uan Chu, the Lord of Szechwan, who was dressed in yellow silk embroidered garments. In the center of his forehead he had a third eye which enabled him to see good and evil, and such invisible creatures as demons. As Ch'uan Chu passed along, people bowed their heads to the ground in reverent worship. After the god came a squad of soldiers to preserve order.

In the parade were people who were strikingly dressed; some had their faces painted. They participated in the procession in performance of vows. When they were sick, or were faced with some dreadful calamity, they prayed to the god for relief, and promised that if they were helped they would participate in this way in the procession on the birthday of the god. The number of people who thus took part in the procession each year seems to the common people to prove the efficacy of the god.

A witness of this procession could see clearly that the people were emotionally thrilled and deeply impressed; that emotions of reverence, awe, and wonder were aroused; and that unconsciously the people received a vivid impression of the greatness of the gods, and were made more loyal to them, the priests, and the religion. The techniques used are admirable for making such impressions on the minds of the simple people, and are evidently the result of centuries of experience.[6]

It is interesting to note that the Chinese case is no exception to the general rule that theatricals are originally closely connected with religion. Although the contents of the plays that have been popular on the boards in China for the past several centuries are not in themselves religious, the performances are thought to entertain the gods as well as their human audiences. Therefore, no festival should be without its theatricals, and in a temple of any pretensions, there will be a place for these, even if it is only a small courtyard.

Because the Chinese drama requires very little in the way of properties, there is no difficulty in the arrangements. A makeshift stage is quickly erected, and cloth backdrops are suspended on bamboo poles. The audience clusters at the front and sides, standing to watch and listen, coming or going at will. A band of perhaps a half dozen instruments, with percussion predominating, supports the singers and directs their highly stylized movements. The stories are all well known to the most rustic audience, consisting of traditional plots from history and fiction, and they always

Wooden vase containing divination slips, a standard feature of all temples of any size in Taiwan. This rather pleasing antique-looking example has the name of its temple, the Palace of the Turquoise-blue Hills, and the word ch'ien, meaning bamboo slips. Above these labels is the omnipresent word for longevity (shou). Other symbols include two knots indicative of the shape of the swastika because of their four ends. The swastika in turn is used for the graph wan, or 10,000—that is, innumerable—implying the hope that one's wishes may come true in all things. (Ch'ing Shan Kung, Wanhua, Taipei, Taiwan)

emphasize the triumph of the conventional morality. The principal actors are appreciated for their skill in the prescribed pantomiming, for their acrobatic feats in the case of plays of military action, and above all for their singing—the drama being something of a blend of ballet and opera. Naturally the troupes that play the countryside and perform for the temple festivals are but crude facsimiles of the artists popular in the great cities of culture; but then, their rural audiences (and the gods themselves) probably enjoy them at least as much as the pampered critics enjoy the most refined productions.*

---

*In a recent technological "breakthrough" in Taiwan, the deity, enthroned in his temple, is provided with a television set for his entertainment.

CHAPTER 5

The State: Emperor and Officials

STATE RELIGION AND THE LITERATI TRADITION

From the functional point of view, the religion of the Chinese State may be seen to have fulfilled two purposes. One was the religious purpose per se, deriving from the belief that the emperor, and by extension his official servants, had an essential part to play in mediating between the forces of nature and the lives of the people; the other was the political and social purpose, in which temples and rituals and the conferring of official titles on important national deities were means, consciously used, to fortify the position of the ruling dynasty and strengthen the prestige of the government. It would be naive to overlook the latter purpose, but it is being overly cynical to deny the former.

The State religion has often been equated with "Confucianism." However, its essential features long antedate the adoption of Literati teachings as the official orthodoxy during the Former Han dynasty[1]—or even Master K'ung himself (551–479 BCE). The sacrificial rituals, and the sorts of deities to which the sacrifices were offered, can be traced back as far as archaeological evidence is found, into the Shang dynasty. These deities were either the more conspicuous phenomena of nature or else the ancestors. A third category of official deification seems to have come into the official liturgy during Former Han times: the public worship of the souls of great men. Although Master K'ung himself was the "great man" par excellence, he obviously would not have approved of this sort of worship. We have earlier quoted his dictum that "sacrifices to spirits which are not those of one's own dead is [mere] flattery."

What is meant by the statement that the Literati teachings were adopted as the State orthodoxy? To put it as simply as possible, it means that the ancient writings identified with the Literati School were exalted above all others, that the basis of all formal education was this Literati Bible, that entrance into the privileged class of scholar-bureaucrats was almost limited to those having some mastery of this literature, and that ultimately all these conditions molded the Chinese State and much of Chinese culture. So far as religion was concerned, it means that the whole weight of the rationalistic, humanistic character of Literati thought was thrown against the development of institutionalized religions such as Taoism or Buddhism. Certainly the State could not do without religion, but the religious ideas and forms were those inherited from antiquity as preserved in the Canon of the Literati.

It was a religion in which the emperor personally officiated at the supreme sacrifices, and his Literati bureaucrats officiated at the lower level throughout the land; thus there was no separate estate of priests. Insofar as the scholars who codified the worship and rituals were of the Literati School, and insofar as the operation of the State cults was a part of the duties of all officials, the religion of the State can of course be described as "Confucian." But like their Master, the Literati thought of themselves as "transmitters rather than creators," and their writings on sacrifices and rituals were but refinements of the doctrines inherited from high antiquity.

One component of the State religion was the cult of Master K'ung himself, who was naturally regarded by the Literati as their patron saint. Every craft and occupation in China had its patron deity, and Master K'ung might therefore be considered as just another of these—except that the craft of the scholars was governing the people and their occupation was official service. The significance of the adoption of Literati teachings as the State orthodoxy was thus that the rulers of China recognized the unique usefulness to government of the Literati theories and training. Or at least, if they actually found other methods more useful in many cases, it was expedient for them to give lip service to the high ideals of Literati teachings. Consequently, they saw the desirability of exalting the Master as a pillar of support for the imperial power. The sacrifices to him were always, and appropriately, the responsibility of the Literati officials, but they were incorporated into the State cults and were even included in the limited group of sacrifices personally performed by the emperor, for what may be called political reasons.

As for the imperial sacrifices, they were so important, and so colorful and dramatic, that they have sometimes been described as if they actually constituted the State religion of China. The sublime sacrifices performed by the emperor at the altars of Heaven and Earth particularly captured the attention of foreign writers in the nineteenth century, who furthermore, because most of them were missionaries, were most concerned with the question about whether the object of this worship was the same as the true, Christian God. It is apparent that the imperial worship was indeed an important component of the State religion, but it was one component only. In this chapter we shall first discuss this imperial worship; next we shall consider the workings of the official religion in general terms; and finally we shall give particulars concerning the official religion as it operated at the local level.

KINGSHIP AND IMPERIAL WORSHIP

In ancient China, as in all early societies, there would have been no meaningful distinction between the "political" and the "religious." The authority of chief or king could not exist without the sanction of religious qualifications claimed and acknowledged. An aura of divinity was indispensable to the charisma of a king. Such an inseparable association of ideas characterized not only primitive societies and the ancient world but continued to the recent past. The religious basis of kingship is proved, if such proof were necessary, by the rapid decline and virtual extinction of the institution once the "divine right" was no longer taken seriously.

We cannot doubt that the origin of kingship in China shared this character. We have already noted (see Chapter 3) that certain passages in the *Shu Ching (Scripture of Archaic Historical Documents)* speak of the king's ancestors as dwelling with the Supreme Ruler in Heaven and as being able to influence the latter. We also mentioned the propagandistic intent manifest in a number of documents in this book, the purport of which was that the overthrow of the Shang and the establishment of the Chou kings constituted the will of the Supreme Ruler in Heaven. Much later, this concept of a "mandate of Heaven" was incorporated into orthodox Literati political philosophy, its classical expression being given by Master Mêng (particularly in *Mêng Tzû,* book VA, Chapters 5 and 6).

The peculiarity of this Chinese version of the divine right is that from the beginning, as found in *Shu Ching,* it was qualified in such a way as to preclude the divinity of the ruling house. To put it in a word, what Heaven gives, Heaven can also take away. No man could establish himself and his line on the Dragon Throne unless he had been accepted by Heaven as the True King; but no dynasty could continue to be acceptable to Heaven unless its kings *actually were* True Kings. There was no mystery about the reading of Heaven's will in the matter: This was manifested in the upshot of revolution. When unbearable conditions or vaulting ambition brought rebels up in arms against the government, if the government was able to put down the rebellion and execute its leaders, it was evident that the emperor still retained his mandate; but should one of the revolutionary leaders overthrow the government and set himself on the throne, it was, on the contrary, evident that Heaven had withdrawn its mandate from the former dynasty and conferred it upon a new one.

In the Chinese system, therefore, divine right meant that the emperor held his office by virtue of a commission from Heaven, but it did not mean that the emperor was himself a divinity. It is remarkable that this theory of the mandate of Heaven retained its vitality throughout Chinese history in a polity that was an absolute despotism. The explanation is that the theory was embodied in the sacred texts of the Literati, who in their capacity as bureaucrats were the indispensable mainstay of every emperor's administration. Although it is going too far to characterize this theory as a "democratic force" in Chinese history, it was at least a factor of real significance in limiting the imperial will, for ultimately it was a justification of the right of revolution. Heaven was on the side of the righteous, whether that side represented the entrenched regime or the rebels.

In order to avoid loss of his mandate, the ruler must benefit the people and give them a secure livelihood. Aside from the mundane policies required to carry out this responsibility, there were the moral and supernatural duties. As for morality, Literati precept held that the people were the grass and their betters the wind—that good or bad behavior of the people was a reflection of the moral example set by the ruler and his officials (see Chapter 1). As for the supernatural, the ruler was held to be the leader and representative of Man, who formed a ternion with Heaven and Earth. This resulted from the gestalt cosmology that we discussed in our chapter on the worldview: Man was inseparably a part of nature, and therefore there was an interplay, a mutual reaction between the two. The function of the emperor was to play his proper part in maintaining the smooth coordination of this cooperative process, which meant ensuring that men were properly and beneficially governed and that they in turn did their (agricultural) work at the proper times and seasons and in the proper way.

The emperor's unique contribution to the coordination of man and nature, aside from supervising the administration of government, was to pay the appropriate ritual respects to the great powers of the universe. The latter was represented in the large by Heaven and Earth, which stood for the *yang* and *yin* forces and were spoken of in homely metaphor as male and female, husband and wife, emperor and empress of the universe. To these two great symbols of Nature the lord of all men sacrificed as the only Powers above his human power. To them he paid the utmost reverence, the threefold kneeling and ninefold prostration, and them alone he acknowledged as his own lord, in his prayer styling himself "your subject." To other impressive but obviously subsidiary powers of nature—the sun, the moon, and other heavenly bodies, the deities that controlled meteorological phenomena, the great mountains and rivers—he also sacrificed, but without humbling himself.

The emperor's humility before the altars of Heaven and Earth was the ultimate sign of his legitimacy as ruler of the people. Only the rightful ruler could perform this ritual, and its imitation by any other person was a declaration of rebellion. It is no wonder that it was made rich with a fascinating symbolism and designed to produce an overwhelmingly impressive effect.

Heaven and Earth were the emperor's symbolical parents, but he also had real, human parents. To them he owed the same obedience in life and worship after death that every Chinese son owed his parents. The imperial ancestors were naturally worshiped in more elaborate style than those of lesser persons, but the practices were essentially the same—dressing, coffining, entombing, setting up of the spirit-tablet in the ancestral hall, and all else. The *fêng-shui* of their tombs was a matter of vital concern to the State because their occupants exercised influence over the reigning sovereign. These spirits dwelt in Heaven, where they presumably had the ear of the Supreme Ruler. This idea was clearly pictured in the arrangements at the altars of Heaven and Earth. At the top of the altar where the spirit-tablet of Heaven or Earth was placed to receive the emperor's worship, the tablets of the imperial ancestors stood at the left and right hands, as if in attendance. This arrangement corresponds to that found in all temples, where the chief deity is flanked by subordinates. Or, if one prefers to think in terms of a Chinese feast—and *the sacrifice is essentially a feast for the divinity* (not an act of atonement)—it is like the guest of honor flanked by what the Chinese call *p'ei-k'ô*, or accompanying guests. But, in fact, it is a representation of the ancient theory we cited from *Shu Ching* (see Chapter 3, p. 41), and the spirit-tablet of Heaven still, in the nineteenth century, bore the ancient name: It read in full, *Huang T'ien Shang Ti*, which may be understood either as Shang Ti [in] August Heaven or as August Heaven: Shang Ti.

THE OFFICIAL RELIGION

We said above that the principal objects of the State worship were very ancient, long antedating even Master K'ung. According to archaeological evidence, in the late Shang or Yin age (roughly 1300–1100 BCE), the following deities were worshiped in addition to the all-important ancestors:

> First of all, there was the Supreme God, the highest of all deities, that was called *Ti*. The position of *Ti* in heaven was somewhat like that of the king on earth. *Ti* was also called *Shang Ti*. . . .
> There were also God of Wind, called "Ti's Messenger," and God of Cloud, called "Six Clouds"—meaning the clouds in the East, West, South, North, above the earth and below the earth. The God of Sun was worshipped at sunrise and sunset. There was a God of Moon; and the lunar eclipse was considered as a portent of evil. Some of the conspicuous stars and constellations were also worshipped, for instance, Aldebaran or alpha of the Hyades.
> In many of the oracles, the worship of Yüeh and Ho was mentioned. Though the two characters have been interpreted as names of ancestors, yet the reading of the contexts convinces us that we should take them at their literal meaning: i.e., *Yüeh* means the mountain and *Ho* means the yellow River. There were gods for the four directions of the compass, as the worship of them is mentioned in the oralces [sic]. Gods of different localities and gods of certain big rivers, for instance, the Hwan, near the capital were constant objects of worship.[2]

For comparison, here are the deities named in the Ch'ing government regulations of the seventeenth century as recipients of official worship:

> Following the ancient classification the beings worshipped were arranged in three ranks.
> In the first rank were placed *Huang T'ien Shang Ti*. . . . The Empress Earth, the Imperial Ancestors, and the Guardian Spirits of the Land and the Harvests [*shê chi*]. To these in the year 1907 there was added the great Sage Confucius, who had previously been placed in the second rank.
> Others of the second rank were the Sun, the Moon, the Emperors and Kings of preceeding [sic] dynasties, the patron saint of Agriculture, the patroness of Sericulture, the Spirits of Heaven, the Spirits of Earth, and

the Year Star, that is to say, the planet Jupiter, by whose revolution around the sun the Chinese calendar was regulated.

In the third rank of this pantheon were the patron saint of Medicine, the God of War, the God of Literature, the North Star, the Eastern Peak, the tutelary deity of Peking, the God of Fire, the Dragon of the Black Dragon Pool (near Peking), the dragon of the Jade Fountain (near Peking) and that of the *K'un Ming* Lake (at the Summer Palace), the God of Artillery, the *Hou T'u* or God of the Soil, the *Ssu Kung* or patron of the Mechanic arts, the God of the Furnace, the God of the Granary, the door gods and a number of canonized patriots, whose company has increased from generation to generation.[3]

All these deities receiving official worship of the first two ranks in modern times were worshiped during the Shang, or at the latest during early Chou times, with the exception, of course, of "Confucius." The third rank includes mostly deities who became popular after the Han dynasty (ended 221 CE) and those (such as the dragons) who are especially connected with Peking as the capital during the reign of the Manchu dynasty.

The calendar of official sacrifices was determined by the Board of Astronomy according to divinatory procedures and was published well in advance by the Ministry of Rites (*Li Pu*). This ministry was from the most remote times one of the major organs of government. Traditional accounts take it back to the as-yet legendary Hsia dynasty, which is supposed to have preceded Shang in the eighteenth century BCE. The feudal courts in Chou China would, of course, have required the services of specialists in sacrifices and protocol. With the formation of the imperial polity in Ch'in and Han times, the Ministry of Rites essentially assumed the form it was to retain until the end of the empire. Its head was one of the nine great ministers of the administrative departments. Under him came various subdepartments and bureaus, most important of which was the Imperial Academy. "In so far as he supervised the Imperial Academy the Minister of Ceremonies performed the same duties as a Minister of Education in the present Chinese Government." But he could also be "described as a chief priest in the government," because he "is said to have been 'in charge of the ceremonies in the Imperial ancestral temples' and 'in charge of the worship of Heaven and Earth.'"[4]

During the latest (Ch'ing) dynasty, the Ministry of Rites performed the same sorts of functions as in Han times. Its educational responsibilities were still most important, but one of its five bureaus was the Bureau of Sacrificial Rites, "for state sacrifices and funerals, conferring of posthumous favors, editing the calendar, and miscellaneous sacrifices. . . . [The Ministry] kept records of all ceremonies the emperor attended, records of the descendants of Confucius, of Buddhist, Taoist, medical and astronomical officials in addition to those connected with education. It is [*sic*] reported to the emperor for rewards all cases of filial piety, righteousness, or loyalty."[5]

The performance of the official worship was regulated by detailed instructions circulated to all government offices (*yamen*) throughout the empire:

Worship of the various gods and saints of the pantheon consisted in bathing, fasting, prostrations, prayers, and thanksgiving offerings of incense, lighted candles, gems, fruits, cooked food, salted vegetables and shew bread, libations of wine, sacrifices of whole oxen, sheep and pigs, sometimes deer and other game and, on certain occasions, a burnt sacrifice of a whole bullock, accompanied by music, and posturing or dancing.

All sacrifices to deities of the first rank had to be preceded by three days of fasting, those to deities of the second rank by two days of fasting. . . . Fasting did not mean entire abstinence from all food, but from *hun*, i.e., from flesh and strong-smelling vegetables, such as leeks, garlic and onions; also from wine and all strong drink. No criminal proceedings were to be held; no invitations to feasts issued or accepted. There was to be no music. No inquiries after the sick were allowed and there must be no mourning for the dead. One was especially forbidden to enter the death chamber of a woman, to sacrifice to spirits and to sweep the tombs. All association of any kind with the sick and the mourner was prohibited. . . .

Special officers were appointed also to visit and inspect the various yamens, and any officer found neglecting the fast was punished according to law. . . .

The object of the bathing and fasting was to make oneself pure in body and heart and worthy to approach into the divine presence.[6]

Aside from those personified forces of nature whose worship had come down from archaic times, and aside from the imperial ancestral spirits, the deities on the official registers had achieved their position by a process with which our previous discussion of the popular religion has made us familiar. The efficacy of a spirit, manifested by deeds, would bring it fame over a widening area until it impressed the officials as being important enough to recommend it to the Throne. Eventually the emperor would confer a rank and title on the spirit, exactly as on a meritorious human subject. The government's patronage would extend further to bearing the cost of founding or renovating temples to the deity. In this way, what had been only a local cult would become a part of the official religion. The process clearly exemplified the dual religious and political purpose of that religion: Certainly the State was anxious to have whatever supernatural assistance might be available, while at the same time, by its patronage of the deities, it tacitly asserted its control over them. In other words, the fact that the emperor could confer ranks and titles and assign posts to the spiritual beings was clear-cut evidence that his authority extended over the spiritual dimension as well as the world of human beings.

OFFICIAL RELIGION AT THE LOCAL LEVEL*

Strictly speaking, there were no "local" officials in the Chinese empire. That is, all officials were members of the imperial government, appointed usually after passing competitive civil service examinations and then posted, shifted about, and given assignments at the discretion of the personnel department in the capital. To guard against the interference of family connections with an official's duties, it was the practice not to assign

*This section describes post-Han China in generalized terms.

him to his home region, so that every official was a stranger in the territory over which he had jurisdiction.

At the local level government was very simple. It was administered by a single magistrate sent down by the central authority and assisted by his staff, who were mostly local personnel of clerical or lower status. This one official would have complete charge over the populace of an entire county. Such a task was possible to perform only because government in those times was not expected to render services to the people. The magistrate was there to see to the collection and forwarding of taxes, to keep a sharp lookout for subversive activities, to quell any banditry or insurrection, and to try criminal and civil cases. As for the latter, both government and people expected that disputes would be settled whenever possible by the elders of family, lineage, and village—and woe betide unfortunate litigants who resorted to the harsh arbitrament of the magistrate's court. The Chinese attitude was that the peace and order of a district directly reflected the moral character of its magistrate. The saying of the Master expressed the ideal:

> Lead them with laws and keep them in order by punishments, and the people will avoid [the laws and punishments] without shame. Lead them with moral example and keep them in order by the rules of proper ritual deportment, and they will have [a sense of] shame and will become [good]. (*Analects* II.3)

The moral influence of the magistrate was reflected not only in the behavior of people but even in the reactions of nature. The magistrate, as deputy of the emperor, played the same role of intermediary between human and natural forces in the small territory under his control. The State cults to be maintained in each local capital were prescribed by government regulations, and performance of the appropriate rituals was the personal responsibility of the magistrate. The local people, on their part, expected the magistrate to use his official authority on their behalf and to intercede with the appropriate spiritual powers in the event of flood, drought, or pestilence.

The official religious facilities required in every local capital were of three types: memorial halls, of which the "Confucian temple" was by far the most important; altars; and official cult temples.

THE TEMPLE FOR MASTER K'UNG
AND THE MOST EMINENT LITERATI

The temple for Master K'ung was known in recent centuries as *wên miao*, which may be translated as "temple of literature," "temple of culture," or, most appropriately, "the civil temple." All these translations reflect the meaning of *wên* and the specific place occupied by Master K'ung and his followers, the scholars or Literati, in Chinese culture. For Master K'ung was the great patron of learning, of the high culture, and consequently of the scholar-bureaucrats who ruled the civil government of China. It is most interesting that these educated elite resisted all efforts to deify their Mas-

Tomb of K'ung Tzû (Confucius) in his native town of Ch'ü-fu, Shantung province (northern China).

ter and that in a land where it was commonplace to turn men into gods, Master K'ung remained a human figure. Perhaps he could most aptly be called the spiritual ancestor of the Literati.

The temple for Master K'ung and his most eminent followers was built to the same architectural design as all other temples, generally speaking (see Chapter 4). The main hall contained the spirit-tablets of the Master and four attendant sages: Yen Hui (his favorite disciple), Tzû Ssû (his grandson and supposed author of *Chung Yung*), Master Tsêng (another prominent disciple), and Master Mêng. The tablet of Master K'ung, which stood in the center of the hall facing the entranceway to the south, was inscribed with the title he still bears: Most Holy Former Master, The Philosopher K'ung. Along the east and west walls of the main hall were the tablets of twelve men honored with the title *chê*, the Wise. Eleven of these were personal disciples of the Master, and the twelfth was Chu Hsi (1130–1200 CE), great synthesizer of the Sung School of the Principle, whose interpretations of the Canon became the orthodoxy of the State. In each of the cloisters forming the east and west sides of the temple compound, the tablets of thirty-five eminent Literati were arranged in order of seniority through the centuries. North of the main hall was a separate building housing the tablets of the ancestors of Master K'ung for five generations.

The entire complex was thus a memorial hall rather than a palace of gods; it was designed to perpetuate the fame of the greatest Literati throughout Chinese history. Its resemblance to the ancestral temples of private clans was especially due to the spirit-tablets; however, prior to 1530 CE the look of the temple for Master K'ung would have been more like that of Buddhist, Taoist, or other cult temples since images were then used instead of spirit-tablets.

The sacrifices in the *wên miao* were held twice yearly, in mid-spring and mid-autumn, during the second and eighth lunar months. At the fourth watch (the night was divided into five watches), the sacrifice was offered to the ancestors of Master K'ung, and at the fifth watch, the sacrifice in the main hall commenced. This would be just at dawn. The senior officials of the prefecture were in attendance, the chief celebrant being the magistrate himself. The officials lined the sides of the courtyard below the hall, while in the center, six ranks of young students in their traditional costume held long wands tipped with pheasant feathers. In the hall itself, and out on the broad porch, were arranged the sacrificial articles, each in its prescribed vessel. Directly before the high tablet of Master K'ung was placed a roll of silk, behind it three chalices of wine, behind them three bowls of two kinds of soup; then came two rows of eight vessels, each containing its appropriate viand, and behind these two more rows, each with four dishes. In the next row were the large animals—in the center an ox and to the left and right a pig and a sheep. These were backed by four small candles in their holders, and in the last, or outermost, row stood an incense brazier flanked by large red candles in their holders.

Before each of the four subordinate tablets in the main hall there were similar arrangements of offerings, and the tablets in the cloisters likewise had their sacrifices—all in appropriately descending degrees of elaborateness. The arrays of edibles constituted a banquet for the honored souls, the more sumptuous in quantity and variety giving more honor in accordance with the rank of the spiritual guest.

The beat of drums marked each stage in the ceremonies. An orchestra played an ancient melody in long-drawn-out whole notes, and the ranks of students postured sedately with their wands. A herald cried out instructions for each action, and the chief celebrant and the rest of the officials followed these instructions silently. The celebrant offered incense, dishes of food, and goblets of wine, each offering being accompanied by the kotow and a hymn of praise.

> The great drum boomed upon the night, the twisted torches of the attendants threw uncertain shadows across the lattice scrolls, and the silk embroideries on the robes of the officials gleamed from the darkness.
>
> The flutes sounded, and the chant rose and fell in strange, long-drawn quavers.
>
> "*Pai*," [make obeisance] and the officials fell to their knees, bending forward till their heads touched the ground.
>
> "*Hsin*," [arise] and they were erect again.
>
> Within the hall, the ox lay with his head toward the image [the scene recalls Yüan times] of Confucius. The altar was ablaze with dancing lights, which were reflected from the gilded carving of the enormous canopy above. Figures moved slowly through the hall, the celebrant entered, and the vessels were presented toward the silent statue of the sage, the "Teacher of Ten Thousand Generations." The music was grave and dignified. . . . The dancers struck their attitudes, moving their wands tipped with pheasant feathers in unison as the chant rose and fell. . . .
>
> . . . It is in reality one of the most impressive rituals that has ever been devised. The silence of the dark hour, the magnificent sweep of the temple lines, with eaves curving up toward the stars, the aged trees standing

*Celebration of the birthday of Master K'ung, now called Teachers Day,
at Taipei Wên Miao. Young students are pantomiming to music on the
foreporch of the main hall in accordance with traditional ritual.*

in the courtyard, and the deep note of the bell, make the scene unforget-
table to one who has seen it even in its decay.[7]

The formal prayer read at this service went as follows:

Wei! On K'ang Hsi [reign period 1662–1722] such-and-such a year,
month, and day, the official N. of such-and-such a *yamen,* and others,
venture to announce to the Most Holy Former Master K'ung Tzû:

Wei! The efficacy of the Master matches that of Heaven and Earth, and
his Way excels all others past and present. He revised and wrote the Six
Scriptures, he has handed down the model polity of our state for ten
thousand generations.

Wei! At this mid-spring (or, mid-autumn), respectfully, with animals
and silk, with sweet wine, with vessels of millet and every other kind of
offering, in reverent observance of the ancient ritual prescriptions, we
spread before thee this divine sacrifice. Accompanying [thee in the recep-
tion of the sacrifice] are the Secondary Sages Yen Tzû, Tsêng Tzû, Tzû
Ssû Tzû, and Mêng Tzû.

Deign to receive it! (*Gazetteer of Taiwan County,* 1720 edition; *Taiwan
Hsien Chih*)

The Altars

The temple for Master K'ung and his most eminent followers and other,
lesser memorial halls served primarily a commemorative and inspirational
function, whereas the union of the human and the supernatural, the mesh-
ing of this-worldly and otherworldly power, was centered at three altars
located in their own compounds. These altars were dedicated respectively
to the gods of land and grain, the gods of the mountains and rivers, and
the souls of those who had been deprived of their ancestral sacrifices—the

bereaved spirits. The origin of the first two groups goes back into Shang times, and the third resulted from native theories of the soul.

A local history of Taiwan describes the altars in the prefectural capital in the early eighteenth century. The altars to the gods of land and grain and to the gods of the mountains and rivers adjoined each other in the same enclosure and were similar in construction. They faced west, were square, measured more than twenty feet each way, were about three feet high, and had three steps on each side. They were bounded by a brick wall having a picket gate on the west. The courtyard between altars and walls was more than twenty feet in width. The total effect, in the words of the history, was that "although it was not completely in accord with the ancient regulations, yet it did not fail to carry on the ancient tradition" (*Gazetteer of Taiwan County*). The only difference in the two altars was that the land and grain altar had a stone pillar buried in its exact center, one foot one inch square, two feet five inches long, its top bell-shaped and protruding.

The altar to the gods of the mountains and rivers held three tablets: In the center place of honor was the tablet to the "*Shên* (god or spirit) of Wind, Clouds, Thunder, and Rain"; on the left, next in rank, was the tablet of the prefectural "*Shên* of Mountains and Rivers"; and on the right was the tablet of "*Shên* of Walls and Moats"—that is, the spirit magistrate of the prefecture. All the tablets of the altars were normally kept in the latter's separate temple and were brought to the altars on the occasions of sacrifice. The spirit magistrate (*ch'êng huang*) played a central role in the official religion of the locality, as the counterpart in the spiritual realm of the living magistrate in this one. He was, in fact, usually a deceased official thus appointed to his new term by imperial commission. He had charge over the bereaved spirits, who were enjoined to report to him all instances of either good or evil deeds performed by people that would otherwise remain unknown and thus go unrewarded or unpunished. According to regulations, every magistrate on arrival at a new post was to spend the night prior to formal assumption of his office in the temple of the *ch'êng huang*, purifying himself and praying for the assistance of his spiritual colleague. This procedure was also followed by magistrates baffled by a law case, and numerous instances are recorded of the *ch'êng huang* revealing the solution to his opposite number in a dream.

Official Cults

We have already described the process by which a cult would extend in importance until the government recognized it and bestowed imperial sanction and patronage. Any cult thus recognized and patronized would be included in the official worship to be performed by local officials.

Whatever gods might be on the official roster at any particular time, one was sure to be worshiped: the local earth god. As we know, he was ubiquitous in the folk religion, and of course a deity so close to the lives of all the people could never be omitted from the official cults. As *hou-t'u* we saw him in the third rank of the official pantheon. Whether or not the local histories mention him, it is to be assumed that his shrines are most numerous of all. Every government office had such a shrine, as did every village

and city subsection. The local guardian spirit is so essential in the Chine
view that even strictly Buddhist monasteries include such deities und
the name *ch'ieh lan*.

In every *yamen* "incense was to be burned [at the local earth god's
shrine] on every new and full moon, while those who held official responsibility were to pray for the welfare of the people" (*Gazetteer of Taiwan
County*). The usual spring and autumn sacrifices given to the gods included offerings to the local earth god. A prayer accompanying the sacrifice was short and simple but eloquently indicates the deity's important
position:

> *Wei!* The efficacy of *shên* extends so far as to transform and sustain, to
> preserve and protect all [within these] city walls. *Shên* defends the nation
> and shelters the people, and all we officials rely upon him completely.
>
> Now, during the mid-spring (or, mid-autumn), we respectfully offer
> animals and sweet wine in this ordinary sacrifice.
>
> Deign to accept them! (*Gazetteer of Taiwan County*)

CHAPTER 6

Three Ways to Ultimate Transformation: (1) Taoist Tradition

Thus far we have considered the most general features of the ancient and traditional Chinese worldview—the occult arts, or pseudosciences, related to religion; the universal family system, with its religious character; the "diffused" religion of the communities; and the religious system that supported the Chinese State until the twentieth century.

Now we will look at the Ways taken by those Chinese for whom religion was a matter of personal salvation, the self-conscious quest of "ultimate transformation."* This ultimate transformation led, in the Taoist Way, to immortal transcendency. It led, in the Buddhist Way, to enlightenment and *nirvāṇa*. It led, in the Literati Way, to sainthood.

As Ways to ultimate transformation, these are voluntary religions, or religions of personal choice. But at the same time, they became institutionalized, with organizations and professional specialists. Taoism and Buddhism resembled religions with which Western students are familiar in that they had ordained priests and eremites, whereas the Literati were secular scholars whose profession was government service. The teachings and rituals of Taoism and Buddhism were universal in the sense that they were adapted to the popular as well as to the professional level. The Literati Tradition, on the other hand, was by definition confined to the elite level, although the ethical principles of which the Literati were the custodians were widely spread among the populace.

We shall take up each of the Three Traditions in turn, beginning with what is undeniably the original native religion of China: Taoism.

---

*This term is fully discussed by its original proponent, Frederick Streng, founding editor of *The Religious Life of Man* series (now *The Religious Life in History* series), in his core volume, *Understanding Religious Life*, 3d ed. (Belmont, CA: Wadsworth, 1985).

TAOISM AS RELIGION

It is essential to understand that Taoism is not the same as "popular religion."* The pervasive influence of various Taoistic principles in the popular culture should not obscure the special features that set Taoism apart as an organized, specialized religion. Such special features include a nearly two thousand-year-old tradition of ordained priesthood; the accumulation of an enormous "Bible" of esoteric texts comprehensible only to those with special competence; a grand liturgical tradition based on the ritual texts; a well-defined eremitic tradition; and many distinctive techniques conducive to the ultimate goal of transformation to transcendent immortality. We shall attempt, in what follows, to delineate the features of Taoism as a Way to ultimate transformation and then to depict the nature of its interactions with religious life in the communities.

The premise of religious Taoism is that life is good and to be enjoyed. The individual self is not set apart from the rest of nature but is, like all things, a product of *yin* and *yang* as the creative processes of *tao*. Neither the ego nor the rest of the phenomenal world is illusory—both are completely real. *The religious quest is for liberation of the spiritual element of the ego from physical limitations, so that it may enjoy immortality or at least longevity.* In other words, the goal is the triumph of the *yang* over *yin*. When one has attained this liberation, this triumph, one may choose either to remain in the physical body to enjoy mundane pleasures or to wander freely in the realm of space, to visit or dwell in one of the fabled abodes of the immortals.

It may seem difficult to reconcile this religious Taoism with the whole purport of the classic Taoist texts *The Old Master (Lao Tzû)*, i.e., the *Scripture of the Tao and Its Individuating Power (Tao Tê Ching)*, and *Master Chuang (Chuang Tzû)*. And yet, although the authors of these profoundly philosophical works would certainly have been bemused by many of the theories and practices of the religion that later claimed them as founders, it is, in fact, easy to find in their writings numerous passages that lend themselves to mystical and even esoteric interpretations. A literal, as opposed to a symbolic or poetic, reading could find both the goal of immortality and some techniques for attaining it in such passages as the following:

> One who does not lose his [proper] place endures for long; One who [apparently] dies but does not perish is long-lived. (*The Old Master* 33)
>
> . . .
>
> I have heard that one who is good at taking care of his life will not encounter wild bulls or tigers when traveling by land, and will not [be wounded] by weapons when in the army. [In his case] wild bulls will find no place in which to thrust their horns, tigers no place in which to put their claws, and weapons no place in which to insert their points.

---

*This point must be mentioned because even today there is considerable confusion of the two among writers on Chinese religion.

And why? Because in him there is no place (literally, no ground) of death. (*The Old Master* 50)

. . .

Attain utmost emptiness and preserve earnest stillness. (*The Old Master* 16)

. . .

Block the road, shut your gate, subdue your ardor, do away with your inner divisions, dim your light, and become one with the dusty world. (*The Old Master* 56)

. . .

[Controlled] exhaling and inhaling; disgorging old [breath] and taking in new; bearlike lurchings and birdlike stretchings are performed solely for the sake of longevity. These are what specialists in guiding [the vital breath] and men who nourish the form [in hope of attaining] the longevity of Ancestor P'êng like to do. (*Master Chuang*, scroll 15, "The Will Constrained"; *Chuang Tzû, K'ô Yi*)

. . .

Master Lieh traveled by charioteering on the wind with light and wonderful skill. (*Master Chuang*, scroll 1, "Taking It Easy"; *Chuang Tzû, Hsiao Yao Yu*)

. . .

In the mountains of Miao-ku-shê (supposedly in the Northern Sea—i.e., an island of the immortal transcendents) there live spiritlike men with flesh and skin like ice and snow, gentle and weak as unmarried maidens. They do not eat the five grains but inhale the wind and drink the dew. They ride on the breaths of the clouds and chariot on flying dragons, traveling beyond the Four Seas. (*Master Chuang*, scroll 1)

. . .

My Master, Master Lieh, asked the Guardian of the Pass,* saying, The Perfect Man (i.e., the Taoist adept) walks under water without hindrance, treads on fire without being burned, and moves about on the heights without fear. May I ask how he has attained to this? The Guardian of the Pass replied, It is by the safeguarding of his pure vital breath. (*Master Chuang*, scroll 19, "The Fulfillment of Life"; *Chuang Tzû, Ta Shêng*)

. . .

The True Man (another term for the Taoist adept) breathes from his heels, while the masses of men breathe from their throats. (*Master Chuang*, scroll 6, "The Great Master"; *Chuang Tzû, Ta Tsung Shih*)

. . .

When he succeeded in transcending his own being, apprehension [of the true condition of things] dawned on him, and when that apprehension had dawned, he was able to perceive the One. When he succeeded in perceiving the One he was able [to understand] the nonexistence of "past" and "present." Understanding the nonexistence of past and present he was able to enter into the awareness of no death or birth. (*Master Chuang*, scroll 6)

The historical relationship between this sort of thinking as found in the first Taoist philosophers and the formulation of specific techniques for

---

*Kuan Yin, the officer in charge of the frontier pass where the Old Master departed from China. The Guardian of the Pass asked the Old Master to leave some written evidence of his wisdom; this is what we know as the *Scripture of the Tao and Its Individuating Power*. Kuan Yin is, of course, not to be confused with Kuan Shih Yin, the bodhisattva *cum* popular goddess.

achieving the goals at which it hinted is obscure. The goal itself must, of course, be as old as humankind, but the kinds of practices characteristic of the religious Taoist system in China were perhaps developed no earlier than three to four centuries BCE. These practices have been divided into two inclusive categories: The first was called "outer elixir" (*wai-tan*); this involved the concoction of a drug of immortality. The second was called "inner elixir" (*nei-tan*), which was the refining by various means of the spiritual essence within the body in order to liberate this spiritual essence from its physical shackles.

Wai-tan

The search for the elixir of immortality, closely related to, or identical with, "the philosopher's stone," apparently began in China and eventually spread to the West. The alchemical elixir, when ingested, would prolong life indefinitely; the alchemical philosopher's stone would be able to transmute base metals into gold. Gold was the common denominator. In the case of the elixir, the symbolism of gold was that of indestructible, incorruptible life. The hope of making cheaper ingredients into the most valuable needs no symbolism.

The earliest literary reference to the elixir is found in the first great history of China, written by Ssû-ma Ch'ien* in the mid-second century BCE:

> At this time [133 B.C.] Li Shao-jün was also received in audience by Emperor [Wu], because, by worshipping the Stove and by a method of [not eating] grain [products], he said he knew how to avoid old age. . . .
> [Li] Shao-jün spoke to the Emperor, saying You should worship the Stove and then you can make [spiritual] beings present themselves; when [spiritual] beings have presented themselves, cinnabar powder can be metamorphosed into gold . . . ; when this gold has been made, it can be used for vessels for drinking and eating, and will increase the length of your life; when the length of your life has been increased, the immortals of Peng-lai in the midst of the ocean can thereupon be given audience; when they have been given audience, by [making the sacrifices] *fêng* and *shan* you will never die. The Yellow Lord† did this. Your subject has traveled on the ocean and had an audience with Master An-chi. Master An-chi fed your servant jujubes as large as melons. Master An-chi is an immortal who is in communication with those on [the isle of] Peng-lai. When it suits him, he appears to people, and when it does not suit him, he remains hidden. . . .
> Whereupon the Son of Heaven [Emperor Wu], for the first time worshipped the Stove in person, sent gentlemen [possessors] of recipes . . . out into the ocean to seek for Master An-chi and similar [beings from the isle of] Peng-lai, and paid attention to metamorphosing powdered cinnabar and potions of various drugs into gold.[1]

The activities of the alchemists were of direct concern to the State, which was anxious to prevent counterfeiting of gold money. For this reason such

---

*Double surname hyphenated: Ssû-ma.

†The mythical Emperor Huang Ti.

activities were proscribed on penalty of public execution. The alchemists, therefore, to avoid prosecution and to protect an esoteric lore, kept their operations secretive, relaying their formulas orally or writing them down in a language so occult and obscure that none but initiates could find them intelligible. One rare text, dating from the mid-second century CE, contains the following explanation of the elixir theory:

> *Tan-sha* (Red Sand, cinnabar, mercury sulfide) is of wood and will combine with gold (metal). Gold (metal) and water live together; wood and fire keep one another company. [In the beginning] these four were in a confused state. They came to be classified as Tigers and Dragons. The numbers for the Dragons, which are *yang* (positive, male), are odd, and those for the Tigers, which are *yin* (negative, female), are even.
>
> The blue liver is the father and the white lungs are the mother. The red heart is the daughter, the yellow spleen is the grandfather, and the black kidneys are the son. The son is the beginning of the *wu-hsing* (the Five Elements). The *three* things are of the same family and they all are of the ordinal numbers *Wu* and *Chi*.[2]

Another passage from the same work pictures the alchemist at work, his ingredients in the cauldron, and explains the efficacy of the elixir:

> Circumference three-five, diameter one tenth of an inch, mouth four-eight, two inches, length one and two-tenths feet, and thickness equal throughout. With its belly properly set, it is to be warmed up gradually. *Yin* (negativeness) is above and *yang* (positiveness) runs below. The ends are strongly heated and the middle mildly warmed. Start with seventy, and with thirty, and two hundred and sixty. There should be thorough mixing.
>
> The *yin* . . . fire is white and produces the *huang-ya* (Yellow Sprout) from the lead. Two-seven gathers to bring forth the man. When the brain [head] is properly tended for the required length of time, one will certainly attain the miracle. The offspring, living securely in the center, plies back and forth without coming out of doors. By degrees he grows up and is endowed with a pure nature. He goes back to the one to return to his origin. . . .
>
> Respectful care should be accorded, as by a subject to his ruler. To keep up the work for a year is indeed a strenuous task. There should be strict protection, so as not to get lost. The Way is long and obscurely mystical, at the end of which the *Ch'ien* (positiveness, male) and the *K'un* (negativeness, female) come together. The taking of so small a quantity of it as would cover the edge of a knife or spatula will be enough to confer tranquility on the *hun-p'o* (man's animal spirit), give him immortality, and enable him to live in the village of the immortals.
>
> . . . Careful reflection is in order, but no discussion with others should take place. The secret should be carefully guarded and no writing should be done for its conveyance. . . .
>
> When the aspirant is accomplished, he will ride on the white crane and the scaled dragon to pay respects to the Immortal Ruler in the Supreme Void. There he will be given the decorated diploma which entitles him to the name of a *Chên-jen* (True Man).[3]

Had alchemy been no more than a technique for producing the elixir, it could be considered as simply protoscience and not as religion; but, in fact, the adepts of this technique were never simply experimenters with material substances. The major treatise of the alchemical school, written by one Kô Hung (253–333?) under the pen name Pao P'u Tzû, or The Master Who Holds in His Arms the Uncarved Block, contains many specifications such as the following:

> The rules of immortality demand an earnest desire for quietness, loneliness, nonactivity and forgetfulness of one's own body.
> The rules of immortality require that one extend his love to the creeping worm and do no harm to beings with the life-fluid. . . .
> The rules of immortality require that one entirely abstain from flesh, give up cereals and purify one's interior.
> The rules of immortality demand universal love for the whole world, that one regard one's neighbor as one's own self.[4]

As in all religions, there is a moral imperative in this search for immortality through alchemy:

> He who aspires after immortality should, above all, regard as his main duties: loyalty, filial piety, friendship, obedience, goodness, fidelity (all good "Confucian" virtues). If one does not lead a virtuous life but exercises himself only in magical tricks, he can by no means attain long life. If one does evil, should this be of a grave nature, the god of the fate would take off one chi (300 days, according to translator's note), and for a small sin he would take off a suan (three days) of one's life. . . .
> If the number of good actions is not yet completed, he will have no profit from them, although he takes the elixir of immortality.[5]

The life to be led by the aspirant is described by the same authority:

> This Way is of utmost importance. You must teach it only to those who are wise and virtuous. . . . Whoever receives this instruction, must as a pledge throw a golden effigy of a man and of a fish into a river which flows eastwards. He must smear on his mouth the blood of a victim to pledge allegiance to the cause. . . . One must compound the cinnabar in a famous mountain, uninhabited by human beings, in the company of not more than three persons. First, one must fast for a hundred days, washing and bathing in water mixed with five odoriferous substances and thus effect absolute purity. Avoid strictly proximity to filthy things and observe isolation from the vulgar crowd. Furthermore, disbelievers of the Way should not be given any information, for these would slander and spoil the elixir, and thus the Medicine will fail.[6]

Nei-tan

The quest for the elixir continued on for centuries, becoming increasingly conceived more in spiritual than in physical terms. This development is summed up by Waley, who calls *nei-tan* "esoteric alchemy":

> *Exoteric alchemy* [i.e., *wai-tan*] . . . uses as its ingredients the tangible substances mercury, lead, cinnabar and so on . . . [whereas] *esoteric alchemy* . . . uses only the "souls" of these substances. . . . Presently a fresh step is made. These transcendental metals are identified with various parts of the human body, and alchemy comes to mean in China . . . a system of

mental and physical re-education. This process is complete in the *Treatise on the Dragon and Tiger* (lead and mercury) of Su Tung-p'o, written *c.* 1100: "The dragon is mercury. He is the semen and the blood. He issues from the kidneys and is stored in the liver. His sign is the trigram *k'an*. The tiger is lead. He is breath and bodily strength. He issues from the mind and the lungs bear him. His sign is the trigram *li*. When the mind is moved, then the breath and strength act with it. When the kidneys are flushed then semen and blood flow with them."

In the thirteenth century alchemy (if it may still so be called) no less than Confucianism is permeated by the teachings of the Buddhist Meditation Sect [i.e., Ch'an]. The chief exponent of the Buddhicized Taoism is Ko Ch'ang-kêng, also known as Po Yü-chuan. In his treatise . . . he describes three methods of esoteric alchemy: (1) the body supplies the element lead; the heart, the element mercury. Concentration supplies the necessary liquid; the sparks of intelligence, the necessary fire. "By this means a gestation usually demanding ten months may be brought to ripeness in the twinkling of an eye." . . . (2) The second method is: The breath supplies the element lead, the soul [*shên*] supplies the element mercury. The cyclic sign [*wu*] "horse" supplies fire; the cyclic sign [*tzu*] "rat" supplies water. (3) The semen supplies the element lead. The blood supplies mercury; the kidneys supply water; the mind supplies fire.

"To the above it may be objected," continues Ko Ch'ang-kêng, "that this is practically the same as the method of the Zen Buddhist. To this I reply that under Heaven there are no two Ways, and that the Wise are ever of the same heart."[7]

Although *wai-tan*, an alchemy of substances, thus becomes more and more a technique for cultivating the "inner chemistry" of the body, it must not be assumed that this latter was historically an outgrowth of the former. On the contrary, as several of the excerpts quoted earlier in the chapter from *The Old Master* and *Master Chuang* show, inner cultivation was already a feature of ancient Taoist philosophy. From these hints, the later adepts of religious Taoism developed a variety of yoga, based on a theory that may be called "spiritual physiology." This in turn formed the foundation for the protoscience of traditional Chinese medicine. The objective of Taoist yoga was, as we have said, liberation of the *yang* soul (that is, the *shên*) from the hindrances of the *yin*, or gross physical body, and thus it was, in fact, a development of the ancient concepts. That is, it had always been presumed that such a liberation was accomplished by death, but the religious Taoists believed it could be accomplished in this very life.

In the spiritual physiology of religious Taoism, the life-force was identified with such obviously vital components as breath, blood, and semen. To preserve life these components must be conserved, and the obstructions to their continuing nourishment of the *shên* must be reduced and finally eliminated. The peculiarity about the religious Taoist notion of breath was that it was not merely inhalation and exhalation of an exterior substance but that it was a progressive "using up" of the allotment of life-spirit with which one was born. Taoist yoga therefore endeavored to conserve the breath. In the same way exhaustion of the semen was equivalent to exhaustion of the life-spirit; therefore, adepts used a technique to retain it instead of ejaculating it during the sexual act. Not only did this prevent exhaustion of the life-spirit, but the method of retention was positively beneficial as well. It was believed that pressure on the urethra at the moment of ejaculation forced the semen back up through the spinal passage to the brain, where it nourished the "Field of Cinnabar" supposed to be located there. Through this circulation of the semen (as of the breath) throughout the various passages and organs predicated by Taoist physiological and anatomical theory, the practitioner was continually rejuvenated.

The same purpose lay behind the various gymnastic routines of Taoist devotees, some of which have been widely adopted in East Asia. The so-called Chinese boxing (*t'ai-chi ch'üan*), a slow-motion ballet performed by countless men and women every morning in China, is like the setting-up exercises used in the West. Its rationale, however, is that just described. Such Taoist gymnastics, when combined with the injunctions of the Old Master to be nonassertive, "weak, like water," and so forth, further led to techniques of bodily combat that have recently become popular among some Westerners, particularly that called the "yielding way" (*rou-tao* in Chinese, or *jūdō* in Japanese).

The Taoist adept attempted to reduce his intake of food as far as possible, because the consumption of food merely contributed to maintenance of the physical body and produced excreta that clogged the various interior passages, which were to be kept open wide for circulation of the life-forces. Even cereals were to be avoided because the body was inhabited by maleficent spirits (*kuei*), who were nourished by cereals.

The notion of the body being inhabited by both beneficent and malevolent spirits was further extended to the conception of the body as a microcosm corresponding to the macrocosm of the universe. Such an imaginative conception might have had its origin, at least in part, in certain passages of *Master Chuang*, where the relativity of things is most powerfully delineated:

> There is nothing in the world larger than the tip of an autumn down; but Mt T'ai is small. There is no life so long as that which is cut off in youth. Ancestor P'êng (the Chinese Methuselah) may be considered to have died prematurely. Heaven-and-Earth were created together with me. The myriad things-and-beings and I are one. (*Master Chuang*, scroll 2, "An Essay on the Relativity of Things"; *Chuang Tzû, Ch'i Wu Lun*)

However, the same sort of thinking was stimulated by the paradoxes beloved of the philosophers of the sophist type who flourished in the fourth and third centuries BCE. And even in the more socially oriented thought of Master Mêng, one finds this curious passage: "The ten thousand things (i.e., all things) are complete within us."[8]

At the highest level, among Taoists of superior intellectual and spiritual attainments, the religious quest led not only to the goal of immortality but to a mystical absorption in *tao* itself. Although the meditational techniques of Taoism were strongly influenced by Buddhism in later times, ultimately resulting in the Buddho-Taoist techniques of Ch'an, it seems certain that some form of meditation was already practiced in China long before the arrival of the Indian religion. What is hinted at in *The Old Master* seems to become explicit in *Master Chuang*:

[Yen] Hui said, May I venture to ask about "fasting the mind"? Chung-ni (i.e., Master K'ung)* replied, Concentrate the will. Do not listen with the ears but listen with the mind. Do not listen with the mind but listen with the vital breath. Hearing stops at the ears, the mind stops at tallying [with a stimulus], but the vital breath is empty and awaits something. It is just the *Tao* that gathers in this emptiness, and this emptiness is the "fasting of the mind." (*Master Chuang*, scroll 4, "Society and the Times"; *Chuang Tzû, Rên Chien Shih*)

. . .

Sloughing off limbs and trunk, driving out intellectual apprehension, abandoning form and rejecting knowledge, identifying with the Great Pervader: this is what is meant by sitting in forgetfulness. (*Master Chuang*, scroll 6)

. . .

Light is produced in the empty room and felicity stops and abides there. If for a time it does not, this is called galloping about while sitting. When the eyes and ears are directed inward and the "knowledge" of the mind is cast out, the very spirits will come to lodge. (*Master Chuang*, scroll 4)

INSTITUTIONALIZATION OF TAOISM

The quest for transcending the limitations of the flesh that has been described thus far was based on esoteric interpretations of certain ancient texts and carried on by means of various techniques that Western scholars have called alchemy. These interpretations and practices constituted the essence of Taoism as a religious Way and required no professional ordination. Indeed, lay devotees of the arts of longevity or immortality must always have been far more numerous than the professional religious. By itself this sort of effort—corresponding in general intent to the search in the West for the "philosopher's stone" or the "fountain of youth"—would not have produced an institutionalized religion. That Taoism did become institutionalized may be ascribed to two major historical developments. On the one hand, the solitary retreats of recluses evolved into whole communities of aspirants living under the guidance of renowned masters, and as one result of this situation, the teachings of the latter were written down to become gospel texts of a Taoist Canon. On the other hand, a new type of religious specialist emerged in the "theocratic" regimes that arose during the time of troubles of the Later Han dynasty, in the second century of the common era.

By far the most important of these regimes for the history of Taoism was that established in the far western province of Ssuch'uan by one Chang Ling or Chang Tao-ling. It is Chang Tao-ling who must be identified, if any one figure can be, as the founder of Taoist religion in the institutionalized form. He stands conveniently for this purpose at the borders of history and legend, and in the latter area he has been deified as one of popular Taoism's most puissant spiritual powers. Historically, it seems

---

*It is hardly necessary to point out that Master K'ung and his favorite disciple are here being made to express Master Chuang's own ideas.

that he did gain political control over a considerable territory, which he administered through a bureaucracy whose officials were more religious than secular in authority. These officials, although deriving organization- ally from the practices of the Han imperium, are said to have acted most importantly in the capacity of parish priests. They, like Chang Tao-ling, were evangelists of a new religion of faith healing and ritual adapted to the needs of the masses. Apparently this addition to the age-old popular religion was eagerly embraced by the multitudes, perhaps because it was the first time that their rulers had concerned themselves with the common people. Now, the services of common mediums, shaman-exorcists, and sorcerers were in a sense brought under the aegis of respectable, literate priest-officials, who could bring an unprecedented spiritual power to bear in popular religion. It was this literacy, or mastery of texts, that distin- guished the Taoists (we shall use this term hereafter to designate the pro- fessional religious and not "believers" in general) from lower-level religious practitioners. At the same time, it was the involvement of the Taoists in the communities that made their services an integral part of the popular religion.

The original chief of these community priests, Chang Tao-ling, assumed a title that was to endure as the most prestigious both within and outside the Taoist institution: **T'ien Shih.** This title, obviously derived by analogy with the imperial title of T'ien Tzû (Son of Heaven), meant the Master Des- ignated by the [Three] Heavens. It remained the hereditary property of the Chang lineage, was given official recognition by many imperial regimes throughout history, especially since the Sung dynasty, and is still acknowl- edged to have unique authority.[9]

The great majority of Taoists remain in society to act as ritualists for the communities in which they live. They are identified as receiving a number of different ritual traditions, but that purporting to trace back to Chang Tao-ling, called the T'ien-Shih Chêng-yi Tao, or Way of the Orthodox One of the Master Designated by the Heavens, holds pride of place. Most im- portant, it has been the T'ien Shih who has been the recognized source of orthodox ordination, which he would confer on aspirants in accordance with their mastery of specific texts from the whole range of sectarian tradi- tions. On the other hand, Taoists who chose to leave the world and live se- cluded in monasteries in order to pursue the alchemical techniques that would gain them personal immortality might be said more closely to re- semble Buddhist monks (see Chapter 8). The major tradition of this style of Taoist career was the Ch'üan-chên Chiao, or Sect of Total Perfection.

THE TAOIST AS EXORCIST AND RITUALIST

The two main functions of the Taoist are exorcism and protection of the well-being and security of the mortal world against the attacks of *kuei*, and performance of rituals on behalf of clients and community. Although both of these functions are also carried on by lower-level religious specialists, the Taoist is recognized to have more effective power under his control for exorcism and protection, and only he knows the complicated rubrics of the major liturgies. He is, to put it in brief, a better-educated specialist than those others, especially by virtue of his book learning. This was, of course, an outstanding qualification in those days when the mere ability to read and write made a person exceptional and constituted the very basis for qualifying one to enter elite status in the society. It should be stressed that the profession of Taoist is very much more demanding in its preparation than those of medium, shaman, or the like. While these latter may have literally no preparatory training but simply be "possessed" by their familiar deity—or even substitute only a convincing assertion of their occult powers for such possession—the Taoist has to undergo a long period of textual studies, supplemented by the oral instructions of his mentor. The latter is customarily his own father as, in common with most professions involving specialized technical knowledge in traditional China, the professional secrets were kept within the family.* Following this long apprenticeship, the aspirant would seek service under an eminent master, in order to become his successor. His ordination was an impressive ceremony, preceded by many days of isolation and fasting and publicly performed during a sacrificial "mass" called *chiao*, which lasted a minimum of three days.

The exorcising work of the **tao-shih** (ordained Taoist) has already been illustrated in the vivid example quoted in Chapter 2 from the pen of Peter Goullart. The basis for the Taoist's control over *kuei* and *shên* was a form of "name magic," an interesting survival, in a sophisticated religion, of a very ancient, even primitive, notion. He could summon and dismiss the deities of **macrocosm** (the universe) and **microcosm** (his own body) by virtue of his knowledge of their names, true descriptions, and functions. He further controlled them by means of cabalistic writing, the talismans or charms called *fu* (see example pictured on p. 92). These *fu* were, in effect, orders or commands issued by the Taoist by virtue of his authority in the spiritual realm, and thereby they kept away *kuei* and invoked the beneficence of *shên*. Other, more dramatic—perhaps even entertaining—techniques and instruments were exampled in the case noted above, which all combine to make the Taoist's performances exciting and impressive to the lay public.

It should be noted that there is generally understood to be a distinction between those Taoists (commonly called "Red-heads" in Taiwan) who are found practicing exorcism and other popular rites in the busy temples on an everyday basis and the supposedly higher-class Taoists (called "Black-heads" in Taiwan) who alone are competent to perform the extended liturgies of the *chiao*. The former will wear a red scarf tied about the head (or waist) and carry a buffalo horn, which they blow in loud blasts, while the latter are seen attired in their formal sacerdotal vestments complete with black "mandarin cap" with gold-colored knob. The essential distinction between the two types is that the former (called *fa-shih*, or occult specialists), knowing only the more rudimentary texts, are ordained in low rank and cannot perform the greater liturgies, while the latter have mastered

---

*J. J. M. de Groot suggests another reason for transmission from father to son: "That same magical power, but for the possession of which ceremonies, formulae, charms and spells are, if not totally useless, at least of little effect, is positively hereditary by birth, since it is homogeneous with the *ling* or power of the *shên* or *yang* soul which a child receives from his father." *The Religious System of China*, vol. 6, p. 1245.

"Black-head" Taoist assisting devotees in Matsu Temple at Kuan-tu, Taiwan.

the texts qualifying them to perform those greatly more complex and religiously profound rituals. However, the superior ranked *tao-shih* (Taoist masters) are, of course, able to carry out the popular rites that are the specialty of their inferiors and often do not disdain to do so in consideration of the pecuniary rewards.[10]

The greater rituals whose liturgies are set forth in the advanced texts are known as *chiao* and **chai**. There apparently was not much difference between these two forms historically. A contemporary Chinese scholar, Liu Chih-wan, has suggested the following distinction: "Taking the broadest view, the difference in the results sought by the two [forms of ritual] is simply that their emphases are not the same: The *chai* places its emphasis upon the prayers of the individual for blessings and the salvation of the dead; whereas the emphasis of the *chiao* is upon the prayers of the public (i.e., the community) for averting calamities and ensuring tranquillity. [Thus] each has its special emphasis."[11] According to the American authority Michael Saso, himself an ordained *tao-shih,* although the two sets

*Taoist talisman in
memorial hall for re-
builders of Matsu tem-
ple in Kuan-tu,
Taiwan. The talisman
is for good fortune,
combining graphs for
prosperity, longevity,
and king.*

of rituals are both performed during the several-day festivals in the communities in Taiwan, the *chiao* has as its purpose "to win blessing from
heaven and union with the transcendent Tao," whereas the *chai* is intended
"to free the souls from hell."[12] A special feature of the latter is that it concludes with a great feast for the souls of those in purgatory, called by the
Buddhist term ***p'u-tu*** (see Chapter 10, the section titled "Seventh Month").

The *chiao* has both esoteric and exoteric levels of meaning. For the Taoist
himself, it is a procedure whereby he personally attains mystical union
with Tao, or in other words, a form of *nei-tan*. To the public it is an impressive ceremonial and magical performance whereby the supreme powers
of the universe are called down into the temple for a State visit and peti-
tioned to give their spiritual support to the community.[13] At the same time,
while these highly formalized, canonically prescribed events are being enacted within a temple—which, incidentally, is only for this occasion made
off-limits to the public—the people are themselves participating in the rituals according to traditional lay roles, and the joint efforts of priests and
people comprise a total community "happening," a great festival both sacred and profane.

In Taiwan today such *chiao* are the most exciting and colorful affairs
carried on in the communities. Like medieval European fairs, they combine the religious, the aesthetic, and the purely sensual, and they last for at
least three days and nights. Large structures called ***t'an***, or altars, are
erected in vacant lots or fields, dedicated to major deities, and at night
brightly illuminated. They are facades or skeletons of bamboo covered
with cloth and paper, colorfully decorated with all sorts of ingenuous folk
art. Every so often the Taoist retinue emerges from the temple to perform
some public section of the liturgies, much to the enjoyment of the people.
Huge crowds arrive, many from distant places, to share in the excitement.

Altar (t'an) erected in a field in connection with the elaborate Taoist
chiao, *or Rite of Cosmic Renewal. Structure is of bamboo, cloth, and
paper, and the lower level has a walkway for the thousands of visitors
who will examine it closely and pay reverence to the several deities enshrined within. Note the naive "folk art."*

Everywhere the local people have set out their household offerings on tables at the roadside, of which pride of place goes to monstrous pigs that
have been fattened for just this occasion and that are spread-eagled in hair-
less nudity on special stands. There are noisy theatricals, fortune-telling
booths, hawkers of every kind, and carnival amusements. Day and night
this animated scene astonishes by its vitality and the prodigality with
which these people of so little material substance spend for their festival.
The persistent theme of the festival as a whole is the dominance of the
dead. Not only are canonical texts of merit and repentance for salvation of
souls constantly being read by the Taoists during the entire *chiao,** but all
of that mountain of food and drink set out by the households of the entire
community is for the souls of the dead. The ancestors are of course expected to enjoy this feast, but there are many souls who must be appeased
for fear of their vengeance—the spirits of those who have been deprived
of their due sacrifices and the spirits of those who must suffer punishment
in purgatory. Dominating the scene before the temple stands the figure of
Ta Shih, the metamorphosed Kuan Shih Yin as King of these Ghosts,

---

*Chiao and *chai* are thus invariably combined in the liturgy, but to the people these
grand celebrations are inclusively known simply as *chiao.*

charged with keeping them in order when they flock to the feast prepared for them by the community. To that feast they have been invited by signal lamps and pennants hung on tall posts and by paper boats sent burning out on the waters. Not until these dangerous spirits have been respectfully banqueted on the essences of the sacrifices can the community feel secure and the hoped-for benefits of the *chiao* be assured.

We may seem here to have left the topic of the religious vocation and to have returned to religion in the community. But it will be seen that it is in fact the roles of exorcist and ritualist for the community that have constituted the profession, the raison d'etre, of the Taoist and ensured the continuing vitality of his public vocation through the centuries.

CHAPTER 7

Three Ways to Ultimate Transformation: (2) Literati Tradition

Like Taoism, the Literati Tradition was an original, native Way.[1] The pervasive influence of the teachings of Master K'ung and his School in formulating the ancient Chinese ethical norms and the Chinese code of ritually proper deportment, as well as the official rituals of the State, was discussed in Chapters 1, 3, and 5. Some students are not convinced, however, that these teachings, important though they were, were "religious" in nature, and "Confucianism" is still often described as "merely humanistic and rationalistic." Such an understandable judgment is reinforced by the undeniable fact that the main concern of the Literati as a class—the career of the scholar-bureaucrat—was secular and by the equally undeniable fact that they frequently condemned the religious beliefs and practices of the common people as "foolish superstitions," unworthy of intelligent and educated men.

Close examination of the Literati over a long span of history shows us that their education did not, in fact, necessarily mold them into materialists or skeptics. Although class pride would usually make them contemptuous of the common herd, they nevertheless believed in the gestalt cosmology with its interactions of the spiritual and human dimensions. They not only were practitioners but also were the mainstays of the ancestral cult, and as officials on local assignment, they had the duty of mediating between people and spirits. Aside from this, they were very often friends with Buddhist and Taoist monks and adepts, and many of them were actually lay devotees of those Ways. One must conclude that intimate familiarity with the contents of the Literati Canon did not in any way conduce to antagonism to religion. In fact, because Literati texts emphasized personal integrity, ethical uprightness, and empathetic concern, familiarity with the Canon might be more likely to produce men of religious character. One must conclude, therefore, that the Literati Tradition was religious in nature—especially if we take a broad view of the term *religion*.

What militates against this latter assumption is the fact that study of the Literati Canon was, for the majority, simply instrumental in their ambition for entrance into the elite class with its power and prestige. Unlike those who would devote themselves to study of the Buddhist or Taoist texts, students of the Literati Canon were motivated not by religious interests so much as by secular goals. It is presumably this very situation that led many Literati to look for religious satisfaction in the Ways of Buddhism and Taoism. This became more compelling during the four post-Han centuries when China was divided in many complicated ways and governed in part by "barbarians" (i.e., non-Chinese), so that the career of the Literati was more or less frustrated. The most intelligent and best educated, as well as the more unintelligent and least educated, turned to Taoism or Buddhism as Ways of salvation or escape.

It was not until the Sung period (960–1279) that the Way of the Literati came to develop an aspect of religiosity comparable with the other Ways. The impetus of this development was, first, restoration of a great imperial State that gave the Literati back their status as elite bureaucrats and, second, the powerful attraction of Buddhism and Taoism that required the Literati to respond with a religious and philosophical sophistication unknown to their predecessors. The Literati who were sensitive to the needs of their times found in the ancient concept of the Saint or Sage (*shêng-rên*) the counterpart or alternative to the True Man of Taoism and the Bodhisattva of Buddhism, and they found the Way to sainthood in their own Canon. In the discussion that follows, we shall outline this "Neo-Confucian" Way to ultimate transformation.

THE RENASCENT LITERATI TRADITION

The earlier form of the Literati Tradition did not survive the collapse of the Han dynasty (c. 200 CE). Buddhism, arriving in China in mid-Han, and Taoism, gradually taking shape as an institutionalized religion as Han disintegrated, were the major popular and elite movements for four centuries. China being politically fragmented, there existed no State well enough entrenched fully to restore the Literati bureaucracy to its old position. Not until T'ang (seventh through ninth centuries) did this situation begin to change. The beginnings of a system of written examinations for official service once again gave Literati a privileged status, as T'ang required a large bureaucracy to administer its vast realm. As it became established that elite status was to be won through the examination system, the brightest talents naturally gravitated into Literati studies. During T'ang, the *Ru* were not yet supreme, but in the following Sung period (mid-tenth through mid-thirteenth centuries), they established their dominance in both the political and intellectual spheres. The work of certain brilliant thinkers gave the Tradition philosophical and religious dimensions that enabled it for the first time to satisfy minds that would previously have found Buddhism or Taoism more congenial.

In the ancient Literati Tradition as molded by Master K'ung, the stress was on perfecting one's moral qualities to become a *chün-tzû*, or noble man. The *chün-tzû* was to seek office as adviser to an intelligent ruler and by guiding this ruler's policies make him morally prominent. Moral prominence would exert irresistible attraction on the people of the world, who would flock to become his subjects. Thus he would be able to reunite the kingdom and put an end to the long era of political and social disorder.

The ideal of the *chün-tzû* and his duty to serve the ruler was still basic in later times. But the situation was different. The Literati had to reckon with the appeal of highly developed systems unknown to the ancient Chinese; in addition, it had become much more difficult to maintain the moral stance required in serving one's ruler. Now the latter was the absolute despot over a vast empire, his court a busy center of factional intrigue of a scale far surpassing the minicourts of late Chou. In the *realpolitik* of power struggles at the imperial court, the Literati were more servants than moral mentors to their lord. The man of principle found his career chancy, dangerous, or even impossible. Needless to say, under such conditions most scholars sacrificed principle to expediency and attempted to further their personal careers. The men we call "Neo-Confucians" were a small minority, who usually found themselves in trouble when they were in office and commonly retired to private study and teaching—in this following the example of their Master.

Beyond the ideal of the *chün-tzû* lay an even loftier goal, which was proclaimed by the philosophers of the New Literati Movement. They set out to rescue their Tradition from the obscurity into which it had been cast by Buddhism and Taoism and to save it as well from the scholars who studied the hallowed texts simply to find official employment or to impress their fellows. The Tradition, according to these revitalizing thinkers, was in fact the Great Tao of Chinese civilization, the Truth that had been revealed by certain saints (*shêng-rên*) of misty antiquity and firmly established by Master K'ung. The line of saints continued only briefly after the Master, including the two disciples Master Yen and Master Tsêng, Master Tzû Ssû—grandson of Master K'ung and putative author of *The Central and Universal Moral Law* (*Chung Yung*), and the chief formulator (in the eyes of the reforming Literati) of the doctrine, Master Mêng ("Mencius"). The Literati philosophers of these later ages proposed to renew and revitalize the succession, indeed, to strive to become saints of *tao* in their own time. The *shêng-rên*, as they conceived him, was one who not only possessed the moral virtues of the *chün-tzû* but who embodied a much more profound metaphysical—even ontological—reality: That is, only he was a *shêng-rên* who had reached the ultimate potential of true humanity by complete identification with all Creation, his every thought and action flowing in effortless harmony with the Cosmic Tao.

Such an ideal has obvious similarities to, and certainly was influenced by, the **bodhisattva** ideal of Buddhism and the ideal of the Perfected Man (*chên-rên*) in Taoism. The Literati needed, of course, to find scriptural authority for their version in their own Canon, and they devoted much scholarly acumen to interpreting their texts accordingly. Two small works were lifted from their original places as chapters of the *Li Chi* (*Records of Rituals*) and ranked with the very records of the teachings of the Master and Mêng Tzû in a group called the Four Books, or the core of the latter-day Literati Bible. The first of these was *The Central and Universal Moral Law*, an eloquent essay on the relationships of moral man to a moral universe. This essay gave the sanction of ancient scripture to the reforming Literati ideal of the *shêng-rên*. The other text was *The Highest Form of Learning* (*Ta Hsüeh*), which had to do with the Great Objective of the Noble Man's Learning (to give a free interpretation of the title). In this brief work, the Literati philosophers found a succinct but complete program for the aspirant to follow. We have earlier quoted the key passage of *Ta Hsüeh* (see Chapter 1, p. 12), but it will be helpful here to repeat one part of it, which speaks of "the men of old who wished to make their bright virtue shine throughout the world":

> When they studied the nature of things then their understanding became complete; when their understanding was complete then they resolved sincerely upon their goals; when they were sincerely resolved upon their goals then their minds (or hearts) were rectified. When their minds were rectified then they were able to discipline themselves; when they could discipline themselves then they could regulate their families; when they could regulate their families then they could put in order their own states; when their own states were in order then they could bring peace to the world.

By Sung and later times, putting the state in order and bringing peace to the world must have seemed more often than not rather utopian hopes; but the Literatus could nevertheless work at the more personal goals outlined by the text. In other words, he could devote himself to the tasks of *how to study the nature of things in order to arrive at understanding, how to resolve sincerely upon the goal, how to rectify the mind (or heart), and how to discipline oneself.*

RELIGIOUS STRUCTURE AND PRAXIS (PRACTICES) OF THE RENASCENT LITERATI TRADITION

Simple though this program may appear, its explication extended over many centuries and filled innumerable volumes of scriptural commentary, letters, and conversations between masters and pupils. Common Literati ideals did not preclude differences of opinion about basic philosophical questions and practices. The lines were drawn most sharply between two schools in particular. The School of Li (the Principle), whose great spokesman was the Sung scholar Chu Hsi (1130–1200), held a position that in Western categories would be termed "philosophical realism." It viewed man and the world as being what they seem to be—distinct and separate entities. Man's mind as subject attempted to understand the world as object. "To study the nature of things" therefore meant to study the Principle in the myriad phenomena of the world and through this process eventually to arrive at true understanding. The School of Hsin (Mind), formulated definitively by the Ming sage, Wang Yang-ming (1473–1529), was, in Western terms, a school of "philosophical idealism." In this view there was no distinction between subject and object; the phenomena of the world, which appear to be "out there," are actually within the mind. "To study the nature of things" therefore meant to grasp the Principle that is innate in the mind.

It is essential to be clear that what these schools were concerned with was not scientific understanding of the physical universe. Their motivation was to understand the *tao:* that is, to be able *to act as moral agents in a universe that operated on moral principles*—as laid down in *Chung Yung.* The Li School sought those moral principles in the world outside, but the Hsin School believed that moral principle must be found within one's own mind.

In either case, the seeking was always difficult and must be carried on with unremitting effort. The task must be undertaken with *dedication,* according to the Li School, which stressed this term (*ching,* also meaning "reverently" or "respectfully"). Wang Yang-ming thought that the term *moral steadfastness (ch'êng),* as used in *Chung Yung,* already described the attitude of resolution. The difference may be rather negligible in our eyes, but we should mark the essential thing, which is dedication to the task. This is easy to talk about but supremely difficult to maintain over months and years. The true Literatus must unflaggingly keep at the work, determined to perfect his moral character so as to realize his true self, taking every changing situation in life as a test and a challenge.

The task involved most specifically rectification of the mind (or heart—the Chinese term having both mental and moral-emotional connotations). Rectification refers to the objective of becoming wholly one with all Creation, from which our alienation is unnatural. The moral universe produces human beings endowed with nature that is good (according to Master Mêng, the great authority for these Literati). It is selfish desires and passions that obscure this good nature and place man in conflict with the *tao,* or Cosmic Principle. The Li School taught that the Literatus was to work to project his mind empathetically upon the world. Understanding the Principle in the world, he would come to feel in sympathetic harmony with it. The person who comes to look on all Creation as his very self comes to love it as he loves himself. One whose love (*rên*) extends so far becomes, in effect, identified with the Cosmos, or Cosmic Principle. The teaching of Wang Yang-ming, on the other hand, is that *rectification* refers to rectification of the mind itself, which is nothing more nor less than Cosmic Principle. There is no Principle of things in the world to understand; there is only the mind, which must be purged of its self-destructive passions and desires. The mind that is thus purged is identical with the Mind of Heaven, or Cosmic Principle, and thus perfectly good.

Such rectification of the mind, or heart, whichever the school of the aspirant, required specific praxis, called in the Chinese terminology, "discipline of the self." We already know that an essential aspect of self-discipline is never-flagging zeal. The zeal must be manifested in diligent attention to one's problems, in study of the scriptural authorities, and in cultivation of the traditional Literati moral virtues. Meditation was encouraged by both schools, the Literati version being called "quiet sitting" (*ching-tso*). The *Ru* were at pains to distinguish their meditation from that of Buddhists and Taoists. It was not aimed at destroying the personality or realizing the emptiness of all things, nor was the student to aim at putting a stop to discursive thought. Instead, he was to calm his mind, purify it, become aware of its original goodness, and sensitize it to the arising of selfish desires and evil passions. The mind was thus to be used as a positive instrument of advancement.

It may be asked why, in a moral universe, the originally good human nature stands in such need of purification. In other words, we meet here the problem of the existence of evil. For the answer to this question, we must glance at the basic metaphysical and ontological premises of the Literati philosophical schools. To begin with, they fully accepted the ancient worldview as we have outlined it in Chapter 1, but they refined it in accordance with the greater sophistication of their age. They thus postulated two additional factors essential to the appearance of the phenomenal world: *li* and *ch'i*. The first we have been rendering as the Principle. It is another way of saying the *tao*. The second is "vital breath," an age-old concept associated with the phenomenal creation in both macro- and microcosm. Lacking the Principle, the *possibility* of the thing does not exist. Lacking vital breath, there is no way for the Principle to manifest itself in phenomenal things.

Both of the major Literati philosophical schools upheld the dogma of Master Mêng that human nature is inherently good. The Li School accounted for the arising of evil in man by the fact that his *ch'i* is sullied to a greater or lesser extent by the physical matter of his body. Here we have a notion reminiscent of the traditional Western opposition of body and soul. The flesh, in other words, by the domination of its desires and passions, corrupts the nature. Wang Yang-ming, on the other hand, denied vehemently that human nature was of itself corruptible. It could not be, because it was exactly the same as the Cosmic Principle itself. Evil arises because material desires and passions *obscure* the incorruptible nature.

The philosophical distinctions between these two positions are real, and they gave rise to endless quarrels between the schools, but for religious purposes they come down to the same thing. That is, human nature has lost its inherent perfection, and the task of the person who wants to attain his true potential humanity is to restore it. A person succeeding in this arduous quest would be called *shêng-rên*. The degree of the evil in which the nature is sunk could be gauged by the fact that so few ever did succeed. The goal of the *shêng-rên* was thus just as illusory, and as beckoning, as the goals of Buddhahood or sainthood in other religious traditions.

The Way of the latter-day Literati schools is most apparently a Way to ultimate transformation. But it is not a universal Way. It is limited both in the sense that it was confined to a small minority of the elite class and that it was concerned only with ethical transformation. It had no contribution to make to the salvation of the common people, nor did it address itself to the broad range of human problems. Buddhism and Taoism likewise had their elite level of transformation, but unlike the latter-day Literati schools, they had forms suited to the masses as well. These can be seen not only as diffused throughout popular culture but also in the beliefs and practices of devout laypersons and their sects.

CHAPTER 8

Three Ways to Ultimate Transformation: (3) Buddhist Tradition

Buddhism,* the only alien tradition both to infiltrate and to modify Chinese culture, arose in India at about the same time (sixth through fifth centuries BCE) that Master K'ung was enunciating the moral law. Buddhism developed in India during the half-millennium before it was brought to China by missionaries at the very beginning of the common era. This long period of development meant that its theories and doctrines were in large part already formulated in numerous Indian schools before the Chinese encounter. The radical dissimilarity of Indian and Chinese ways of thinking, as well as the utterly dissimilar Chinese and Indian languages (Pali and Sanskrit), made it difficult for the Chinese to comprehend the new religion. The early centuries of Buddhism in China were perforce marked by efforts to translate the sacred texts and penetrate their true meaning. Many Indian and Central Asian missionaries and their early Chinese converts devoted their lives to this task. The determination of Chinese monks to acquire as many as possible of the texts in the original languages drove many of them to attempt the long and frightfully dangerous pilgrimage to the Buddhist homeland during those early centuries. According to Chinese records, some 121 missionary translators came to China, and 164 Chinese pilgrims made the round trip to India during the centuries between Han and T'ang. However, because translation was often carried on by whole teams of missionaries and Chinese converts with their numerous assistants, these figures do not give us a real picture of the ferment of activity.

The transplantation of Buddhist thought to China is one of the great intercultural movements of history. Among the many lessons we may draw from that movement is that accommodation of a foreign culture is accomplished only as a result of many modifications and reinterpretations that make it comprehensible and eventually naturalize it. In the case

---

*For a full treatment of Buddhism, the reader is again referred to Richard H. Robinson and Willard L. Johnson, *The Buddhist Religion*, 3d ed. (Belmont, CA: Wadsworth, 1982).

of Buddhism, one must recognize that first there was Indian Buddhism; then there was Indian Buddhism in China; and finally, after many centuries of adjustments, there was Chinese Buddhism.

MAHĀYĀNA: THE CAPACIOUS VEHICLE

The Chinese, while becoming acquainted with all of the Indian schools, were drawn by decided preference to those upholding Mahāyāna views. The philosophical formulation of Mahāyāna is found in the abstruse treatises of Nāgārjuna and his pupil Āryadeva at a time corresponding to the end of the Han dynasty, and these Indian treatises were translated into Chinese by the great scholar Kumārajīva at the beginning of the fifth century. The work of these Buddhist doctors founded the Mādhyamika, or school of the Middle Way.

In the fourth and fifth centuries, Asaṅga and Vasubandhu, dissatisfied with certain of the Mādhyamika premises, proposed their own revisions to found the Yogācāra (or Vijñānavāda), or school of Consciousness Only. Their works were translated into Chinese by the greatest of all the pilgrim-scholars, Hsüan Chuang, in the mid-seventh century. The treatises of these two schools became the "systematic theology" of the whole Mahāyāna movement, resulting in a Buddhism that differed widely from the Buddhism of the Pali texts, both in theory and in practice.

The difference in theory centered on the ontological problem. That is, if there was no ego (as the Buddha had taught), then *what* was it that accumulated and carried on *karma* from one existence to another? What was the relationship of this to the nature of ultimate Reality? (Reincarnation as such was not in question; it was an accepted premise in all of Indian religion.)

The discovery of the Buddha Śākyamuni concerning this ontological problem was the law of interdependent causation, expressed in the formula: This being so, that comes to be. . . . this ceasing to be, that ceases. In the Buddhism of the Pali texts, which the later Mahāyānists called Hīnayāna,* this formula sums up a simple and straightforward doctrine: Existence is caused by the unceasing accumulation of *karma*; existence involves all sorts of suffering; salvation means putting an end to the suffering by putting an end to the accumulation of *karma*. One begins to put an end to the accumulation of *karma* when one realizes that every mental or physical action has its proportionate result and that *karma* is, in fact, the sum of these results. Our *karma*-producing actions are caused by the delusion that we are *real selves*, that the ego is a *permanent identity*—and therefore this self or ego is dominated by egoistical desires or attachments. It is desire, passionate attachment (or its converse, revulsion and hate), caused by ignorance concerning the truth about this so-called self, that shackles us to

*Hīnayāna is a pejorative term, contrasting the Small Vehicle of Salvation with the Great Vehicle of Mahāyāna. But these terms are always used in Chinese.

the ever-revolving wheel of birth-life-death-rebirth, through the continuously replenished motive force of accumulating *karma*. Therefore, the key to release from this wheel is the understanding that there is no self or ego and consequently that desires and the satisfaction of desires are the illusory products of ignorance.

Although this theory is simple and coherent, the problem of just what the illusory self or ego was, and the relationship of this to ultimate Reality, bothered the analytical minds among later Buddhists, and the answers proposed gave rise to a number of schools. Hīnayāna schools seem to have been more realistic, in the philosophical sense, accepting the existence (at least the temporary existence) of a number of elements and aggregates, which they exhaustively cataloged. The elements, called *dharmas*, included such things as sensation, form, memory, space, and energy. The aggregates, called *skandhas*, included material form and the spiritual items of sensation, ideas, concepts, and understanding. Salvation was attained by realization, or enlightenment, concerning the truth that self or ego was merely a temporary association of these *dharmas* and *skandhas*.

But more profound analysis, most notably by the second-century philosopher Nāgārjuna, showed that this Hīnayāna view was still naive. Not only did self or ego not exist, but the hypothesized *dharmas* and *skandhas* did not exist either. It was just as illogical to posit the existence of numerous components that would come together to form a temporary individual as it was to think that the individual was a thing-in-himself. A thoroughgoing analysis therefore led to the conclusion that there was literally nothing that had true existence, nothing that could be called a thing-in-itself. The Middle Way of Mādhyamika thus, by a relentless dialectic, destroyed completely the illusion that anything exists. So-called existence was equated with nonexistence. In the Chinese formulation, this result was expressed as follows:

> No production and no extinction; no enduring and no cutting off; no unity and no diversity; no arriving and no departing.

Since "existence" and "nonexistence" are in the last analysis identical, a name must be given the true condition. To avoid all characterizations (which would ipso facto be false), the name given is Void, or Emptiness (*śūnyatā* in Sanskrit, *k'ung* in Chinese). As one looks at the phenomenal world, one observes the "existence" of "things," and such observation has a relative validity. But when one attains enlightenment, one understands that from the level of absolute truth it is equally meaningless to think of any "thing" as either existing or nonexisting. In this paradox, the only true statement is that reality is "not this, not this"—and perforce one calls reality *k'ung*. This is strikingly reminiscent of the opening lines of *The Old Master (Lao Tzû)* (see Chapter 1, p. 4).

The Mādhyamika dialectic destroyed any ultimate "reality" to which one could cling, and in this sense it carried the mission of the Buddha to its logical conclusion. *Śūnyatā* became the central philosophical tenet of East Asian Buddhism. At the same time it provoked a reaction; by its complete denial of any conceivable reality, Mādhyamika seemed to go beyond logic and credibility. For this reason Asaṅga and Vasubandhu argued that *thought* at least must exist. Their Yogācāra school took a position similar to the general thesis of philosophical idealism in the West. "Knowledge" was explained on three levels: the illusory "commonsense" level; the relative level at which things are conceived as having temporary existence through a combination of components; and the true level, which is in fact the same as Mādhyamika. The distinctive feature of this school was its postulation of an "eighth kind of consciousness" (the *ālaya-vijñāna*) that was responsible for storing up and producing all *dharmas* and hence for the transmigratory cycle of *saṁsāra*, or suffering. Because of its assumption of the existence of this kind of consciousness, the school was known in China as Consciousness Only (*Wei Shih*). Its abstruse philosophical formulations made it less than popular among Chinese Buddhists.

By itself, this profounder philosophical analysis of the Mahāyāna (that is, Mādhyamika) would not have created a form of Buddhism distinctively different from that based on Pali texts. In our typically Western concern with the philosophical aspects of Buddhism, we must always remind ourselves that Buddhism is a religion, not a philosophy. The intellectual work of the Buddhist doctors was not, after all, the seeking of theoretical truth for its own sake; their purpose was to clarify various points concerning the meaning of, and the way to attain, the religious goal of enlightenment. The abstruse writings of these theorists, like the works of Christian theologians, provided the foundation for systematic doctrine but not the substance of the religious life. Probably only a very few Chinese Buddhists, either in the **Saṅgha** or lay devotees, ever thoroughly understood or even studied such difficult formulations of doctrine.

More pertinent to Buddhism as a religion is the Mahāyāna development in which Buddha, from the original signification of an enlightened human being, became in fact the equivalent of the Godhead in other religions. A form of docetism (the doctrine that the savior's mortal semblance was only illusion) interpreted the earthly career of Śākyamuni as a compassionate expedient for the salvation of humans, and this same explanation of expedience (*upāya*) became a general feature of the Mahāyāna movement. *Upāya* accounts for the variant teachings of the schools and justifies all the techniques whereby the Buddhist Law brings salvation to sentient beings.

Salvation in the earlier Buddhist teachings had been explained as the hard-won fruit of countless incarnations during which the aspirant disciplined himself to extinguish the passions tying him to the flux of existence. Its goal, called *nirvāṇa*, although never defined by Śākyamuni, seemed to be something negative, in the sense that it was the termination of one's connection with life. *Nirvāṇa* was earned by unremitting striving; it was a personal victory over ignorance. The teachings of Śākyamuni were a signpost, but one had to make one's own way to the goal.

Salvation in the Capacious Vehicle of the Mahāyāna was presented on two levels: To the man capable of the highest understanding, it was enlightenment about the Voidness of Reality and thus release from the torments of egoism; to the ordinary man it was pictured as a paradise where,

105

*Three Ways to
Ultimate
Transformation:
(3) Buddhist
Tradition*

*Kuan Shih Yin's saving power. By calling the bodhisattva's name in
faith, one will be saved from any disaster. Note demon causing fire and
believer standing in lotus, symbol of Buddhism. Wood-block print from a
popularly disseminated devotional tract.*

among the most beautiful and uplifting surroundings, the souls of believers heard from the Buddha Himself the words that would bring them to true enlightenment. Moreover, ordinary men were not left to their own feeble resources in the religious quest. Buddha was not just a sage who had left wise teachings for the guidance of his followers; He was an eternally subsisting Being, a Deity, and He actively succored all beings who longed for salvation.

In this great work, according to the Mahāyāna scriptures, Buddha Śākyamuni was assisted by countless **buddhas** and bodhisattvas. On the highest level, the Godhead (or Ultimate Reality, or Void) was of course One and ineffable. But on the relative level, the Principle of Buddha might be conceived as infinitely multiple. At the level where expedience (*upāya*) sought to meet the limitations of popular understanding, the buddhas and bodhisattvas became individualized deities, comprehensible and approachable by the ignorant masses. The bodhisattva, a being who had attained enlightenment and the limitless powers that enabled him to become Buddha, was the specific ideal of Mahāyāna. The individual, personal salvation won by the Hīnayāna *arhat* was denigrated as a selfish, limited ideal and was contrasted with the Mahāyāna ideal of the saint who—although he had won salvation—yet vowed to devote all his religious power to helping others along the way. In the Mahāyāna ordination, the monk therefore took the vow of the bodhisattva.

MONKS AND MONASTERIES

Monachism (monastic life) was a distinctive feature of Buddhism from the start. If one sought to follow the prescription of Śākyamuni, that the way to escape the wheel of rebirth and never-ending suffering was to cool the flames of desire into the ashes of nonattachment, one obviously had to leave the world of the home and the society in which desire and attachment were the motivating forces. The followers of the Buddha grew into a vast community, and it was necessary to devise rules for the government of this community. These rules, codified as the **Vinaya**, became one of the major divisions of the early Buddhist Canon. They were believed to have been promulgated by the Buddha Himself, and because of this belief they retained binding authority over all the Buddhist monastic communities through the centuries. Thus the Saṅgha, or monastic community, in China was under the same regulations as the Saṅgha everywhere, with only minor differences brought about by local conditions.

One difference was that Chinese monks often did not follow the original Indian tradition of mendicancy. The Chinese Saṅgha tended to live in settled fashion, grouped in individual monasteries that were usually supported by landholdings. Their economic base was the income from lands worked by tenant peasants. This more sedentary character of the Chinese Order was perhaps a result of the climatic difference from India, where only during the rainy season were the monks unable to wander freely. In part it would also have resulted from the difference in social traditions, that of China having little place for the wandering mendicant, in contrast to the age-old custom of India. Even more than in India, then, the monastery was in China the center of Buddhist life.

Chinese monasteries varied from huge to tiny, their population numbering hundreds or even thousands in the former case but including only the hut or cave of the solitary anchorite in the latter case. Some were famous centers of pilgrimage, noted for great teachers and honored by the State, but far more were isolated, obscure, and humble. Ideally they were built in places far from the contamination of the dusty world, where the quiet beauties of nature provided an inspirational setting for the religious life. In any Chinese landscape painting we can find one or more such Buddhist (or Taoist) retreats located in the sheltered valleys, admidst soaring peaks, rushing streams, and hoary pines. Not the least of their functions was to serve as hostels during the visits of lay devotees or ordinary persons seeking temporary refuge from the noise, the strife, and the tensions of society. To all their doors were open and their simple hospitality freely given. To layman and casual visitor alike they also offered the unaggressive evangelism of their physical arrangements: They were not only monasteries, or homes for the Saṅgha, but also temples, housing the icons of Buddhism that were deities to the simple and symbols of the Buddhist Truth or Law to the sophisticated.

It would be impossible to know what proportion of the Saṅgha were true seekers after religious salvation and what proportion were members for fortuitous reasons. There is no doubt that many were given by parents in fulfillment of religious vows. There is also no doubt that because of the structure of Chinese society, in which there was no place for unfortunates who for one reason or another had been displaced from their families, the Saṅgha served as a refuge. This "social security" function, although of course bringing into the Saṅgha many who were not religiously motivated, should not be deprecated on that account. It was certainly one aspect of Buddhism that contributed to its survival in the later ages of the Literati State, as may be indicated by the following remark typifying the attitude of the Literati:

> Buddhist monks and nuns are heretics among the people; yet throughout history they have not been abolished. For by this means the widower and the widow, the childless and the orphan, have available succor to save them from death. (*Gazetteer of Taiwan County*, 1720 edition)

A person often joined the Saṅgha by applying, or being given as a child, to the master of some small temple. Here he would receive training as a novice. A peculiarly Chinese aspect of this practice is that the relationship of master and novice was often considered the equivalent of the natural father-son relationship. Thus even in the celibate Buddhist Saṅgha, the Chinese family system retained its hold, with monk "families" continuing through many generations.

After preliminary studies, the novice would travel to some monastery noted for its great tradition of famous masters, and there he would apply for ordination. Only certain State-approved monasteries were authorized to issue the ordination certificate—which was thus, from one point of view, a license granted by the imperial government. Ordination involved

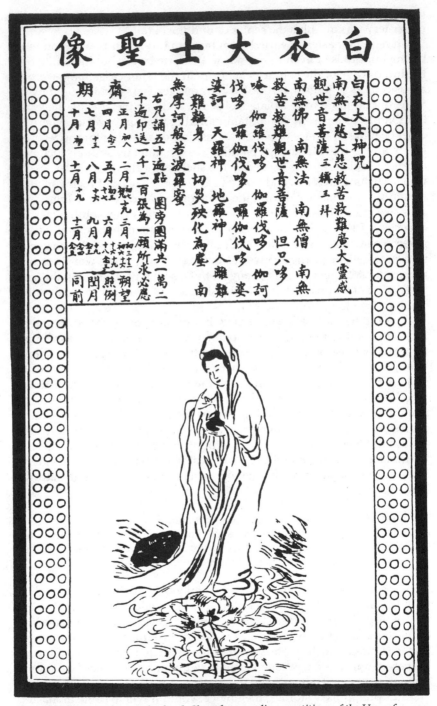

*Buddhism at the popular level. Sheet for recording repetitions of the Vow of
the White-Robed Bodhisattva, Avalokiteśvara (original Sanskrit for the Chinese Kuan Shih Yin or Kuan Yin). One of the circles is filled in for every
fifty repetitions. There are thus 12,000 repetitions recorded on this sheet. By
completing 1,200 sheets one's prayers will be answered without fail.*

109

*Three Ways to
Ultimate
Transformation:
(3) Buddhist
Tradition*

a longer or shorter period of study and training and was conferred in three stages. In later times these three stages, each originally requiring extensive preparation, were for practical reasons combined into a three-part ceremony concluded within a period of a few weeks or days. The bodhisattva vows were, as we have indicated, the important ones. These were (1) to lead all beings to salvation, (2) to seek to put an end to all pain and suffering, (3) to study all teachings of the Buddha, and (4) to seek to perfect oneself. After pronouncing these vows in impressive rituals supervised by duly authorized senior monks, the candidates were branded by burning incense on their shaven pates and became *hô-shang*, or full-fledged monks.

The newly ordained monk might either return to his original master to serve in the local temple and eventually to take over its administration, apply for permanent service in the monastery in which he had been ordained, or take to wandering from one monastery to another in order to visit all the holy places throughout the country. Any monk would be accepted for a few days' stay in any monastery on presenting his ordination certificate. The peripatetic career of such wandering monks is indicated by the picturesque name given to the monastery dormitory in which they were housed: the *yün-shui t'ang,* or hall of clouds and waters.

The life of the monk in the monastery was strictly regulated by the *Vinaya,* as we have said, and in addition each monastery had its local administrative routine. Duties were divided into various areas. These usually included study of the canonical literature (one or several sacred texts were often emphasized, according to the particular monastery or master),

Newly ordained Buddhist nuns.

meditation or yogic concentration, officiation at public or private worship services (especially the soul-masses) on request, and the daily housekeeping tasks. The more menial chores were performed by lay servants. Government of the monastery was in the hands of the abbot, who was elected by the monks, and his appointed officers. The abbot of an important monastery would be confirmed in office by the State—another indication of the State's close supervision of religious institutions. The power of the abbot within the monastery was, like that of the senior person in any Chinese institution, paternalistic, and it extended to the expulsion of any monk who committed a grave sin or who was incorrigibly nonconformist.

The monastery-temple, although open to visitors and even to long-term guests, was in no sense a church, nor were its resident monks engaged in religious work in the community. As we know, their major contact with the community nearby was in connection with the mortuary rites. The soul-masses might be performed in the home of the deceased or they might be held on the premises of the monastery itself. Occasionally, also, a patron of the monastery might request a lecture or a series of lectures on the Buddhist Dharma by a renowned scholar-monk, and at such times a congregation of sorts would assemble.

These scholar-monks, called *fa-shih* (or Dharma masters), were the elite among the Saṅgha. They were educated men with special competence in the highly technical literature of the enormous Buddhist Canon, and as such they often commanded great respect at the highest levels of Chinese society. But it is probable that in all ages the rank and file of the Saṅgha were only semi-literate, trained in the *Vinaya* ordinances, taught to perform the necessary rituals, and able to recite by rote a smattering of Chinese versions of the sacred texts and the unintelligible Sanskrit formulas. This is not, of course, to imply that such monks were necessarily inferior in religious attainments.

CHINESE BUDDHIST SCHOOLS

Most of the Indian Buddhist schools, as represented by their texts, came into China during the first five or six centuries CE. These schools, whose differences were mostly philosophical, must have presented a perplexing problem to the Chinese, who were not only faced with the difficulty of reconciling conflicting doctrines but were also unprepared by their own traditions to engage themselves in the sort of speculation that intrigued the Indian mind. In the upshot, what we shall call Chinese Buddhism, as opposed to Indian Buddhism in China, reflected the harmonizing, compromising temper of the Chinese mind, with its interest in practice rather than theory.

This harmonizing, compromising tendency is exemplified in the two great schools called T'ien-t'ai and Hua-yen. Both were founded in the latter part of the sixth century by Chinese masters, and both had as their rationale the thesis that the differences in Buddha's teachings as found in various texts were explainable as expedience, or *upāya*. Thus the Buddha, as a great teacher, understood that different approaches are necessary to meet the needs of different people. The task undertaken by the founders

of the Chinese schools was to find the order in the myriad scriptures and
to identify the progression of the Buddha's teaching from most elementary to most refined, from simplest to most comprehensive, and thus to
see the whole Canon and the various schools as one great system. Kenneth
Ch'en has summarized as follows:

111

*Three Ways to
Ultimate
Transformation:
(3) Buddhist
Tradition*

> The T'ien-t'ai School represented the Chinese attempt to establish a great
> eclectic school recognizing all forms of Buddhism. Through its compre-
> hensive and encyclopedic nature it had a place for all the Buddhist scrip-
> tures; it considered these scriptures as being gradually revealed by the
> master when he found that his audience was gradually beginning to
> understand his message better and better. The school saw no antagonism
> between the Hīnāyāna and Mahāyāna; all sutras were to be accepted as
> true words of the Buddha if they were considered as being taught during
> a certain period. The school, however, did believe the *Saddharma* [*Lotus
> Sūtra*] to contain the essence of all the teachings, and also taught that all
> men could become the Buddha, since all possessed the Buddha-nature.[1]

The T'ien-t'ai school's own theoretical standpoint has been called a sort
of pantheism: "there is no noumenon besides phenomenon; phenomenon
itself is noumenon. . . . All things have no reality and, therefore, are void.
But they have temporary existence. They are at the same time mean or
middle, that is true state, Thusness."[2] We recognize here the basic Mahāyāna position as formulated in the Mādhyamika treatises of Nāgārjuna.
According to T'ien-t'ai, as all beings are of the same Buddha-nature, all are
to attain Buddhahood eventually.

The Hua-yen school also arranged the teachings of the Canon in systematic progression but decided that the pinnacle of the Buddha's thought
was found in the *Avataṁsaka,* or *Garland Sūtra.* The philosophical conclu-
sions of the Hua-yen were similar to those of the T'ien-t'ai, but even more
universal:

> There is a world of *li* or ultimate principle* and a world of *shih* or phe-
> nomena, which are perfectly interfused with each other. At the same
> time each individual phenomenon is also unimpededly identified with
> every other phenomenon. A totalistic system is thus established, with
> everything leading to one point, the Buddha, in the center.
>
> Since all phenomena are manifestations of one immutable noumenon,
> they are in perfect harmony with one another, like the different waves of
> the same water. From the religious point of view everything in the uni-
> verse, animate and inanimate, are [*sic*] all representations of the same
> supreme mind, and can perform the work of the Blessed One.[3]

It will be seen that the establishment of these two Chinese schools, far
from compounding the sectarian division of Buddhism, in fact worked for
ecumenism. Neither claimed a monopoly of truth, and both acknowledged
the necessity of various teachings to suit various needs. They did try to de-
fine the highest truth, but they recognized the value and the validity of
what they considered to be only relative truth.

---

*This *li* is a different word from the *li* meaning ritually proper deportment.

The emphasis of the foregoing schools was on the universality of Buddhist salvation, based on the philosophical tenet that all creation shares in the Buddha-nature. But in their scholastic work of systematizing the order of the Canon, they did not yet arrive at a practical way of fully implementing this universal salvation. That way was developed by a third Chinese school, the Ching-t'u, or Pure Land. This school held that all men were capable of salvation and not just the few fortunate enough to be able to devote their whole lives to religion in the Saṅgha. The basis for this belief was, first, the universal Buddha-nature, and, second, the assertions in certain scriptures, notably the *Lotus Sūtra* and the *Larger* and *Smaller Sukhāvatī-Vyūha Sūtras* (translated in Chinese as *Sūtra of Limitless Longevity*), that unlimited mercy was available to the cry of faith. Specifically, the Pure Land was the realm established by the Bodhisattva Dharmākara in fulfillment of his vows on attainment of buddhahood as Amitābha or Amitāyus:

> When I have become a Buddha
> May my country be the highest,
> Its people rare and excellent,
> Its field-of-Truth superlative,
> The land as good as Nirvāṇa,
> Matchless and incomparable.
> Then in pity and compassion
> I will liberate all beings.
> Men from ten quarters who, reborn,
> Their hearts rejoicing and unstained,
> Have arrived inside my country
> Will dwell in peace and happiness.[4]

Entry into this paradise of Buddha Amitāyus* was won by devotion to the Buddha and by meritorious deeds but above all (and, in some interpretations, exclusively) by faith. The arduous practices of self-discipline, study, and yogic concentration were not required. The pietistic form of Buddhism, carrying the conception of the boundless compassion of the Savior to the logical extreme, went so far as to declare that the most sinful of men, if struck with contrition at the moment of death and able to call the name of the Savior only once in genuine faith, would be taken to the Western Paradise (as Amitāyus's kingdom was called). The practice of this school reduced itself to the reaffirmation of faith through frequent repetition of the sacred formula, *Nanmo Amit'o Fo,* Hail to Amitāyus Buddha! An important feature of the pietistic school was the evolution of the Bodhisattva Avalokiteśvara, the principal helper† of Amitāyus, into the most prominent deity not only of Ching-t'u but of the popular religion as well. As we saw in our discussion of the major deities of Taiwan (see Chapter 4), Avalokiteśvara is called "Kuan-yin" or "Kuan Shih Yin" in Chinese and has become a compassionate mother-figure in this popular religion.

It is easy to see why the Pure Land became the most popular school of Chinese Buddhism. It is perhaps not so easy to see why the fourth of the

---

*We believe *Amitāyus* is preferable, although the word *Amitābha* is generally used to render the Chinese term.

†In fact, Avalokiteśvara may be better described as an avatar of the Buddha.

great Chinese schools gained its dominant position. This was the school called Ch'an (a Chinese transliteration of the Sanskrit *dhyāna*, meaning "yogic concentration"), better known under its Japanese pronunciation and color, Zen. Like Ching-t'u, Ch'an was a reaction against the scholastic and formalistic preoccupations of other Buddhist schools, but unlike Ching-t'u, Ch'an offered no "easy road" to salvation through faith.

In one sense Ch'an was a return to the sort of Buddhism the Mahāyāna had deplored in Hināyāna schools: It taught that salvation was enlightenment concerning the true nature of Reality or Void (that is, the Mādhyamika *śūnyatā*) but that it had to be fought for and won in the Hināyāna way, through personal striving. The great mission of Ch'an was to reiterate the message so often proclaimed by Śākyamuni—namely, that the problem was suffering and that the only goal was the elimination of suffering. In other words, philosophy was not the essence of religion, scripture reading was not the method of religion, and there were no other powers (buddhas and bodhisattvas) "out there" to help the sufferer escape his predicament. Further, good deeds in themselves—although admirable and necessary—had nothing to do with achieving enlightenment, and no amount of ritual or magic could contribute an iota to salvation.

The adherents of Ch'an sought to cut directly through to the solution by means of the meditational techniques that would lead to the realization of truth, and in this also they may be said to be following the traditional account of the attainment of enlightenment by Śākyamuni. The tenets of Ch'an were summed up in a typically laconic Chinese formula:

> By mind transmitting to mind. No establishment of the written word. Transmission [of the teachings of the school] outside of the [orthodox] religion. Pointing directly to the human mind, and seeing the innate nature, one becomes Buddha: this mind is already Buddha.

Ch'an was thus a method, or one might say *the* method, to attain enlightenment, and its utter frankness in exposing the futility of all the other methods has sometimes led to accusations that it is actually not Buddhism at all. But as we have pointed out, not only was Ch'an in a real sense a return to the basic Buddhism of the Founder, but the Ch'an method was practiced to some extent in all schools. Besides, enlightenment was by no means the sole goal of Buddhism as a religion, and Ch'an monks led the same life of discipline, asceticism, and virtue as all their fellows in the Saṅgha. In the end, the centrality of the Ch'an technique was accepted in Chinese Buddhism, and it assumed the leading position among the Saṅgha schools.

Having briefly described the major Chinese schools, we should emphasize that Chinese Buddhism is, after all, essentially nonsectarian. The most striking thing about these Chinese schools is not their individualism but their harmonization. If to the four schools discussed above we add the Indian *Vinaya* school (called *Lü* in Chinese), which stressed the task of living up to the code enacted by Śākyamuni for cenobitic (monastic) life and was thus neither a philosophical school nor a school stressing particular techniques of enlightenment, we may see Chinese Buddhism as a whole in the following terms. The religious life has various requirements, even though one school may emphasize one aspect over another. These requirements are (1) intellectual understanding, or Buddhist wisdom (T'ien-t'ai and

Hua-yen), (2) faith (Ching-t'u), (3) meditation, or inner striving to enlightenment concerning *śūnyatā* (Ch'an), and (4) the life lived in moral self-
control under the discipline of the rules given by the Buddha Himself (Lü).
Thus in the Chinese view there was no real incongruity in the fact that adherents and practices of several schools were found under the same roof
in many monasteries. It should be emphasized that "school Buddhism"
was in China of concern only to the professional religious and that the ordinary Chinese would neither know nor care about such distinctions.*

In sum, the premise of Buddhism is that life is suffering, that suffering
arises from desires or passions, and that desires or passions arise from the
erroneous conviction that the ego exists. In Mahāyāna the religious quest
leads to enlightenment not only concerning the nonexistence of ego but
also concerning the illusory condition of all the phenomenal world. When
one has attained enlightenment, one is fully aware of the transcendental
character of ultimate Reality, one is "dead" to the desires of this world,
and one attains the wisdom and compassion of the bodhisattva.

---

*Most writers stress that in the recent millennium the living Chinese Buddhism has,
practically speaking, been reduced to Ching-t'u and Ch'an.

CHAPTER 9

Their Separate Ways: Cults and Sects

We now turn our attention to a significant form of religious life not comprehended under ancestor worship, community religion, the well-defined Three Ways, or religion of the State. We refer to cults, centered on charismatic leaders and often filled with messianic expectations. These were usually low-profile groups in the Chinese religion, but on occasion they developed into widespread sectarian movements. Such cults and sects were considered by the Chinese State as at best "unorthodox," and presumptively as "heterodox." But it has become increasingly apparent to scholars that large numbers of Chinese throughout history were drawn into such cultic groups. Even the Literati would sometimes become active in them, particularly those devoted to receiving communications from the gods through "spirit-writing" on the planchette. In this chapter, we shall briefly characterize the cults and sects.

CHARACTERISTICS OF LAY RELIGION

The number of persons of pious inclinations who were able to "leave the home" and take up the career of professional religious was, of course, always small. For a very much larger number, the satisfaction of religious needs was a matter of devotions practiced privately in the home or in the company of other like-minded householders. (The reader will keep in mind that we are now speaking of a level of religious concern beyond that of customary participation in communal activities.) Because the organized religions with which the Chinese were familiar were Buddhism and Taoism, those furnished the model for "nonprofessional" religion. The religion of devout laypeople thus tended to be a mixture in some proportion of Buddhist and Taoist beliefs and practices, of the universal ancestral cult, and of the persisting, age-old traditions of the peasantry. Literati influences were present in this mixture also, spread abroad by the ubiquitous storyteller, the popular drama, morality tracts, and a rich repertoire of proverbial sayings.

Because we are already somewhat familiar with these ingredients, it will not be necessary to spell out in detail the characteristics of lay religion. It is obvious that the degree of devotion would vary from individual to individual. Some, particularly among the old, perhaps, who had both fewer social responsibilities and more personal concern because of the imminence of death, would go as far as to retire completely from normal life and spend most of their time at their devotions, praying, chanting sacred texts, burning incense before their favored icons, and, in general, cultivating a sanctity calculated to win salvation in the coming existence. Others, with less leisure and more worldly responsibilities, would try to accumulate merit through good deeds and economic support of Buddhist and Taoist institutions. Vegetarianism was commonly practiced in the belief that all life was sacred and the killing of animals a cause of "bad *karma.*" Many laypeople regularly performed some variety of yogic meditation, whether for religious advancement or simply as a measure for promoting personal health and longevity.

RELIGIOUS SOCIETIES AND SECTS

Laypeople frequently banded together in religious societies, which would sometimes become identifiable as sects. Societies might have as their objective some limited purpose such as accumulating a joint fund to support group pilgrimages to famous holy mountains or to give special service in a temple of choice. Sometimes societies would be cultish in nature, centering about the worship of a particular deity or growing up around the charismatic personality of some self-proclaimed seer or healer. Most such cults were local and would have remained quite unknown in the historical record. Some were recorded by officials because they were considered to be dangerous to the State. Sects of this sort were usually persecuted ruthlessly.

In the Chinese polity there were few institutions standing between the State and the lineage with its families. Those that did exist, such as local communities, guilds, and Buddhist and Taoist monasteries, functioned only with permission from the State and were always responsible to the State. The imperial government interfered as little as possible with existing institutions, but institutional leaders were answerable for the behavior of members, and the government always held in reserve its absolute authority to intervene as it might see fit.

Any group of persons coming together privately to hold meetings, to celebrate rites and ceremonies, and to promote beliefs and practices not sanctioned by recognized precedent was automatically suspect in the eyes of the State. Such sub-rosa organizations were guilty of heresy in the official view, no matter how innocuous, or even benevolent, their beliefs and practices actually were. Even worse than heresy was the presumption that the true motives of an extralegal group were revolutionary. It was a fact, in this vast country, poorly connected by arteries of transportation, where

premodern communications were measured in days, weeks, or even
months, that a revolutionary movement could develop to dangerous proportions before the government could suppress it—or even learn of its existence. This suspicious and sometimes even paranoid attitude on the part
of government was responsible for the secrecy of many groups. That government's attitude was not entirely unjustified can be seen from historical
cases such as the so-called Yellow Turban insurrection of late Han, the activities of the White Lotus Society during Ming and Ch'ing times, and the
devastating Taiping Revolution of the mid-nineteenth century. These were
all cases where purely religious concerns eventuated in insurrectionist political aims. Religion cannot be discounted as a strong factor in Chinese
secular history.

A point of special note in this regard is the intimate connection, in the
Chinese tradition, between natural calamities, the sufferings of the people,
and the holding of the imperial sovereignty. Major disasters called into
question the Mandate of Heaven and gave plausibility to the claims of
messianic leaders that Heaven was about to dethrone the ruling house and
institute the reign of peace and prosperity so ardently hoped for by the
people. Texts were found and produced that were interpreted as fore-
telling such events, even to the arrival of the Millennium and the concomitant descent of a Buddha. It was Buddhism, in particular, that seems to
have provided such popular, **millenarian** ideas, and in evaluating the nature of Chinese Buddhism, we should take note of this aspect. Such popular, sectarian forms of Buddhism were, of course, aberrant from the
"orthodox" Buddhist tradition of the Saṅgha, but they were nevertheless
genuinely Buddhist in inspiration and iconography.

Despite the secrecy of most unorthodox groups and the frequent connection of religion and political rebellion, we should also note the interesting fact that some religious sects were bold enough to operate openly and
to propagandize their beliefs both orally and in writing. In this lies one feature that distinguishes religious sects from the well-known secret societies
of China, whose activities were antidynastic and, in modern times, often
criminal. It is worth remarking, in other words, that religious sects and secret societies had different motivations, at least when they started out.[1]

The religious teachings of societies and sects would range from lay
devotees' vows of Buddhism or Taoism to the most novel and ludicrous
rantings of self-proclaimed prophets. The range is comparable to that familiar in the West, where the layperson may belong to an old, established,
conservative denomination; may be caught up in the emotionalism of a
fundamentalist revival; or may be drawn to the peculiar doctrines of an
extremist cult. Whatever the case, the widespread occurrence of cults and
sects is ample testimony to the universal longing for material and spiritual
salvation shared by the Chinese people.

CHAPTER 10

The Festival Year

Cutting across social groups and voluntary institutions is the series of annual festivals observed by the entire nation. Although many of these have in the course of time become drained of religious meaning (just as few of our present holidays are still holy days), almost all of them derived from religious origins, and the majority continued to carry at least some religious significance.

The almanac told the people when the festival days were to occur each year, and the traditions of ages prescribed how they were to be celebrated. Still, there were any number of customs that varied from place to place. For this reason every gazetteer or local history had a section in which the festival calendar (*sui-shih*) of the particular locality was described in detail. Here we shall list only a few of the outstanding festivals that were universally observed and some of the typical ways in which they were celebrated.

NEW YEAR

The concept of the New Year is, of course, of great symbolic meaning among every people. In China it was by far the most important and elaborate of all the universal festivals. It actually began in the twelfth month when, about ten days before the end of the year, government offices (*yamen*) throughout the country closed down (literally, "sealed up their seals," *fêng-yin*), not to reopen for business until about a month later. Then, on the twenty-third day of the twelfth month, in every home the God of the Cooking Stove (Tsao Chün or Tsao Wang) was sent off to heaven to report to the Supreme Emperor of Jadelike Augustness (Yü-huang Shang-ti), celestial ruler in the Taoist and popular pantheons.

Tsao Chün, like the local earth god, has an importance in the lives of the people out of all proportion to the humbleness of his icons. He is ordinarily represented by a cheap and gaudy print that is pasted on the wall above the stove. This deity, whose worship dates back to the mid-second century BCE, is both guardian of the hearth and arbiter of longevity (in which role he is called Ssû-ming Fu-chün). His place behind the stove is strategically located for him to carry out the important function of keeping a daily record of the words and actions of the family, the sum of which it is his duty to report on his annual visit to Heaven. A detail that writers are fond of mentioning is the custom of smearing his mouth with some sugary substance before transmuting him to the ethereal realm by burning, so that he will have only "sweet" things to tell.

As arbiter of the length of life that will be enjoyed by each family member, his function naturally seems a more serious one. How seriously this function is actually taken no doubt varies according to individual belief. But it is in his role as deity of the kitchen range that he seems most significant. Because, whatever the "historical" background for this role, it is the stove that in fact stands for the unity of the Chinese family. As a number of recent studies have pointed out, "division of the stove" is both a symbolical and an actual event marking the splitting of the family, that is, the establishment of separate households by brothers after the death of their parents.

Tsao Chün returns to the home on New Year's Eve, when a new picture is pasted up over the stove. His is not the only symbol of renewal that goes up at this time: During the days preceding the New Year, every household puts up new "spring couplets" on either side of the gate and across the lintel. These are written on lucky red paper and consist of mottoes expressing the pious hope for blessings of all kinds to descend on the household during the coming year. And then on the leaves of the gates themselves are pasted bright pictures of fierce warriors who serve as guardians of the gate.

Rituals of New Year's Eve are for the family to observe within its own doors, which are sealed until the following morning. These rituals include the worship of Heaven and Earth, of the tutelary deities of the home, and of the ancestors. At the conclusion of these rites comes the family feast, which is attended by all members who can possibly be there—but by no outside guests. This ecumenical meal is another of the numerous practices by which family unity is reaffirmed. It is followed at midnight by an even more explicit ritual—all family members come forward in order of precedence to prostrate themselves and touch their foreheads to the floor (kowtow) to the family head and his wife.

The religious and familial rites having thus been performed, the first few days of the New Year are devoted to pleasure and relaxation and to paying courtesy calls on one's seniors and superiors. All business is at a standstill, even nowadays for as long as a week and in past times for almost the entire first month.

Two religious ceremonies of importance that occurred during the first two weeks were the family and communal worship of Ts'ai Shên, God of Wealth, and the official performance of the rituals connected with the beginning of spring (*li ch'un*, first of the twenty-four "seasons" of the lunar calendar). In imperial times the emperor himself opened the agricultural year by ceremonially plowing a special field in the capital, this being emulated by the chief officials in every locality. Then came the religious procession headed by the "spring ox," an effigy whose color predicted the climatic conditions of the coming year (based on information contained in the newly published almanac). Many other symbolic items and actions connected with this procession had to do with hopes for a prosperous agricultural year.

The first (new moon) and fifteenth (full moon) are naturally to an agricultural people the most noticeable markers of time in the lunar months, and it is not surprising that many ritual observances fall on one or both of these days. In the case of the New Year, it is the first full moon that marks the end of the celebrations. This is the time for the lantern festival, originally of religious derivation, but in later centuries mostly a holiday in which enjoyment of the beauty and ingenuity of the lanterns is the principal feature, along with parades featuring the dancing of lions and dragons accompanied by a hubbub of music and drumming.

THIRD MONTH

The second of the great universal festivals falls 105 days after the winter solstice or, in recent times, on the third day of the third month. This is the fifth of the twenty-four lunar seasons, whose climatic character in north China gave it the name "clear and bright" (*ch'ing ming*). It is the most important of the three special occasions of the year for visiting the ancestral tombs, renovating them, and sacrificing to them. As such it is part and parcel of the complex of continuing sacrifices to the *manes*, which we have discussed in our chapter on the family. Here we should point out that in all these ancestral rites there are specific foci of interest. The vast majority of the ancestors inevitably pass into oblivion, or at least are only lumped together as the "common ancestors," while the attentions of the living center either on their immediate, rememberable generations or else on the most important figures of the past—notably the founding ancestor of the lineage. It is to these tombs that the family goes on *ch'ing ming* and other days of remembrance, as it is from these tombs that "good *fêng-shui*" may be sought.

The twenty-third day of the third month is the birthday of T'ien Hou, Imperial Consort of Heaven (see p. 57). Having been adopted into the official calendar of sacrifices, her birthday was marked everywhere in the empire. However, because she is primarily the protector of seafarers and her cult developed south of the Yangtze River, the great popular festivals are found in the southeastern coastal provinces.

FOURTH MONTH

The supposed birthday of the Buddha Śākyamuni occurs, according to Chinese calculations, on the eighth day of the fourth month. This is an occasion celebrated primarily by the Saṅgha. The principal rite is the "bathing of the Buddha," in which the Buddha image is laved with scented water.

The temples will be filled, and there may be elaborate processions with the Buddha image borne in state by the monks.

FIFTH MONTH

The third major universal celebration is that popularly known as the dragon boat festival, placed (in accordance with another Chinese propensity) on "double five," or the fifth day of the fifth month. The dragon boat races may very well represent the fighting of dragons in the skies and hence be related to abundance of rainfall, for which the dragon is responsible in Chinese lore. The festival is quite different in the north, which lacks the rivers and lakes on which such spectacles can be staged. The rationale of the boat races has long been understood as a reenactment of the search for the drowned poet Ch'ü Yüan, who committed suicide in ancient times because his honest counsel was spurned by his lord. The triangular-shaped dumplings traditionally eaten on this day are likewise supposed to stand for the food that the sorrowing people dropped into the water for Ch'ü Yüan's spirit.

But it would seem logical to seek the true origin of this important festival in the occurrence of the summer solstice, which falls at about the same time. This, of course, marks the highest expansion of the fructifying influence of *yang* and the beginning of its gradual displacement by *yin*, an event of great significance in the Chinese worldview. However, the double-five festival is one of those that has declined into a mostly secular occasion.

SEVENTH MONTH

The seventh month sees the second of the major periods in the annual round that focuses on the ancestors. During this entire month, the gates of purgatory stand open and the souls of those who have no ancestral sacrifices—the bereaved spirits—are free to wander about in the invisible dimension that impinges upon the mortal world. During this month, many special measures are taken by the living to placate these ghosts and avert harm. The fact that a whole month is involved in this problem of bereaved spirits is eloquent testimony to the profound importance of ancestral sacrifices.

But though this is, as we know, a native cult of the highest antiquity, it has, like most aspects of the mortuary rites, been largely taken over by Buddhism (and to a lesser extent Taoism). The bereaved spirits are identified with the Indian *preta*. The great services of sacrifice that take place in the middle of the month are called *yü-lan hui*, which is a Chinese rendering of the Sanskrit term *Avalambana*. The officiants are monks who recite from the canonical Chinese text that tells of the filial piety of Mu-lien (Maudgalyāyana), who rescued his mother from the torture of the hell in which souls cannot eat. This he was able to do by the grace of the Buddha, who instructed him to make offerings on the fifteenth day of the seventh month to seven generations of ancestors. The ritual is called "ferrying across [to the other shore of salvation] all [souls in limbo or purgatory]" (*p'u tu*), a Buddhist term. The populace participates in the extensive ceremonies, particularly through their generous offerings.

EIGHTH MONTH

No festival is more common, throughout the world, than the celebration of the autumn harvest. In China this has been transformed into a celebration of the beauty of the harvest moon, at its most perfect on the fifteenth night of the eighth month. Although its religious element long ago faded, this festival is one of the most popular in the year. The traditional gift is circular "moon cakes," and the people feast outdoors, enjoying the glorious moon until late at night.

NINTH MONTH

If the moon festival celebrates the most conspicuous *yin* force in the heavens, the "double *yang*" (*ch'ung yang*) is, in name at least, the polar opposite. Alas for our hope to find some significant symbolism; the name simply reflects the fact that the unbroken lines in the diagrams of the *Yi Ching* are technically called nines, and this festival falls on the ninth day of the ninth month. No religious element seems to remain in what is a minor event in the festival calendar, marked only by picnics (preferably in the hills) and kite flying.

TENTH MONTH

On the first day of the tenth month, the ancestors are especially remembered for the third time, as the family pays ritual visits to their tombs. In addition to the usual sending of mock paper money, the family provide the dead with paper effigies of warm clothes for the winter and any other articles it is thought they might want. The ritual is called "sending cold weather clothes" (*sung han yi*).

TWELFTH MONTH

Various observances during the twelfth month are, as we have seen, a prelude to the great festival of the New Year. The winter solstice is marked by sacrifices as the day on which the potency of *yin* reaches its extreme, to be gradually replaced by the life-nurturing power of *yang*. On the eighth day of the month, it is the custom to serve friends with a special gruel made of many ingredients, which is also presented as an offering to the Buddha. This is called *la-pa chou*, and the entire month is sometimes designated by the first word of the term. (*La* was the name of a sacrifice connected with the winter solstice in antiquity; *pa* means the "eighth [day]"; and *chou* means "gruel.") Then come the "sealing up of the seals" and the ritual of sending Tsao Chün to Heaven, and the old year gives way again to the new.

All the festivals are timed in accordance with the lunar, agricultural calendar, and even official adoption of the solar calendar decades ago and its everyday use have not affected the universal usage of the old calendar in governing celebration of the festival year; it is this calendar that is still printed in the almanac.

CHAPTER 11

Traditional Chinese Religion as Means of Coping

In the preceding chapters we have attempted to analyze the various characteristics of religion in the traditional Chinese culture. In the present chapter we shall endeavor to synthesize these—what we have called, in the aggregate, "Chinese religion"—in order to show how they make up an unpremeditated "system" that comes to grips with life's unavoidable problems. The responses to these problems, on the other hand, we have claimed to be manifestations of the Chinese culture, and which we believe in fact to constitute the essence of that culture. Although these responses are "functional," we prefer to consider them on the model of what Arnold Toynbee, in his *A Study of History*, calls "challenge and response." In this chapter, then, we change our focus from Frederick Streng's concept of religion as "means to ultimate transformation" to religion as "means of coping with existential problems."[1]

What are the problems to which we allude? Our list includes suffering; the unpredictable quirks of Fate; human inadequacy in vital tasks; the meaninglessness of life; authority and submission; the omnipresence of evil; and, of course, death. Man is driven by circumstances to seek an end to suffering, courage to meet his unavoidable trials, superhuman help in his most urgent responsibilities, assurances that existence is meaningful, ultimate sanctions for conditions of power and subservience in his society, comfort in the thought that eventually good will triumph despite the flourishing of evil today, and at the last, salvation, or the victory of the self over pitiless Time. In addition, one cannot overlook what seems to be the nearly universal longing to worship and surrender to a higher Power—what in Indian terms is called *bhakti.* Now let us take up each of the foregoing challenges in turn and briefly describe how the Chinese responded to them religiously.

SUFFERING

125
*Traditional
Chinese
Religion as
Means of
Coping*

"... Oh! suffering world
Oh! known and unknown of my common flesh,
Caught in this common net of death and woe,
And life which binds to both! I see, I feel
The vastness of the agony of earth,
The vainness of its joys, the mockery
Of all its best, the anguish of its worst;
Since pleasures end in pain, and youth in age,
And love in loss, and life in hateful death,
And death in unknown lives, which will but yoke
Men to their wheel again to whirl the round
Of false delights and woes that are not false ..."

Thus, the future Buddha, as Sir Edwin Arnold imagines him to cry out when he has felt the full import of the Four Signs.[2]

As we know (see Chapter 8) Buddhism is the religion that arose in response to the perception that existence itself is suffering, and Chinese Buddhism is thus the most direct Way of dealing with this category. However, the Buddhism of the Chinese masses was the Mahāyāna, in which suffering beings were succored by divine power. How much the Chinese conceptions of divine power are derivative from the Buddhist bodhisattva, and how much they had already arisen independently, is a problem to which we do not have the answer. But certainly the Buddhist influence was important.

What we do know to be a fact is that Buddhism brought the Indian idea of karma to China, and along with karma came the notion of "karmic justice," which involved postmortem punishment in purgatories as well as rebirth in a form commensurate with one's good and evil acts in the previous existence. Such ideas, which came to permeate the Chinese culture, served both as "carrot-and-stick" influences on behavior, and as morally satisfying explanations of apparently immoral existential situations. The fear of postmortem punishment and degradation in rebirth impelled Chinese to call upon the liturgical expertise (or magical power) of the professional religious, both Buddhist and Taoist, to influence the supernaturals to overlook sins and raise the future status of their deceased seniors.

Suffering is not conceived as always karma-induced, of course. One had to reckon with malevolent spirits and displeased ancestors. One performed divination to discover where the problem lay and again called in religious specialists to perform the appropriate rituals (see Chapter 2). Supplication, sacrifices, the making and carrying out of vows of propitiation, and exorcism were methods of dealing with malevolent spirits. As for displeased ancestors, one discovered through divination that they were not being given the appropriate sacrifices (as necessary for them as food is for the living human) or were consigned to an unacceptable tomb.

Since "suffering" is really an all-inclusive category, it would be tedious to specify its endless particulars. We may limit our consideration to the conspicuous case of disease, always and everywhere one of the most devastating causes of suffering. Technical means of coping with disease notwithstanding, in no time or place has disease been eliminated. For those in dire straits, the only recourse has often been supernatural help. In many cultures, including the traditional culture of China, the cause of disease has been thought to be as likely supernatural as physical. The expertise of the physician trained in traditional Chinese medical lore was effective only for the latter; when the disease appeared to be cosmic (caused by the sufferer's particular place in the Great Scheme of Things), karmic (caused by the sufferer's own behavior in a previous existence), or the result of the attacks of malevolent spirits, religious expertise was called for.

In fact, healing in human cultures is never a monopoly of physicians. Whether their skills are trained in one of the traditional systems or in modern scientific schools, they are always in short supply, and people turn to faith healing either by necessity or by choice. Of course for many thousands of years all healing was essentially faith healing, its practitioners shamans or similar specialists who claimed to transmit supernatural power to the healing of the sick. It is perhaps not irrelevant to remind ourselves that faith healing is still, in the modern scientific milieu of the West, a conspicuous phenomenon—whether practiced by religious specialists or by psychiatrists.

QUIRKS OF FATE

Religious responses are evoked above all when the particular worldview of any group of people is suddenly faced with anomalies, when expectations of regularity and dependability systematized in that worldview are confounded. Conditions of extreme emergency call forth deep-seated hopes for supernatural succor. Crises such as earthquake or flood, drought or famine, war or pestilence, arouse people to their utmost efforts to ward off disaster, but when human beings have done their best, the rest is, as the saying goes, in the lap of the gods.

The Chinese have responded to these unexpected crises, or quirks of fate, just like everyone else, praying for the mercy of whatever gods there be. One special feature of the Chinese case should be pointed out, however. According to the Chinese worldview, such quirks of fate were due to the failure of Man, especially as represented in the person of the Son of Heaven—the Emperor—to do his part in maintaining the blend and balance of natural operations. More than this, the manifestations of maladjustments in natural operations were ominous of Heaven's displeasure with the rule of its human representative, and thus of a possible "change of the Mandate." In other words, it was a time of great danger but also of great opportunity: The will of Heaven was unsettled, and the legitimacy of the ruling dynasty in question. Such readings of crisis events must be counted among the most common causes of the many uprisings against established authority in Chinese history, including the eruptions of rebellions by millenarian sects.

HUMAN INADEQUACY

Human inadequacy is obviously another broad category that might subsume almost all challenges and religious responses. However, we use it here to refer to those situations in which people undertake activities whose outcome is of vital importance but remain uncertain of success because of factors beyond human control. An evident example of such an undertaking is an activity whereby the group obtains its basic necessities. In a hunting culture life depends upon finding and killing game; in an agrarian culture like that of traditional China the crops must thrive if existence is to be assured.

Because agriculture, especially in premechanized conditions, is always perilously dependent upon nature, it was to the powers of nature that the farmer addressed his supplications. Much of the peasant's religious preoccupation is thus with warding off the blights of weather and crop disease, which he could only assume were supernaturally caused.

Similarly, the artisan, such as the caster of bronze or iron or the firer of ceramics, was conscious of the limitation of his own ability to guarantee success. His undertakings were therefore carried out under the auspices of deities whose special province was that of the particular craft (or business) concerned. Without the patronage of supernaturals, every occupation was hazardous. In the traditional cultures people had not yet attained a sense of self-confidence in their unaided efforts.

MEANINGLESSNESS OF EXISTENCE

Existence is inherently meaningless. Meaning is something human beings, presumably alone among the creatures, somehow create and project upon their environment and themselves. Meaning is individually thought and felt, yet in many ways socially expressed and nurtured. Even when it seems to be purely individual, it has been, as we know, to a great extent "socialized" into us. This is obvious, for example, in our ethical values, which we absorb from our family and community long before we give them any self-conscious deliberation. It is also true about the notions we hold of the relationships between humans and the rest of the world, including supernaturals. The creation, transmission, and reinforcement of certain meanings that have been accepted within a culture as incontrovertible—"We hold these truths to be self-evident"—is studied in anthropology and religion as myth and ritual. Myth and ritual may in turn be subsumed under the comprehensive rubric of symbolism, a mode of expressing meanings more concisely, immediately, and impressively than by verbal definition. Those kinds of meanings that are not expressible in words may find expression in the arts, whose products themselves never cease to evoke by their intriguing ambiguity additional inexpressible meanings. In general, one may say that profundity of meaning is in a spectrum that goes inversely to verbal clarity: from words through visual representation through kinetic and musical revelation. From the point of view

of religion, the extreme end or ultimate form of this spectrum is just si-
lence. In the highest truth of Mahāyāna Buddhism this is enlightenment as
to the essential "emptiness" of all things whatsoever. It was already set
forth in the *Lao Tzû* (chapter 56):

> One who knows the Tao does not talk about it;
> One who talks about it knows it not.
> Block the road, shut your gate, subdue your ardor, do away
> with your inner divisions, dim your light, and become one
> with the dusty world. This is called realizing the original
> identity of all things. . . .

Meaning seems to involve two interrelated kinds of mental constructs:
worldview and value. By the former we mean the work of the mind that
makes sense of, or confers order upon, a universe of an infinite variety of
phenomena. By the latter we mean the assigning of relative value to social
relationships and to all of the other products of a culture. For life to have
meaning in the religious sense of the word, the world must be recognized
as a cosmos, a system in which the place of humankind is not only defined,
but in some way important.

We have already (in Chapter 1) shown how the Chinese gave meaning
to the world by means of their "gestalt cosmology"; one might say this
worldview enabled them to avoid alienation in space. Similarly (as we
have outlined in some detail in Chapter 3) by means of "familism" they
avoided alienation in time. The ancestor cult, the carrying on of family relationships through time, provided basic psychological security just as the
family organization provided social security. The ancestor cult assured
that the family system in which the individual had been subordinated all
of his or her life was triumphant over death itself. It was a self-fulfilling
cycle of meanings from life to death and back to life. The individual did
not face the endless emptiness of time alone and helpless; one was a link
in the continuous chain of being that was conceived as an organismic reality. This view sanctioned and gave meaning to the elaborate codes of behavior (*li*) that worked to perpetuate the system and thus served the
essential purpose of establishing social values. When a person knew how
to live, and knew that death did not cut him or her off from life, existence
was no longer meaningless.

AUTHORITY AND SUBMISSION

The preceding words will already have indicated the extent to which the
religious view of the Chinese derived from solutions to the problem of authority and submission within the family. This is not of course to say that
the Chinese were always happy about their family system, in which from
the present-day point of view there was an intolerable repression of
women and the young. Nevertheless, it seems to have served human needs
at least as well as any other family system over a very long period of time.
Insofar as psychological security resides in well-defined "rules of the

game," the Chinese system was admirably unambiguous, resting upon the unquestionable authority of males and seniors and the generally accepted submission of females and juniors. In this respect, as we have seen in Chapter 3, the elaborate and detailed codes of *li* not only ritualized the myths, formed the basis for legal and governmental controls, and influenced to a decisive degree the Chinese notions of the Good Society but had already, in ancient times, given religious sanctions for authority and submission in that society. One can see the basic, all-pervasive, religious dominance of these ancient convictions—as summed up in the Literati Tradition—in the seemingly endless struggle to throw off that Tradition in our times.

This reminds us that the interrelationship of religion and society is to be found in the political system as well. Until early in the twentieth century one of the classical cases of "kingship" was to be found in the Chinese polity. This was the archetype in which, unlike in ancient Egypt or Japan, the sovereign himself was not divine, but his authority was divinely sanctioned. However, as we have pointed out, that divine sanction (the Mandate of Heaven) was conditional upon the continuing satisfaction of Heaven with the ruling dynasty, and it could be removed and given to another line for due cause. Submission was not, therefore, unconditional and permanent, and Chinese religious convictions always supported the right of rebellion under unbearable oppression.

OMNIPRESENCE OF EVIL

Like all values, the moral law is a human construct and not something given in nature. In fact, many have pointed to the moral law as precisely that which raises humans above the animal level, where the governing law is simply big fish eat small fish.

Inevitably, it is the very acceptance of the moral law that produces the omnipresence of evil. Whatever contravenes the moral law is evil, and in the nature of things there will always be plenty of contravention. Although society attempts to keep the moral law effective by means of its criminal laws, such efforts are conspicuously limited in success. The religious question arises as to why, in a cosmos that, particularly in China, is conceived to be a moral order, evil should exist. Then there is the even more practical question as to why the moral law should be obeyed when evil people flout it with seeming impunity and benefit to themselves. This is the challenge to the conscience to which Master K'ung refers when he says, "The victory [of right] in the [moral] struggle [within a man's heart] may be called virtue" (*Analects* VI.20).

In many cultures the struggle between good and evil is projected onto the transcendental level and made into a struggle between the ultimate Powers of the universe, God and Devil, who use humans as their pawns. The Chinese did not explain evil in such terms, despite their recognition of spiritual agencies in suffering. They placed it squarely upon the shoulders of man himself, as a morally responsible agent.

The problem of evil received its most satisfactory solution in China with the acceptance of the theory of karma as brought in by Buddhism. As we have already alluded to this theory several times, we do not need to spell it out here.

DEATH AND SALVATION

Dying can be subsumed under suffering, but death itself is indubitably *sui generis* as well as the inevitable, inescapable, unpredictable fate of all living beings. So basic is this fact that some students of religion have attributed to it the very existence of religion. However this may be, it is certainly the case that responses to death in Chinese culture—in the form of rituals, funerals, mourning, sacrifice, and caring for the soul in its postmortem state—have been predominant in the religion. As we have in Chapter 3 already outlined this situation we need not explain it here, and we shall confine our remarks to a few supplemental observations. For one thing, we note that religious responses to the challenge of death are designed to affirm by every possible ritual the continuing, unbroken relationship of deceased and survivors. This is in striking contrast to the purpose of death cults in many other cultures, where the dead are feared, and efforts are made to assure that their separation from the living is total and irrevocable. Chinese religion, for its part, comforts one facing the prospect of death with the knowledge that he or she will, as it were, remain a communicating member of the family. The survivors are in this religious tradition comforted by the belief that they will make such a continuing relationship possible through performing their many rituals.

Here again Buddhism has filled out many apparently previously ambiguous suppositions, with its system of purgatorial examination and punishment, of rebirth in accordance with karmic justice, and above all, of counteracting Saviors of the Dead, the Bodhisattva Kṣitigarbha (Ti Tsang Wang in Chinese) and the Buddha Amitāyus, who by their grace can and will bring the deceased out of purgatory to the Western Paradise in accordance with the teachings of the Pure Land. In this connection, also, one should remark on the adaptation of the Buddha Śākyamuni's disciple, Maudgalyāyana, to the popular cult of the dead, in the shamanic character of Mu-lien, a monk who goes to purgatory to save his mother. The symbolism, as acted out in innumerable funeral dramas throughout China, has had an irresistible appeal in the Chinese familistic culture and in ritual is played out indifferently by Buddhist, Taoist, or even lay performers.

Salvation, the overcoming of Time, thus appears in two guises in the Chinese religion. On the one hand it means subsisting after death as an ancestor; on the other, it means gaining the Buddha's paradise or some form of blissful immortality according to Taoist notions. In either case it depends ultimately upon the filiality of the survivors. This makes their responsibility for performing the appropriate rituals very heavy. It also gives them the satisfaction of feeling that they are able to cope with the crisis of death effectively.

131

*Traditional
Chinese
Religion as
Means of
Coping*

*The First Court of Purgatory, where all the sins of the dead are read to
them from the ledger kept there and the appropriate punishments to be
inflicted therefor are pronounced. From a text produced at a "spirit-writing"
session, in which a deity reveals the details of the supernatural realm (in
this case purgatory) to cult members via the "automatic writing" stick
wielded by a specialist who is in trance. (Taichung, Taiwan)*

BHAKTI

Judging from the religious attitudes found in many cultures, the impulse to worship, to surrender to some Higher Power, is quite universal. At the end of Chapter 4, we quoted a description of the emotional reaction to a religious parade, and those "emotions of reverence, awe, and wonder" may be seen on the faces of Chinese in many circumstances of ritual processions, visits to temples, and other occasions where the images of deities are the focal point of attention. It seems significant that such female deities as Kuan Shih Yin and the Holy Mother in Heaven are especially the objects of fervent devotion, indicating perhaps that male dominance in Chinese society is counterbalanced by a deep underlying dependence upon maternal compassion as exemplified in these saviors. However this may be, we need to recognize the propensity of the Chinese for bhakti, or loving devotion to their gods.

A SUMMING UP

In this chapter on religion as means of coping we have looked at Chinese religion as a set of existential challenges and religious responses, which include the following: *Suffering:* Buddhism's understanding that existence itself is suffering has made a deep impression, and Buddhism's explanation of karmic causation has been largely accepted by the Chinese. Aside from karmic causation, the Chinese have retained the belief that the innumerable forms of suffering are caused by supernatural agents whose attacks can be dealt with by various ritualistic techniques. The problem of disease is a complicated case in which karma, the attacks of spirits, the cosmic situation, and physical factors are all involved. *Quirks of Fate:* When overwhelmed by disasters that upset the dependable regularity of nature, in China as elsewhere people have recourse to supernatural aid. In China, however, natural disasters were sometimes interpreted as signs of Heaven's displeasure with its human deputy, and this might lead to rebellions and millenarian uprisings against the political establishment. *Human Inadequacy:* The limited ability of man to influence the outcome of vitally important activities, particularly in times before technical means permitted confidence in human competence, led the Chinese, like people of all cultures, to seek the favorable intervention of the numinous Powers concerned. *Meaninglessness of Existence:* Without imputing value to one's life and significance to one's existence in this great universe, one is literally lost. In China, human beings were integrated into a "gestalt" universe of Heaven, Earth, and Man that overcame their potential alienation in space. The ultimate value of familism was the social as well as individual response to such alienation in time. *Authority and Submission:* Through their familistic (rather than individualistic) social system Chinese learned well-defined roles, and this generally carried over into the political sphere. Chinese kingship, which gave a ruling dynasty its sacred legitimation, was dependent upon the ruler's carrying out his duties to Heaven and Man and was revokable (something which happened many times in history) when the ruler failed in these basically religious responsibilities. *Omnipresence of Evil:* Evil is flouting of the humanly devised moral law. The Chinese did not personalize evil as a transcendent Power but generally accepted the Buddhist theories of karma, purgatorial punishments, and rebirth as accounting for the moral or immoral situation. For the Literati, in addition to recognition of these Buddhist ideas, there was the obligation of conforming with the ethical teachings of Master K'ung and the great exemplars of his School. These ethical teachings in fact permeated the world of the common people as well. *Death and Salvation:* The mystery and perplexities of death were addressed by both Buddhism and Taoism, and by the ancient native tradition as well. Although Buddhism (followed by Taoism) convincingly showed that all persons must go to the purgatorial realm after death, and there suffer for their many sins, there were ways of saving the soul of the deceased through ritual and prayer, whereby that soul could bypass the unpleasantness of purgatory and its terrible punishments, and go directly to paradise. These rituals and prayers became on the one hand the concern of religious specialists, and on the other the means whereby survivors could take comfort that they had done what should be done to assure their deceased family members' salvation. Perhaps such responses also lightened the fear of death among those survivors, who must anticipate their own demise. *Bhakti:* The well-nigh-universal impulse to worship and surrender to the numinous Power in which one has faith is found in the Chinese religion as elsewhere in the form of ritual acts of devotion.

CHAPTER 12

The Disruption of Tradition

The Chinese civilization was, until the mid-nineteenth century, essentially an original, self-contained system. It was a civilization that historically had been superior to its neighbors and that had indeed been the source of the high cultures of all East Asia.

This Chinese civilization was immensely long-lived, rich, and satisfying to the Chinese. It had the scope and the local variations of a grand continental scale but the pervading unity of a great traditional culture. The only imported influence of significance in this civilization was Buddhism—which in its turn was profoundly modified in its accommodation to Chinese ways. The Chinese view of nature and man, and the Chinese social practices (*li*), have not changed in any great measure since ancient times. That is why in this book we have been able to describe Chinese religion without specifying the historical tense.

During the past century and a half, however, China entered a new era. Its civilization was no longer self-contained, evidently superior, or even satisfying to the Chinese people. By the rude insistence of the aggressive Western powers during the nineteenth century, and by the even more irresistible impact of modern science and technology and all that these bring in their train, China was forced into an unprecedented situation. Part of the problem was the necessity to modernize without the gradual evolutionary process that brought Europe from medieval to modern conditions. Even more serious was the trauma resulting from the realization that the whole position of China had altered so that, far from being the center of human culture, she was now, in fact, a backward culture in a modern world.

THE TURBULENT TWENTIETH CENTURY

During the first half of the twentieth century, the most salient characteris-
of China was turbulent change—political upheaval, rampant mili-
an economy struggling to emerge from medieval limitations, a

dangerously burgeoning population, a succession of tremendous natural disasters resulting in famines and plagues of unimaginable dimensions, a society torn between tradition and modernization. The political and military chaos that had always accompanied the "change of the Mandate" when one dynasty replaced another was exacerbated to unprecedented degrees by the involvement of Western and Japanese imperialistic pressures and interventions, culminating in the full-scale invasion and occupation of much of China by Japanese armies from 1937 to 1945.

There was not one but several revolutions in this era. The revolution of 1911, although militarily a minor incident, accomplished a major change: the overthrow of the imperial system that had existed for two thousand years. The victory of the Nationalists in 1927 brought a first measure of unity to a nation that had since 1912 been torn by sectional strife and warlord rivalries. The revolution of 1949 brought to a successful conclusion the epic, thirty-year struggle by the Communists to impose a socialist system on China. Thus the revolutions of the twentieth century were fundamentally different from revolutions of China's past. Those had changed the dynasty but preserved the system: New actors simply replaced the old, and tradition was restored. The twentieth-century revolutions changed the actors, but much more important, they attacked the whole traditional system.

Although not a revolution in the political sense, another upheaval of the most profound consequence should be mentioned here. That is the New Culture Movement, or Renaissance, which began with an attack on the old literature and education in 1917, erupted into a nationwide student protest in May 1919, and developed on many fronts throughout the following decade. In its original form, the attack was against the persistence of the use of a "dead language"—classical Chinese—in a world in which young Chinese desperately needed to think (and hence to write) in modern ways; it was also against the monopolization of education by the few who could afford the time and effort required to master the classical language in a day when republican and democratic movements called for universal literacy.

The great student demonstrations, which erupted on May 4, 1919, in protest against the "sellout" of China's national interests at the Paris Peace Conference, were significant as the first unified expression of the determination of the younger generation to bring to a halt the almost century-long series of humiliations inflicted on China by the Powers. The New Culture Movement was driven by this strong determination, although there was no unanimity about the best way in which to proceed. But although on the surface the destiny of China seemed to be in the hands of those representing only ignorance and reaction—the warlords—the real wave of the future moving powerfully underneath was the young intellectuals (the term in China meant anyone with so much as an elementary school education) who were going through an agonizing struggle to find China's new Way. What they demanded was national union, restoration of sovereignty, modern education, a new society purged of all the traditional evils, and, in fact, a new China that would take its rightful place as a great nation in the world of the twentieth century. Thousands of these students went abroad to Europe and the United States (whereas a couple of decades or so earlier most went to Japan) and brought back with them the new ideas gained from their experiences in foreign lands. As would be expected, these ideas were varied and often self-contradictory as well as antitraditional. Out of a thousand debates and literary battles, lines were formed; groups advocating one or another position in regard to science, education, politics, religion, literature, and art combined and dissolved, attacked and were attacked. In the decade following the May Fourth Movement, such struggles may have seemed almost fruitless, but they were part of the great effort to overthrow the weight of tradition and found a modern China.

As a part of this traditional system, religion could not, of course, escape this effort. In the discussion that follows, we shall analyze some of the ways in which religion has been subjected to powerful forces for change during recent decades.

The Worldview

The rise of scientific secularism in the West occurred coincidentally with the strongest impact of Western political and economic power on China, at the end of the nineteenth and during the early twentieth centuries. In this period the Chinese were subjected both to a strong barrage of Christian propaganda and to its counterinfluence, atheistic, or at least scientific, materialism. By the 1920s and 1930s this warfare of Western ideas had become the most important factor in the intellectual world of China, where it was, of course, complicated by the existence of native traditions opposed to both foreign creeds. Every shade of opinion, from the most conservative to the most radical, was represented. Slowly but surely the conservative views gave way as the weight of the most able intellectuals shifted to the side of "science"—whether physical or economic (Marxist).

Still, it cannot be said that the worldview of the Chinese as a whole was much affected by the conquests of Western science and philosophy. This particular battle was fought among a tiny handful of intellectuals and hardly touched the thinking of the vast majority of the people. The small number of Buddhist thinkers had no reason to feel any erosion of their basic premises. The higher philosophy of Buddhism, far from being antagonistic to the spirit or methods of science, is readily adaptive to the new ways, regarding as it does all knowledge of the phenomenal world as being on the level of relative truth. No more sophisticated or final theory of Reality is ever likely to be devised by the mind of man than the "non-theory" of *śūnyatā*. The native cosmology based on *tao*, *yin* and *yang*, the five elemental operative qualities, and all their associated concepts were by no means swept away. Perhaps they never will be swept away, since Western science and philosophy can hardly offer more satisfactory alternatives. Even on the formal philosophical level, the victory of Western concepts might ultimately prove ephemeral, since there is apparently a surprising vitality in the New Literati Tradition.

Family Religion

The strong family system of the Chinese was under great stress during this period. As industrialization progressed, the cities drew increasing numbers of workers from the rural environs, and urban conditions of life

tended to break down family cohesion. With economic independence de-
rived from factory wage earning came a certain amount of freedom of choice for the individual and the weakening of the authority of family elders. Modern education furthered this process, both because many students lived away from their homes and because their books were strongly influenced by Western individualistic thought. Even the chaotic conditions brought about by political instability and continual fighting contributed to the same result, as millions of persons became homeless or were pressed into military service.

The result of these and many other factors was the erosion of parental control, the weakening of lineage loyalties, and a sense of isolation and alienation among individuals. When the Communist regime came to power, it was able to capture the allegiance of millions of persons who welcomed a new focus for their loyalties—and of course that regime has given its most determined efforts to substituting loyalty to the Party and State for loyalty to the family. It would be overstating the success of these efforts to claim that the traditional family has already succumbed, but there is no doubt that the regime has succeeded in bringing about a considerable degree of nationalistic feeling and a consciousness of wider social responsibility.

The implications of these developments for the ancestral cult are obvious. If that cult was in essence the symbolic cement holding together a structure of families and lineage, then the disintegration of family and lineage is prima facie evidence of the weakening of the ancestral cult. If our view is correct—that this family cult has been the basic, universal religion of the Chinese—then it is further apparent that its disruption implies the most serious consequences for Chinese civilization. Indeed, it is not difficult to find many examples of profound changes that have already occurred in specific places where the process of dissolution is far advanced.

Community Religion

Community religion, as we have described it, is equally caught up in a vortex of change. Formerly isolated communities are being exposed to many outside influences. Their exclusiveness and unity are breaking down. Their inhabitants travel to the cities, work in factories, serve in the army. Roads and railways bring the world closer. Education arrives, and the efficacy of the gods is called into question. The rudiments of modern schooling spread scientific explanations of cause and effect, and the animistic beliefs lose their rationale. This process has been going on for more than a century, and long before the Communist government pushed its campaigns against "superstitions," temples throughout the country had been allowed to fall into disuse or had been converted to secular uses. However, the persistence of traditional popular religion is remarkable, and against all repression and modernization it was clearly reasserting itself in the late 1980s and into the 1990s.

State Religion

On the collapse of the imperial polity in 1911, the whole structure of the State religion disappeared. Subsequent governments were generally indif-

ferent, if not hostile, to religion. The Nationalist regime in the early 1930s
sponsored a revival of the ancient Literati ethic as a matter of official policy. This included annual observance of the ritual in the *wên miao* on the
birthday of the Sage, the celebration being named Teachers Day, however.
The position of the Communist regime is naturally in accord with the dictum of Marx and Engels, that "religion is the opiate of the people." For a
brief time, during the so-called Great Proletarian Cultural Revolution of
the late 1960s, it seemed that a new "State religion" was being established,
as the nation was flooded with busts of Chairman Mao, and copies of the
Little Red Book of his sayings were in every hand. But the "cult of Chairman Mao" was as transient as other propagandistic movements whipped
up by the Party, and with Mao's death in 1976, it faded away immediately.
By the late 1980s, the general "religious" fervor of Communism in China
seemed to have vanished, one of the many evidences that Communism
could not live up to its utopian visions. With the collapse of the regime in
the Soviet Union, utopianism in China practically disappeared.

On the mainland of China, there is hardly a vestige of "State religion,"
as cynicism about the Party and its ideology has become widespread.
Under the Nationalist-controlled government on Taiwan, the grandiose
memorial hall to the late leader Chiang K'ai-shek and the more modest
memorial hall to the Founder of the Republic, Sun Yat-sen, provide evidence of the persisting tradition of erecting quasi-religious monuments to
great leaders. The ritual of bowing to the portraits of the Leader (Sun Yat-
sen and Chiang K'ai-shek in Taiwan and—at least formerly—Mao Tse-
tung in the mainland) might be considered as quasi-religious in nature,
although such a ritual is better compared to the American practice of
schoolchildren saluting the flag and reciting the Pledge of Allegiance.

Mao Tse-tung will perhaps never regain the status he once had in Chinese eyes because his epic accomplishments as leader of the Communist
struggle to power and his undoubted achievements in the early days of
the Socialist State have been overshadowed by the tragic results of his rad-
icalism during his later years. Chiang K'ai-shek suffered the ignominy of
defeat and loss of the mainland, but during his later years in Taiwan, he
regained considerable stature as a leader. Whether this will be sufficient to
give him lasting status as a "good emperor" entitled to national worship
remains to be seen. It is Sun Yat-sen, acknowledged by Communists and
Nationalists alike as the Founding Father, the man who brought about the
overthrow of the two thousand and more years of the imperial system and
the establishment of the first "modern" government in China, who has
long since acquired, and still retains, the potent mythic qualities of a "semi-
divinity."

Institutionalized Religion

As the more conspicuous of the institutionalized religions, Buddhism is
naturally of special interest when we are considering the travails of religion in the twentieth century. Despite a small flurry of activity during the
first four decades of the century, which sometimes led observers to conclude that they were witnessing a revitalization of Chinese Buddhism, it
has become apparent from more careful study[1] that this was an illusion.

Much of this activity was superficial, an attempt to "modernize" the religion in competition with Christianity, a series of social, political, and economic moves that were more a desperate defense against the forces inimical to Buddhism than a manifestation of re-creative vitality.

The forces referred to are the same ones we have already mentioned, including scientific secularism, Christian propaganda, complex processes of industrialization and modernization, and disruption of the traditional family and social systems. If young Chinese intellectuals turned to any religion it was apt to be Christianity, which was somehow associated with the power and progress of advanced Western nations (despite the incongruity of that association within Western civilization itself). Buddhism, a religion advocating withdrawal from the world rather than struggle within it, was completely unrelated to the urgent needs of China as these young people saw it. The more Buddhist leaders tried to bring their religion and its institutions into some sort of relevance to the situation, the further they took these from their true character. *Irrelevance* to social and political movements was inherent in Chinese Buddhism; a "social gospel" was incongruous. The Chinese ideal of the monk or nun was precisely the recluse devoted to holy ritual and yogic meditation.*

Under Nationalist control the State did not persecute Buddhism, but neither was it interested in nurturing it. As for the Communists, Buddhism fell into the same category as all other religions—an instrument of a "feudal" exploitation of the masses that would not be tolerated. Communist policy toward religious institutions has been to use them when they could be made to serve the interests of the Party line and otherwise to encourage their demise. Because there was some small value in international relations with the so-called Buddhist countries of Southeast Asia for the Chinese to seem to patronize the religion, this game was played. A malleable group of monks was organized into the Chinese Buddhist Association (continuing a name from Republican times), which could "represent" Chinese Buddhism to the outside world and which attempted mollification of international Buddhist outrage at such harsh anti-Buddhist actions as the persecutions in Tibet. A few of the well-known temples and monasteries were maintained as showcases for Buddhist visitors, and a few books and magazines were published for external consumption. All of this could not disguise the fact that Buddhism had ceased to play an institutional role in Communist Chinese society.

During the excess of the Great Proletarian Revolution in the late 1960s, it seemed that practically every monastery in China had shut down. Without the economic basis of land rentals, the monasteries could hardly survive in any case. And in the new society of the People's Republic, it was difficult indeed to justify the monastic life, when all activities must be measured against the obligation of "service to the masses."

As for institutionalized Taoism, until very recently it has received very little attention from scholars in this century. One can only say that its fate has, in general, paralleled that of Buddhism. It had far fewer monastic

---

*But see footnote on p. 142 in "Taiwan and Overseas" subsection.

centers than Buddhism, but, on the other hand, it had a much more intimate association with the popular religion: As we know, most of its professional religious served as priests, mediums, and exorcists. Therefore,
its survival power may be greater than that of the Buddhist Saṅgha.

This close association with popular religion is not an unmixed advantage, however; it brings Taoism under the same rubric as "superstitions"
and causes it to be an object of contempt of the intelligentsia and an object
of persecution by the government. The Communist regime has been even
more outspokenly opposed to superstitions than are the Nationalists: Although article 88 of the constitution of 1954 guarantees "freedom of religious belief,"[2] such freedom explicitly does not extend to "superstitions."

The single most important symbol of institutionalized Taoism was the
Master Designated by the Heavens (Chang T'ien Shih) of the southern
school (see Chapter 6). The incumbent, sixty-third in the line, fled when
Communist forces arrived, and his great ancestral estates in Kiangsi
province were confiscated. Thus was eliminated the only nationally important center for certification or ordination of Taoist priests. However, in
Taiwan a young successor, the sixty-fourth Master Chang, revived the authority of his sect to ordain Taoists; and institutionalized Taoism seemed,
beginning in the late 1980s, to be enjoying something of a renaissance in
Taiwan.

Master K'ung and the Literati Tradition

The most important casualty of these revolutionary times is Master K'ung:
by this is meant the whole religious, ethical, educational, literary, and political backbone of the traditional Chinese civilization based on the Canon
of the Literati. The damage done to the Chinese Great Tradition by the collapse of Literati authority is even more serious than the profound changes
wrought in Western society by the attacks of scientific secularism on traditional religion.

The outward signal of the death of Literati authority was the abolish-
ment in 1905 of the imperial examinations with their degrees, thus doing
away with the very raison d'être of traditional education. Increasingly, as
Western influences penetrated the minds of China's intellectuals, Master
K'ung came to stand for an anachronistic system of values that was a veri-
table millstone about the neck of progress. With the victory of modern education—that is, textbooks written in the colloquial language rather than
the language of the Classics—in the early 1920s, study of the traditional
Literati texts became not only irrelevant to the attainment of status in the
modern society but an antiquarian pursuit of interest only to the limited
number willing to spend the considerable effort required to comprehend
those ancient texts.

It is true that when the Nationalist government in the early 1930s felt
the need to counter the ideological program of the Communists, they
turned to the Literati Classics as the only viable source of an authentic native tradition. But their efforts to inspire youth through required courses
on the Classics in the middle schools and universities cannot be said to
have been successful.

Thus if one takes the most extreme view, one concludes that the Chinese civilization molded by the Literati Tradition is really dead and that some entirely new national character must replace the old tradition. This is, of course, the thesis of the leadership on the mainland. The apparently erratic policies of Mao Tse-tung had as their unvarying goal the extirpation of "feudal" remnants in China's society (most of which are the creation of Master K'ung and the Literati Tradition), the creation of a new people whose ideals are those of revolutionary socialism, not those of the Literati Tradition, and, of course, ultimately, the utopia of a true communistic society. In Taiwan, on the other hand, there is an outspoken challenge to this effort, as the Nationalist government continues—perhaps in a somewhat more effective manner than before—to assert the values of the Literati Tradition as the true Chinese culture, while at the same time pursuing completely modern goals in the social and economic spheres.

Taiwan and Overseas

In considering the religious situation of the second half of this century, one must thus look not only at the mainland but also at the island province of Taiwan and the many millions of Chinese residing overseas (mostly in Hong Kong and Southeast Asia). Although there is great variety in the religious picture from place to place, in general it is accurate to say that traditional religion is flourishing more among Chinese outside than inside the mainland. Certainly in the case of Taiwan, one would need to modify many of the generalities offered above. There one finds a strong family (although not necessarily a strong lineage) system operative. There the popular religion is flourishing. There Buddhism is enjoying a genuine renaissance, both as a popular religion[3] and as a monastic vocation.* Christianity, whose missionaries operate in force on the island, has made a strong impression. Temple building in Taiwan redoubled as if in direct challenge to the iconoclasm of the Cultural Revolution on the mainland, and all the government's stern injunctions against "waste" have failed to dampen the exuberant extravagance of the Taiwanese religious festivals (*pai-pai*).

THE CLOUDED CRYSTAL BALL

We opened our discussion in this book with the statement that we viewed Chinese religion as primarily an expression of the Chinese culture. It is an obvious concomitant of that view that as the culture changes, so must the religion. The future of religion in China is thus integrally bound up with the question of cultural change; therefore, the basic question is the outcome of the gigantic experiment that has been taking place on the mainland of China since 1949. It seems self-evident that it is as much a misjudgment to find that Communist China is something entirely novel as

---

*There seem never to have been any Taoist monasteries in Taiwan. There are, however, many professional Taoists who function at the level of popular religion.

Local opera troupe performing at a pai-pai, *or religious festival, in Taiwan. Notice painted faces and costumes and the very casual attitudes of
stage hands and audience, which does not mean the performance is irrelevant to the religious purport of the celebrations.*

it is to find that it is merely a continuation of the old in a new guise. Yet
long before the Communists established their control, China had changed
and was changing drastically, as our earlier remarks have indicated. It
seems most unlikely that we have yet come to a point of stability in this
process, and indeed it was the most basic premise of Chairman Mao and
his followers that revolution must continue for a long time to come if Communist goals were to be achieved. Although it is still too soon to judge
how much of this philosophy of "continuing revolution" will survive
Mao's death, there is the undeniable fact that the attainment of "modernity" in a society in itself assures a condition that seems part and parcel of
that modernity: ceaseless, restless change.

During the first decade and a half of the Socialist regime, to some observers it seemed that the utopian idealism of Chairman Mao and his more
radical followers had, in fact, brought about a dramatic and unexpected
change in Chinese social consciousness. The shibboleths of welfare of the
people and sacrifice for the good of all seemed to have become a new way
of life for Party and masses alike. But sea changes of this sort are inherently suspect, and the events of the mid-1960s—of which the Great Proletarian Cultural Revolution was the culmination—and the following years
have shown how superficial was the real impact of those idealistic slogans
and movements. The "continuing revolution" of Mao is indeed a prospect,
but it is a different sort of revolution—that of struggles for political power
and not for the victory of Communism as a Way. As far as our subject is

concerned, the most significant fact to emerge in these post-Mao years is the unmistakable vitality of the traditional popular religion and all its cluster of age-old customs—not that the philosophy of the Party has changed in regard to "superstition," but that every moment of relaxation of the repression has seen the practices of popular religion springing up "like weeds."

Any attempt to predict the forms Chinese religion will take in the future, especially in view of these continually new developments, would obviously be foolish. What we can assert is the necessity of understanding the traditional forms in our effort to understand the whole culture of the past and in the broader task of understanding religious humankind in the universal framework. And we can be sure, as we reflect on history, that even the seemingly most drastic changes or suppressions of forms do not guarantee the outcome: Religious forms, like certain plants, can remain dormant for a very long time, only to spring up again when the environment becomes favorable.

APPENDIX 1

The Canons of the Three Traditions

THE CANON OF THE LITERATI

In Chinese civilization the Canon of the Literati occupies a position some-what analogous to that of the Bible and the major works of Greek and Roman literature. If we include with the original texts the innumerable commentaries and exegeses of scholars through the ages, the comparison might be with the Bible and the works of the Church Fathers and theologians. One should understand that the Chinese Classics, as they are often called in English, had both secular and sacred meaning, providing an "orthodoxy" for philosophy, statecraft, ethics, and religion. The scholars of these texts, who memorized and internalized them, made up the true elite class of traditional China. Through the system of written examinations (whose predecessors went back as far as the Han dynasty), the government selected the type of scholar considered most useful for State service. But whether thus selected or not, all who received a bookish education studied these texts as their curriculum. The influence of the Literati Canon in Chinese culture will therefore be understood to be all-pervasive.

Three works preceded the times of Master K'ung: the *Yi*, the *Shu*, and the *Shih*. The Master himself was supposed to have compiled the *Ch'un-Ch'iu*—or rather, to have edited this chronicle of his native state of Lu—to reveal his judgments on historical events and persons. In addition, he was supposed to have added vitally important commentaries (the so-called Ten Wings) to the *Yi* and to have selected the song lyrics to be included in the *Shih* out of an original corpus ten times the size of the final version. Then there were the texts dealing with *li*, or the correct ritual behavior of aristocrats toward each other and the spirits, in many of which the Master is quoted. Although no doubt late compilations (i.e., no earlier than the Han period), these texts on *li* undoubtedly contain a great deal of much earlier material, and there is no reason to be skeptical of the pronouncements of the Master so far as their purport is concerned.

In 213 BCE the First Emperor of Ch'in "burned the books and buried the scholars." That is, he attempted, in what is a paradigmatic way of despots, to make history start with his own dynasty and to stop the mouths of those who objected. The books of the philosophers of the preceding age were in large part lost through this holocaust and were recovered only in part by the discovery of remnants and the extraordinary feats of memory of aged scholars during the early Han. The reconstituted texts were the subject of endless scholarly controversy throughout later ages.

During the reign of the Filial and Martial Emperor (Hsiao Wu Ti) of the Han (mid-second century BCE), the doctrines of the Literati School were proclaimed the State Orthodoxy. A university was established with chairs for professors of each of the Literati texts, and talented young men were brought from all over the empire to study under these professors. In addition to the texts we have mentioned above, the Scriptures of the Han period included the *Chou Li,* or *Chou Kuan,* and the *Three Exegeses* (*chuan*) on the *Ch'un-Ch'iu,* each named for its putative author: the *Kung-yang Chuan,* the *Ku-liang Chuan,* and the *Tso Chuan.* The *Lun Yü, Mêng Tzû,* and *Hsiao Ching* were singled out as basic works of the Master's School. The first dictionary, a glossary called *Êr Ya,* was also given quasi-canonical status.

Because of the dangers of loss and scribal error—not to speak of fraud—in making handwritten copies, the Canon of the times was engraved on stone to fix the texts. This was done first in 175 CE, and again between 240 and 248. Many centuries later (mid-tenth century) the Canon was made widely available by wood-block printing.

In Sung and later times, with the renaissance of the Literati Tradition, the philosophers of the new schools adopted as their Canon the groupings of the Four Books and the Five Scriptures (*ssû shu wu ching*). The Scriptures included the *Yi, Shu, Shih, Li Chi,* and *Ch'un-Ch'iu* with the *Three Exegeses.* The Four Books included two small texts extracted from *Li Chi,* namely *Ta Hsüeh* and *Chung Yung,* plus *Lun Yü* and *Mêng Tzû.* These (except for the *Li Chi* and *Ch'un-Ch'iu*) were equipped with the commentaries of Chu Hsi, the great Sung dynasty synthesizer, and were in this form adopted as standard texts for the government examinations.

The final version of the Canon appeared at the very end of the twelfth century under the overall title *Thirteen Scriptures, with Notes and Commentary.* The texts included were *Yi, Shu, Shih,* the *Three Li* (*Yi Li, Chou Li, Li Chi*), the *Ch'un-Ch'iu* with its *Three Exegeses* (*Kung-yang Chuan, Ku-liang Chuan, Tso Chuan*), *Lun Yü, Hsiao Ching, Êr Ya,* and *Mêng Tzû.* A fourteenth text, the *Ta Tai Li Chi,* may be said to have quasi-canonical status.

Shu Ching: Scripture of Archaic Historical Documents (or Book of History)

These are documents purporting to record words and deeds of ancient rulers and ministers from the legendary Sage King Yao to the early Chou dynasty. Although some of these documents were already recognized as forgeries as early as the Han period, to most Chinese the entire work would have been considered scripture.

See: Bernhard Karlgren, trans., *The Book of Documents* (Stockholm, 1950); James Legge, trans., *The Shoo King* (Oxford, 1865).

Shih Ching: Scripture of Song Lyrics (or *Book of Songs, Odes, Poetry*)

This is an anthology of song lyrics from the feudal states and the court of Chou. It is not only one of the basic scriptural works but also the fountainhead of later Chinese poetry.

See: James Legge, trans., *The She King* (Oxford, 1871 and 1895); Arthur Waley, trans., *The Book of Songs* (London, 1937); Bernard Karlgren, trans., *The Book of Odes* (Stockholm, 1950); Ezra Pound, trans., *The Confucian Odes* (Harvard, 1954); Marcel Granet (English translation by E. D. Edwards), *Festivals and Songs of Ancient China* (New York, 1932).

Yi (or I) Ching: Scripture of Change (or *Book of Changes*)

See Chapter 2 for discussion.

See: James Legge, trans., *The Yi King*, 2d ed. (Oxford, 1899); Richard Wilhelm (translated into German; English translation from the German by Cary F. Baynes), *The I Ching, or Book of Changes*, 2 vols. (New York, 1950); John Blofeld, trans., *The Book of Change* (London, 1965); Hellmut Wilhelm, *Change: Eight Lectures on the I Ching* (New York, 1960); Wei Tat, *An Exposition of the I-Ching, or Book of Changes* (Taipei, 1970).

Ch'un-Ch'iu: Springs and Autumns

This title was originally applied to the annals of the various feudal states in Chou times; its later application is solely to this chronicle of the State of Lu, as edited by Master K'ung. It covers the reigns of the Dukes of Lu from 722–484 BCE. It is so terse that three classical exegeses were written to accompany it: *Kung-yang Chuan, Ku-liang Chuan,* and *Tso Chuan.*

See: James Legge, trans., *The Ch'un Ts'ew with the Tso Chuan* (Oxford, 1872).

Li Ching: Canons of Ritual and Protocol

This title is applied in reference to three works on *li: Yi,* or *I, Li* (*Ceremonial and Ritual*), *Li Chi* (*Records of Ritual*), and *Chou Li,* or *Chou Kuan* (*Institutes or Officials of the [Early] Chou*). We have cited from the first two of these several times (see Chapter 3). There is, in addition, the *Ta Tai Li Chi* (*Records of Ritual [Compiled by] Tai Senior*).

See: James Legge, trans., *The Li Ki,* 2 vols. (Oxford, 1885); John Steele, trans., *The I Li,* 2 vols. (London, 1917). There is no English translation of the *Chou Li* or *Chou Kuan;* one should consult the French version of Édouard Biot, *Le Tcheou-li ou Rites des Tcheou,* 3 vols. (Paris, 1851). There is no translation of *Ta Tai Li Chi.*

Lun Yü: Analects

This includes conversations and sayings of Master K'ung and his personal disciples, presumably compiled by a near generation of followers. The writing is terse, with cryptic fragments.

See: There are many translations, among which those of James Legge, *The Confucian Analects,* 2d ed. (Oxford, 1892); and Arthur Waley, *The Analects of Confucius* (London, 1938) have been most frequently used by those who speak English. More-recent translations to be noted are those of

D. C. Lau, *Confucius: The Analects* (a Penguin paperback, 1979) and the version edited by The Council of Chinese Cultural Renaissance, Republic of China, included in their *English Translation of the Four Books* (Taipei, 1979).

Ta Hsüeh: The Highest Form of Learning (or The Great Learning)

This is a short chapter extracted from *Li Chi* by the Sung dynasty Literati philosophers and given special prominence as one of the Four Books. It dates perhaps from the times of Master Mêng ("Mencius"), that is, the fourth century BCE. Its theme is the ordering of society through individual self-cultivation.

See: James Legge, trans., *The Great Learning*, 2d ed. (Oxford, 1892); E. R. Hughes, *The Great Learning and the Mean-in-Action* (New York, 1943).

Chung Yung: The Central and Universal Moral Law (or The Doctrine of the Mean)

Like the preceding, this is a chapter extracted from *Li Chi* and given special prominence by the Sung Literati philosophers. It is traditionally ascribed to Master Tzû-ssû, grandson of Master K'ung. Its theme is the personal and political implications of human nature and self-cultivation, that is, moral man in a moral universe.

See: James Legge, trans., *The Doctrine of the Mean*, 2d ed. (Oxford, 1892); E. R. Hughes, *The Great Learning and the Mean-in-Action* (New York, 1943); Hung-ming Ku, trans., *The Conduct of Life* (an available reprint is in the anthology compiled by Yutang Lin, *The Wisdom of China and India*, New York, 1942); Wei-ming Tu, *Centrality and Commonality: An Essay on Chung-yung* (Honolulu, 1976).

Mêng Tzû ("Mencius"): Works of the Philosopher Mêng

Mêng Tzû, or Master Mêng, lived c. 390–305 BCE and was one of the two principal exponents of the Literati doctrines as interpreted by Master K'ung (the other being Master Hsün, or Hsün Tzû) during late Chou times. The work bearing his name, unlike the *Analects*, contains lengthy dialogues that give us a good understanding of his thought.

See: James Legge, trans., *The Works of Mencius*, 2d ed. (Oxford, 1892); D. C. Lau, trans., *Mencius* (a Penguin paperback, 1970).

Hsiao Ching: Scripture of Filiality

This is a small work of unknown date and authorship, probably compiled prior to the Han (say, third century BCE). It expounds the cardinal virtue of Chinese ethics, as emphasized by the Literati School, in the form of a lecture by the Master to his disciple Master Tsêng, who was renowned in later ages for his filiality.

See: James Legge, trans., *The Hsiao Ching*, 2d ed. (Oxford, 1899); Sister Mary Makra, trans., *The Hsiao Ching* (New York, 1961).

Êr Ya

This is the first dictionary, compiled at least as early as the early Han dynasty. There are no translations or studies available in English.

A NOTE ON THE BUDDHIST CANON

In Sanskrit the Canon is called *Tripiṭaka,* or Three Baskets. One "basket" contains *sūtras,* which are scriptures or words on Dharma by the Buddha. A second contains *Vinaya,* which are prescriptions for the conduct of members of the Saṅgha, or Buddhist Order (including lay believers). The third contains *Abhidharma,* or treatises called *śāstras,* written by learned "doctors of the Church" to explicate Dharma.

The Indian Canon arrived piecemeal in China beginning in late Han times and included both Hīnayāna and Mahāyāna texts. In Chinese the "Three Baskets" are *San Tsang,* or Three Storehouses or Treasuries, and the Canon is usually called *Ta Tsang Ching,* or Great Storehouse or Treasury of Scriptures. Although it consists mostly of translations from Pali or Sanskrit originals (many of which were subsequently lost in India), it also contains some materials composed by Chinese Buddhists. The Chinese Canon is that used in Korea, Japan, and Vietnam.

The Buddhist Canon is too huge and complex to describe here. We refer the reader to the book in this series by Richard H. Robinson and Willard L. Johnson entitled *The Buddhist Religion,* in which there is "An Overview of the Buddhist Scriptures," as well as much other pertinent material.

It is important to realize that the Buddhist Canon is written in a special technical vocabulary featuring numerous translations and transliterations of the Buddhist technical terms from Indian languages and that it was therefore largely unintelligible, even to otherwise well-educated Chinese, without special study. This means that it was, in effect, open only to professional religious and those lay scholars with a special interest in Buddhism. For this reason alone, its influence in the Chinese culture could not approximate that of the Canon of the Literati, not to mention that it was always regarded as the product of "barbarians" and outside the great traditions of the native culture.

A NOTE ON THE TAOIST CANON

Like the Buddhist Canon, the *Tao Tsang* (Storehouse or Treasury of the Tao) is immense and complex, but it is much less systematically organized. Unlike the Buddhist Canon, all of its heterogeneous contents are the original productions of Chinese minds. Its earliest texts may compete in antiquity with the early Buddhist works, as one substantial group consists of pre-Ch'in and early Han books furnished with Taoist commentaries. Here we see the Old Master as the true Founder of Taoism, with a large number of commentaries on the text that goes under his name. In addition to the more "philosophical" works of antiquity, the Canon contains hundreds of later documents such as texts on outer and inner alchemy, breath-yoga, diet, sexual praxis, rituals, talismans and registers, anatomy and physiology, occult techniques and incantations, biographies of adepts (a major preoccupation), and so forth.

The history of this gigantic "Bibliotheca Taoica" is full of ups and downs, as materials were added, frauds were perpetrated, out-and-out plagiarisms of Buddhist concepts were made, and emperors promoted or attempted to destroy it. There was never any ecclesiastical authority to give formal approval or disapproval of texts, and even after the wood-block edition of the mid-fifteenth century had given the Canon a seemingly fixed form, there were additions to it, as witness the Continuation of this Ming Canon, published in 1607.

It must also be pointed out that at no time in history, until modern mechanical means of reproduction made it possible, was the complete Canon ever available, even to the professional religious. As far as the layperson is concerned, the esoteric language as well as the scarcity of Taoist texts made the Canon literally a sealed book. The professional Taoist community priest was likely to be in possession of a few ritual texts handed down in his family as "trade secrets"; the layperson interested in self-cultivation, breath-yoga, gymnastics, and the like would likewise possess a few texts on those subjects.

The reader interested in learning more about the nature, history, and organization of the *Tao Tsang* is referred to my article "Taoism: Classic and Canon," in *The Holy Book in Comparative Perspective*, edited by Frederick M. Denny and Rodney L. Taylor, 204–223. Columbia, SC: The University of South Carolina Press, 1985.

APPENDIX 2

The Mind or Heart Scripture of Perfect Wisdom

In an introduction such as this, it is impossible to represent adequately the rich complexities of Buddhist doctrines. We have stated that the concept of Emptiness—*śūnyatā* in Sanskrit, *k'ung* in Chinese—underlies the thinking of all East Asian Buddhist schools, and fortunately there is a brief *sūtra* (scripture) that not only exemplifies this concept but was widely read and memorized by clergy and laypeople. We give here a translation of the Chinese text.

> When Bodhisattva of Great Power Kuan (that is, Kuan-shih-yin, or Avalokiteśvara) meditated deeply on the Perfect Wisdom that Leads to Salvation (*prajñā-pāramitā*) He clearly perceived that the Five Heaps (that is, the *skandhas*, or psycho-physical components of beings) are all empty and that [by this Wisdom] all beings will be ferried across [the Sea of Suffering or Rebirth, that is, *saṁsāra*].
>
> [He said to Śāriputra, Śākyamuni's senior disciple,] Śāriputra, form is not different from emptiness, emptiness is not different from form. Form is in fact emptiness, emptiness is in fact form. Perceptible objects, sensations, mental images and memories, mental constructions, and discriminative consciousness (i.e., the Five Heaps, or *skandhas*) are all like this.
>
> Neither do eyes, ears, nose, tongue, body, or mind (i.e., the faculties of the senses) exist. [And so] there are no *dharmas* (i.e., phenomena) of sight, sound, smell, taste, or feeling by physical contact. There being no realm of vision [or any other realm of the senses], including mind consciousness, there is no ignorance [or any other kind of suffering], including old age and death, and there is also no doing away with old age and death. There is no accumulation of suffering, no origination [of suffering], no annihilation [of suffering], no True Way [of escape from suffering].* There is no knowledge and no attainment, because there is nothing to attain.

---

*Thus the Four Aryan Truths, a basic formula pronounced by the Buddha in His first sermon on Setting in Motion the Wheel of Dharma, are negated.

It is because the bodhisattva relies upon Perfect Wisdom that his mind or heart is unimpeded. Because his mind or heart is unimpeded he has no fear and is far from falling into dreamy imaginings. Therefore all the Buddhas of the Three Ages (that is, past, present, and future) rely upon Perfect Wisdom to attain Absolute Enlightenment (*anuttara-samyak-saṁbodhi*). Therefore, knowing Perfect Wisdom is the great spiritual **mantra** (i.e., incantation), the great mantra of enlightenment, the unsurpassed mantra, the unequalled mantra, they are able to abolish all suffering. This mantra is true and real and not empty. Therefore they utter the Mantra of Perfect Wisdom, which goes as follows:

*Gate, gate, pāragate, pārasaṁgate, bodhi, svāhā.**

Such is the Mind or Heart Scripture of Perfect Wisdom.

---

*Edward Conze, in his translation from Sanskrit, renders this mantra as "Gone, gone, gone beyond, gone altogether beyond, O what an awakening, all hail!" (Edward Conze, *Buddhist Wisdom Books* [London: Allen & Unwin, 1958], pp. 101f.)

APPENDIX 3

The Heaven-Honored One of the Primal Beginnings Speaks the Scripture of the Precious Names of the Three Controllers

It will be obvious from our remarks in Appendix 1, "A Note on the Taoist Canon," that there can be no such thing as a "representative" Taoist text. What is presented here is a brief extract from the Taoist liturgical tradition, to illustrate an aspect of the religion that was referred to only in passing in Chapter 6. Some points that may be noted include (1) the concept of a pantheon in the Heavens, (2) the hope of bringing supernatural power to bear on man for his protection and blessing, (3) a faith in formulaic utterances, and (4) a detectable Buddhist influence. Although this particular text is chanted by professional religious, it shows that Taoism is not only a religion of self-salvatory practices, such as alchemy or other regimens leading to immortal transcendency, but a means of saving ordinary folks.*

At that time[1]

The Heaven-Honored One of the Primal Beginnings was in the Palace of the Eight Scenic Views[2] in the Grand Heaven[3] together with the Spirit Kings of all the Heavens, the [deities of] sun and moon, stars and constellations, the Superior Saints and High Venerables—an infinite crowd of

---

*This selection is translated from a manual entitled *Scriptures and Rituals for Matins and Vespers in Taoist Temples,* compiled by Chao Chia-cho, a leading Taoist of the School of the Master Designated by the Heavens, and published in Taipei in 1969.

[1]This is a formula something like our "once upon a time"; but it is, in fact, an imitation of the Mahāyāna Buddhist sūtra opening, as is the whole setting, locating the Lord in a supernatural place surrounded by crowds of divine beings.

[2]Eight Scenic Views is a title applied to descriptive poems, sometimes illustrated with prints, found in many local gazetteers.

[3]The Grand Heaven—Ta Lô T'ien—is said to be like the Pure Land of Buddhism.

Holy Ones[4]; and He spoke the unsurpassed and perfectly true and wonderful Dharma.[5]

There was a True Man[6] named Great Immortal Transcendent Bare Legs who left his place and came out [of the crowd]. He raised his clasped hands to his forehead in salutation, and prostrated himself, saying to the Heaven-Honored One: The people of the world below all suffer distress, whether it be from water or fire, weapons or disease. The devils and bogies who produce [these calamities] ensnare them in Heaven and net them in Earth, and everyone suffers distress. How can they be saved?

The Heaven-Honored One replied: All the spiritual beings and immortal transcendents who have attained the Tao are protected by the Three Controllers (San Kuan). Men born in the lower region, if only they hold to the Precious Names of the Three Controllers, will be able to eliminate distress, to do away with it entirely. I now communicate to you [the Precious Names]. Disseminate them in the world below. Those among men who take care to recite them will get blessings without limit, and all their troubles will be mitigated. Then He spoke the Precious Names:

> In the North Pole [Star], mysterious and lofty,
>   Courtyard of the Purple Invisible Emperor—
> In the [subterranean] prisons of Mt. T'ai,[7]
>   And in the pure cold Watery Country—
> Ruling the Three Realms
>   And governing the myriad spirits—
> The Three Primordials collate the Registers [of life and death]
>   Whereby the good and the evil are divided.
>
> Observe fasting and abstinence and ceremonially chant,
> And do not fail to carry out every vow,
> [Thereby] dispersing calamities and dispelling [the karmic results of] sins
> And bringing down blessings and extending life.
>
> [In accordance with] the perfectly true and wonderful Tao,
>   Whose merits are boundless,
> They have made the Great Vow of Commiseration
>   And have the Great Compassion of the Great Saints.
>
> The First Primordial, of First Rank,
>   Controller of Heaven who confers blessings,
>   Great Emperor of Purple Invisibility;

---

[4]Just like the bodhisattvas, devas, and other saints of Buddhism.

[5]The same Chinese term, *fa*, as the Dharma of Buddhism.

[6]True Man, it will be recalled, is one of the ancient appellations of Taoist adepts.

[7]These are the hells, or more accurately, purgatories, which are taken from Buddhism by Taoism. Mt. T'ai, most sacred of the five "sacred mountains" of China (in Shantung province) was early identified as one of the major centers of judgment of the dead.

The Second Primordial, of Second Rank,
    Controller of Earth who saves from sin,
    Great Emperor of Pure Vacuity;
The Third Primordial, of Third Rank,
    Controller of the Waters who does away with distress,
    Great Emperor of the Grotto of Yin;
The Ch'ien[8] Primordial, of Fourth Rank,
    Controller of Fire, who investigates and compares [human
      conduct],
    Great Emperor of the Grotto of Yang;
Three Primordial Lords,
Three Hundred and Sixty Responding Heaven-Honored Ones,
Feminine-youths True Men[9]—
    [These] will investigate and compare [human] officials.

At that time

The Great Immortal Transcendent Bare Legs together with the Spirit Kings of all the Heavens and the great crowd of True Men and Immortal Transcendents, hearing the Precious Names, greatly rejoiced. They saluted, bowing their heads, and retired. Receiving [the Precious Names] with faith, they carried out [the instructions of the Heaven-Honored One of the Primal Beginnings].[10]

---

[8]*Ch'ien* refers to the pure *yang* hexagram standing for Heaven. (This "Fourth Rank" primordial does not seem to fit the schema, but for whatever reason, he is included.)

[9]Taoism has a special esteem for the feminine (as we see in *The Old Master*); adepts who have the secret of immortal transcendency are eternally youthful.

[10]The Heaven-Honored One of the Primal Beginnings is one of the Taoist Trinity; they are called The Three Pure Ones (San Ch'ing), and as the highest Powers of the Cosmos they are represented on the altar during the Taoist Rites of Cosmic Renewal (*chiao*).

Notes

All translations not otherwise credited are the author's own. The order of Chinese names is surname first, followed by given name.

Chapter 1: The Early Chinese Worldview

1. Joseph Needham has thoroughly developed this theme. See his "Human Law and the Laws of Nature in China and the West," in *Science and Civilization in China* (Cambridge, England: Cambridge University Press, 1956), vol. II, chap. 18.
2. This dating is in accordance with traditional views. More-recent scholarship would put the dominance of yin-yang theory as late as the Han period (202 BCE–220 CE).
3. Ku Hung-ming, trans., *The Conduct of Life* (Taipei: privately published, 1956), p. 25.

Chapter 2: Prescientific Theory and Religious Practice

1. In order to correct this system to accord with the actual number of days in a solar year, the Chinese had already, as far back as the testimony of the oracle bones (described in Chapter 3) takes us, devised the Metonic Cycle, which provided for seven intercalary months within every nineteen years. See Tung Tso-pin, "The Chinese and the World's Ancient Calendars," *A Symposium on the World Calendar* (Taipei: Chinese Association for the United Nations, 1951). Fullest treatment of Chinese astronomic achievements is given by Needham, *Science and Civilization*, vol. III.
2. John Lossing Buck, *Land Utilization in China* (Shanghai: Commercial Press, 1937), p. 392.
3. John Shryock has called attention, however, to one significant difference between the animistic spirits in general and those of the ancestors. It was not uncommon for people to coerce their deities, as when a magistrate would order the image of the god exposed to the broiling sun in case the god had failed to respond to prayers for rain. But no matter what the circumstances, "no Chinese would think of insulting or reproving his ancestors." See *The Origin and Development of the State Cult of Confucius* (New York and London: Century, 1932), p. 91, note 20.
4. For much of the material in the preceding two paragraphs I am indebted to the illuminating discussion in Needham, *Science and Civilization*, vol. II, 13(g).

5. E. J. Eitel, *Fêng-Shui: Principles of the Natural Science of the Chinese* (Hong Kong and London: Trubner, 1873), pp. 22f.

6. Eitel, *Fêng-Shui*, pp. 48ff.

7. Eitel, *Fêng-Shui*, p. 54.

8. For the compass used in *fêng-shui* (and its connection with the history of the navigational compass), see Needham, *Science and Civilization*, vol. IV, 26(i).

9. There were ten "celestial stems" and twelve "terrestrial branches," and they were combined in order in the following manner: IA, IIB, IIIC, and so forth. A complete cycle thus produced sixty combinations. This system, found on oracle bones of the late Shang dynasty, is still used today.

10. One cannot dismiss the purely aesthetic aspects of *fêng-shui*. Aesthetic considerations unquestionably constituted an important component of the theory as it developed. The prescriptions of *fêng-shui* are also undeniably based on practical considerations, such as climatic and sanitary factors. The vitality of the whole pseudoscience was no doubt due in no small measure to these facts.

11. The foregoing is a general characterization of *fêng-shui* in its modern form. The origins of this pseudoscience may be traced back to late Chou times, but it seems that it began to become established as a system during the post-Han centuries (around 300 CE).

12. Alan J. A. Elliott, *Chinese Spirit Medium Cults in Singapore* (London: London School of Economics and Political Science, Department of Anthropology, 1955), p. 161.

13. Condensed from V. R. Burkhardt, *Chinese Creeds and Customs* (Hong Kong: South China Morning Post, Ltd., 1953–1958), vol. II, pp. 144–148.

14. The use of fetishes must be as ancient as magical religion itself, but documentation goes back only to the first century CE (Wang Ch'ung, *Critiques of Theories, Lun Hêng*, "Lan-Shih"). See Alfred Forke, *Lun-Hêng* (London: Luzac, 1907–1911), vol. II, pp. 38f.

15. Burkhardt, *Chinese Creeds and Customs*, vol. II, pp. 142f. Italics supplied.

16. Condensed from Peter Goullart, *The Monastery of Jade Mountain* (London: John Murray, Ltd., 1961), pp. 86–89.

CHAPTER 3: THE FAMILY: KINDRED AND ANCESTORS

1. Tung Tso-pin, *An Interpretation of the Ancient Chinese Civilization* (Taipei: Chinese Association for the United Nations, 1952), p. 19.

2. Tung, *Ancient Chinese Civilization*, p. 19. Quotation from *Chung Yung*, XIX.

3. Tung, *Ancient Chinese Civilization*, p. 21.

4. This is again an oversimplification. In reality, because the ancestral cult is a reflection of the specific history, structure, and functioning of a particular community, it is expressed in widely varying ways. See especially Emily M. Ahern, *The Cult of the Dead in a Chinese Village* (Stanford, CA: Stanford University Press, 1973), Conclusion, pp. 245–266.

5. For convincing evidence of this latter assertion, one may consult the detailed discussion of funeral rites in J. J. M. de Groot, *The Religious System of China* (Leiden: E. J. Brill, 1892–1894), vols. I and II. Here nearly every detail of late nineteenth-century practice is shown to conform to the scriptural injunctions.

6. James Legge, trans., *Li Ki* [*Chi*] (Oxford, England: Oxford University Press, 1885), book one, I, 1, pp. 62ff.

7. Legge, trans., *Li Ki,* book twenty-three, 5–7, pp. 257f.

8. Legge, trans., *Li Ki,* book one, II, 3, p. 116.

9. Legge, trans., *Li Ki,* book one, I, 3, p. 82.

10. Legge, trans., *Li Ki,* book one, I, 2, pp. 71f.

11. Ch'ü T'ung-tsu, *Law and Society in Traditional China* (The Hague: Mouton & Co., 1961), pp. 25f.

12. Legge, trans., *Li Ki,* book ten, pp. 450f, 453, and 458.

13. Legge, trans., *Li Ki,* book ten, I.20, pp. 458f.

14. The most exhaustive treatment of the funeral rites will be found in Groot, *Religious System of China,* vol. I, which devotes 237 pages to the subject. See, for an outline of the rites, my article, "Funeral Rites in Taiwan," in our companion volume of readings, *The Chinese Way in Religion,* ed. L. G. Thompson (Belmont, CA: Wadsworth, 1973), pp. 160–169. More recently, there has appeared a collection of articles by anthropologists and historians entitled *Death Ritual in Late Imperial and Modern China,* ed. James L. Watson and Evelyn S. Rawski (Berkeley, Los Angeles, London: University of California, 1988).

15. J. Steele, trans., *The Yi Li* (London: Arthur Probsthain, 1917), vol. II, pp. 9–12.

16. Chiang Monlin, *Tides from the West* (Taipei: China Culture Publishing Foundation, 1957), p. 9.

17. Chiang Yee, *A Chinese Childhood* (New York: Norton, 1963), pp. 9ff.

CHAPTER 4: THE COMMUNITY: GODS AND TEMPLES

1. From Laurence G. Thompson, "Objectifying Divine Power: Some Chinese Modes," in Spencer J. Palmer, ed., *Deity and Death; Selected Symposium Papers* (Provo, UT: Religious Studies Center, Brigham Young University, 1978), p. 140. For a particularly helpful discussion of this matter, see Murray and Rosalie Wax, "Magic and Monotheism," in June Helm, ed., *Symposium on New Approaches to the Study of Religion* (Seattle, WA: University of Washington, 1964), pp. 50–60.

2. H. Maspero, "The Mythology of Modern China," in J. Hackin et al., *Asiatic Mythology* (New York: Crowell, n.d.), p. 262.

3. Material in this section is based largely on my article "Notes on Religious Trends in Taiwan," *Monumenta Serica,* vol. XXIII, 1964. The figures quoted are taken from a Survey of Temples and Churches in Taiwan Province compiled by Liu Chih-wan and published in *Taiwan Wen Shian* in June 1960. More up-to-date figures have been published by Lin Hêng-tao in his *Conspectus of Taiwanese Temples (Taiwan Ssû-miao Kai-lan),* published in 1978. According to Lin's figures, the total number of temples some fifteen years after the 1960 survey had increased dramatically to over five thousand.

4. C. H. Plopper, *Chinese Religion Seen Through the Proverb* (Shanghai: The China Press, 1926), p. 33.

5. Maspero, "Mythology of Modern China," p. 340.

6. David C. Graham, *Folk Religion in Southwest China* (Washington, DC: The Smithsonian Institution, 1961), p. 154, citing his own earlier article in the *Chinese Recorder,* July 1935, pp. 425ff.

1. The arrival of Confucian doctrines at this dominant position was a gradual process during two centuries BCE. See "The Victory of Han Confucianism," in *The History of the Former Han Dynasty by Pan Ku,* Homer H. Dubs, trans. and ed. (Baltimore: American Council of Learned Societies, 1944), vol. II, pp. 341–352.
2. Tung, *An Interpretation of the Ancient Chinese Civilization,* pp. 18f.
3. E. T. Williams, "The State Religion of China During the Manchu Dynasty," *Journal of the North China Branch, Royal Asiatic Society,* vol. XLIV, 1913, p. 14.
4. Quotations from Yü-ch'üan Wang, "An Outline of the Central Government of the Former Han Dynasty," *Harvard Journal of Asiatic Studies,* vol. 12, 1949, p. 151.
5. Hsieh Pao-chao, *The Government of China (1644–1911)* (Baltimore: Johns Hopkins Press, 1925), p. 142. Material in brackets supplied.
6. Williams, "State Religion of China," pp. 17f.
7. John Shryock, *The State Cult of Confucius* (New York and London: Century, 1932), pp. 176f. Material in brackets supplied.

CHAPTER 6: THREE WAYS TO ULTIMATE
TRANSFORMATION: (1) TAOIST TRADITION

1. Homer H. Dubs, trans., "The Beginnings of Alchemy," *Isis,* vol. 38, 1947, pp. 67ff. Material in brackets by the translator.
2. L. C. Wu and T. L. Davis, trans., "An Ancient Chinese Treatise on Alchemy Entitled Ts'an T'ung Ch'i," *Isis,* vol. 18, 1932, p. 255. Material in brackets and parentheses by the translators.
3. Wu and Davis, trans., "Ancient Chinese Treatise," pp. 260f. Material in brackets and parentheses by the translators.
4. E. Feifel, trans., "Pao P'u Tzû," *Monumenta Serica,* vol. VI, 1941, pp. 158ff.
5. Feifel, trans., "Pao P'u Tzû," pp. 209ff. Material in parentheses supplied.
6. Feifel, trans., "Pao P'u Tzû," p. 9f.
7. Arthur Waley, "Notes on Chinese Alchemy," *Bulletin of the School of Oriental and African Studies* (University of London), vol. 6, pt. 1, 1930, pp. 15f. Material in brackets supplied.
8. *Master Mêng* VIIA.4.1. Material in parentheses supplied.
9. The sixty-third generation Chang T'ien Shih fled from the Communists, who confiscated his ancestral estates on Lung-hu Shan (mountain) in Kiangsi province, going first to Hong Kong and eventually to Taiwan, where he died (in 1970). Burkhardt, *Chinese Creeds and Customs* (Hong Kong: South China Morning Post, Ltd., 1953–1958), vol. II, pp. 132ff., has an article on him, illustrated with a portrait. See also Holmes Welch's article "The Chang T'ien Shih and Taoism in China," *Journal of Oriental Studies* (University of Hong Kong), vol. 4, 1957–1958, pp. 188–212, which includes the author's report of his personal visit to the Taoist leader in Taiwan. A distant relative succeeded him in 1970 as sixty-fourth generation Master Designated by the Heavens.
10. A leading authority puts it candidly as follows: "The Taoists are in fact men who practice a trade, the secrets of which are kept in the family much as the secrets of the professional seamstress, herbologist, or bean-curd maker. An aspirant Taoist novice attaches himself to the troupe of a famous Taoist master, beginning by playing the musical instruments, as-

cending through the ranks of incense bearer, procession leader, assistant cantor, learning by rote memory the various tunes, the steps, the mudras and mantras that go to make a Chief Cantor *(Tu-kung)*, or the Taoist High Priest *(Kao-kung Fa-shih)*, with a titled ordination and grade. . . . Professional Taoism becomes a search for more and more rituals, more methods of performing cures, more ways to increase the demand for one's professional services in the community." (Michael Saso, "Lu Shan, Ling Shan, and Mao Shan . . . ," *Bulletin of the Institute of Ethnology, Academia Sinica* [Taipei], no. 34, autumn 1972, pp. 128f.)

11. Liu Chi[h]-wan, "Chung-kuo Chiao-chi Shih-yi" ("Analysis of the Meaning of the Chiao-Sacrifice"). In the author's collection of studies entitled *Chung-kuo Min-chien Hsin-yang Lun-chi (Essays on Chinese Folk Belief and Folk Cults)* (Taipei: Institute of Ethnology, Academia Sinica, monograph no. 22, 1974), p. 24.
12. Michael Saso, *The Teachings of Taoist Master Chuang* (New Haven, CT: Yale University Press, 1978), p. 195.
13. See Michael Saso, *Taoism and the Rite of Cosmic Renewal* (Pullman: Washington State University Press, 1972), for detailed explication.

CHAPTER 7: THREE WAYS TO ULTIMATE TRANSFORMATION: (2) LITERATI TRADITION

1. The discussion in this chapter derives from my paper "Confucianism as a Way of Ultimate Transformation," published in the report on *East/West Cultures, Religious Motivations for Behavior: A Colloquium* (Santa Barbara, CA: Educational Futures, International, November 17–20, 1977), pp. 1–38.

CHAPTER 8: THREE WAYS TO ULTIMATE TRANSFORMATION: (3) BUDDHIST TRADITION

1. Kenneth Ch'en, *Buddhism in China: A Historical Survey* (Princeton University Press, 1964), pp. 310f. Material in brackets supplied.
2. Junjiro Takakusu, *Essentials of Buddhist Philosophy*, 2d ed. (Honolulu: University of Hawaii Press, 1949), pp. 135f.
3. Ch'en, *Buddhism in China*, pp. 319f.
4. Richard Robinson, trans., *Chinese Buddhist Verse* (London: John Murray, 1954), p. 43.

CHAPTER 9: THEIR SEPARATE WAYS: CULTS AND SECTS

1. The pioneering work in English in this field is by Daniel L. Overmyer, to whose *Folk Buddhist Religion* (Cambridge, MA: Harvard University Press, 1976) the interpretation in the preceding two paragraphs is indebted.

CHAPTER 11: TRADITIONAL CHINESE RELIGION AS MEANS OF COPING

1. The thrust, and much of the content, of this chapter derives from a public lecture that was later published in an article entitled "The Scrutable Chinese Religion," in the book, *China and Christianity; Historical and Future Encounters* (pp. 36–60), edited by J. D. Whitehead, Yu-ming Shaw, and N. J. Girardot, and published by the Center for Pastoral and Social Ministry of the University of Notre Dame in 1979. Permission to utilize this material is gratefully acknowledged.

2. Sir Edwin Arnold, *The Light of Asia,* Book the Third, originally published in 1879 and reprinted in countless versions until the present day. The Four Signs—by encountering which the pampered young prince Gautama was led to his destiny as the Buddha—were an old man, a sick man, a corpse, and a wandering ascetic "truth seeker."

CHAPTER 12: THE DISRUPTION OF TRADITION

1. See especially Holmes Welch, *The Buddhist Revival in China* (Cambridge, MA: Harvard University Press, 1968).
2. What such "freedom" means in practice is clearly spelled out by Richard C. Bush, Jr., in his *Religion in Communist China* (Nashville and New York: Abingdon Press, 1970), pp. 15–22.
3. In the 1990s Buddhism especially has exhibited a phenomenal growth and new sorts of activities. Ministry of the Interior figures show an increase in registered Buddhist temples from 1,157 in 1983 to 4,020 in 1993, while clergy and laypeople alike have become impressively active in a "social gospel" that is new to Buddhism. Other religions have also flourished during the same period. (*Free China Review* 44.12, December 1994, is largely devoted to "The New Buddhism: Religious Renaissance"; figures quoted here are from page 6 of this journal.)

Glossary

arhat One who has attained the goal of no-rebirth. Often used in Chinese contexts to refer simply to personal disciples of Śākyamuni.

bhakti Loving devotion (to a deity).

bodhisattva One who delays indefinitely the final step to Buddhahood out of compassion for the sufferings of others. The bodhisattva is the ideal of Mahāyāna.

buddha One who has attained the perfect condition of enlightenment and liberation from suffering, that is, *nirvāṇa*. Often refers to the "historical" Buddha, Śākyamuni. In Mahāyāna, especially at the popular level, the term is equivalent to God, or a Supreme Deity.

chai A traditional Taoist ritual for salvation of the dead.

ch'i Vital breath. A metaphysical concept that is paired with *li* (2) to account for the phenomenal world.

chiao The most elaborate Taoist communal ritual: the Rite of Cosmic Renewal.

ching (1) The generative essence component of life.

ching (2) Dedication, reverence, respect.

ch'ing ming Clear and bright; the fortnightly division of the spring during which families visit ancestral tombs to renovate them and sacrifice.

chün-tzû The Perfect Gentleman, the noble man defined by moral character, according to the ideals of the Literati texts, especially the *Analects*.

dharmas Elementary constituents of phenomena. Not to be confused with the Dharma, which refers to the Buddhist Truth or Way or Law.

dhyāna Yogic concentration or Buddhist "meditation." Ch'an and its Japanese pronunciation Zen are transliterations of this word.

fa (1) Criminal law; that by which the masses are governed, as opposed to *li* (2), the social codes of the elite.

fa (2) In professional Taoism, occult techniques.

fa-shih (1) Master of the Buddhist Law; often called (more correctly) Dharma-Master.

fa-shih (2) In professional Taoism, the Master of Occult Techniques.

fêng-shui Winds and water, "geomancy." The pseudoscience of siting dwellings of dead and living to assure good fortune.

fu Charm or talisman, written by Taoist or other religious practitioner claiming power over spirits.

hô-shang Ordained Buddhist.

hsiao Filiality or filial piety, the cardinal Chinese virtue.

hsin Mind, heart, or mind/heart, depending on context.

hsing See *wu-hsing*.

hun The "spiritual" one of man's two souls.

karma The concept that what is now is the direct and inevitable result of what was before. In Buddhist theory it is an impersonal "law" of cause and effect; in popular understanding it is the moral law: What you sow you shall reap.

kuei Malevolent spirits.

k'ung Literally, empty or emptiness. Chinese translation of Sanskrit terms *śūnya* and *śūnyatā*, perhaps the most basic concept of Mahāyāna theory.

li (1) Ritually proper deportment in every social circumstance. A code supposedly followed by aristocrats in antiquity and by *chün-tzû* after the time of Master K'ung.

li (2) This term [a different word in Chinese than *li* (1)] in "Neo-Confucian" philosophy denotes the metaphysical concept of the Principle. Paired with *ch'i*, it produces all actual and potential phenomena; the ultimate extension of the concept is the totality of *li,* or Cosmic Principle, which seems identical with *tao.*

ling Spiritual power or efficacy.

Literati The "Confucian" scholars, or *Ru*.

Lü School The Chinese name for the *Vinaya* School, which emphasizes strict adherence to the precepts.

macrocosm The universe.

mantra Verbal formula, usually of Sanskrit syllables having no literal meaning, which is repeated for magical purposes in religious rites.

microcosm The human body.

millenarian Refers to belief in the dawning of the age of human happiness, when the Buddha (usually Mi-lô, or Maitreya) or some other savior will descend in glory to save true believers and destroy their enemies.

nei-tan Inner alchemy; alchemical operations conceived as taking place through meditative techniques inside the body.

nirvāṇa The state attained by Buddhas, left undescribed by Śākyamuni, but in popular conception perfect bliss or even paradise.

oracle bones Instruments of divination in archaic times. Cracks produced when bones were heated gave positive or negative responses from the spiritual dimension.

p'o The "physical" one of man's two souls.

p'u-tu Ritual to assist souls to attain salvation in the "otherworld."

rên The cardinal virtue of the *chün-tzû*. Many translations have been suggested, such as benevolence, altruistic love, man-to-manness. At a less exalted level it is commonly used simply to mean good or charitable. With Master Mêng, and thereafter, it seems suitably rendered as "empathetic concern."

Ru The "Confucian" scholars or Literati.

Saṅgha The order of Buddhist monks and nuns.

shang ti The Supreme Ruler in Heaven.

shên Beneficent spiritual beings; deities; ancestors. The spirit component of life.

shêng-rên Saint, sage.

skandhas Five psychophysical constituents that, along with the *dharmas*, make up all phenomena.

śūnyatā Emptiness, or *k'ung*, in Chinese. It refers to the true nature of all things, according to Mahāyāna theory; which is to say, nothing exists as a thing-in-itself.

sūtra Scriptural texts supposedly uttered by the Buddha Himself. In Mahāyāna, often set in vast, prodigiously elaborate scenes featuring gatherings of innumerable Buddhas, bodhisattvas, and other saints from countless worlds and universes.

t'an Altar. In this text, refers to large temporary structures erected out of doors in connection with the

Taoist Rite of Cosmic Renewal, or *chiao*.

tao Metaphysically, the Cosmic Order or Nature as it functions without any concept of Deity. Humanly, the Way whereby one must live if one is to be in harmony with the Cosmic Order.

tao-shih Ordained Taoist.

t'ien Heaven. A more impersonal concept of Supreme Deity than *shang ti* in the Classical Age (early centuries BCE). Survives in the popular religion as a personal power.

T'ien Shih The Master Designated by the Heavens, title of the most prestigious Taoist, hereditary in the Chang lineage since second century CE.

tsu Lineage.

t'u-ti Local earth god, called by several other names according to time, place, and function, but always most closely associated with everyday life of the people as well as the officials.

upāya Expedient means. The accommodation to the particular level of understanding of the individual sufferer by the Buddha's teaching and hence by the teachings and practices of the various schools.

Vinaya The rules and regulations governing the *Sangha*, one of the three divisions, or "baskets," of the Buddhist Canon (*Tripiṭaka*).

wai-tan External alchemy, the attempt to concoct the elixir that will give the adept immortality, or at least great longevity. Other practices are also associated with the purely "chemical" experimentation.

wên-miao The "Confucian Temple"; literally, the Temple of Culture, Temple of Literature, or Civil Temple. In traditional times it was a State-prescribed memorial hall, established in every administrative capital.

wu-hsing The five elemental operative qualities, or phases, of all phenomena, whose symbols are water, fire, wood, metal, and earth.

yamen The quarters of an official, combining his residence and his official buildings.

yang The male, bright, positive force in the universe. In popular religion, it is Good as contrasted with Evil; in the search for immortality of Taoism, it is what must be nourished to overcome *yin*.

yin The female, dark, negative force in the universe. In popular religion it is Evil as contrasted with Good; in the search for immortality of Taoism, it is what must be eliminated to attain the ultimate triumph of *yang*.

Selected Readings

The following bibliographical suggestions have been made subject to certain limitations—namely, they are all in English, books are preferred to journals, and materials apt to be unduly difficult to procure are not usually listed. This means, of course, that certain important—even definitive—works are regrettably omitted. The objective has been practical usefulness in the service of the text. Even so, there are variations in the level of ease or difficulty of comprehension and sophistication in what is suggested, as I have in mind varying levels of background in readership.

The most nearly complete bibliography in the field is my own *Chinese Religion in Western Languages; A Comprehensive and Classified Bibliography of Publications in English, French, and German Through 1980.* Tucson: University of Arizona Press, 1985. Published for the Association for Asian Studies as their Monograph No. XLI. This should be supplemented by my *Chinese Religions: Publications in Western Languages, 1981 through 1990,* edited by Gary Seaman. Ann Arbor, MI, Association for Asian Studies, Monograph No. 47, 1993.

There are two immense repositories of information about Chinese religion in traditional times that are indispensable to all students. They have in common a certain tone of condescension and even contempt characteristic of Western attitudes toward China during the late nineteenth and early twentieth centuries and for that reason will be objectionable to modern sensibilities. However, they are the work of scholars who spent many years in China investigating Chinese religion and who knew the literary sources, and they are unparalleled mines of useful information:

Doré, Henri. *Researches Into Chinese Superstitions.* Shanghai: T'usewei Press, 1914–1933. Translated into English in part, by several translators, and republished in Taipei by Ch'eng-wen Pub. Co., 1966–1967, 11 vols. in 5. The English translation leaves 7 volumes still untranslated.

Groot, J. J. M. de. *The Religious System of China.* 6 vols. Leiden: E. J. Brill, 1892–1910; reprinted in Taipei by Literature House, 1964.

For a rapid overview of Chinese religion one may read these articles:

Overmyer, Daniel L. "Chinese Religion: An Overview." In *The Encyclopedia of Religion,* edited by Mircea Eliade, vol. 3, pp. 257b–289a, with extensive bibliography. New York and London: Macmillan, 1987. Historical survey.

Thompson, Laurence G. "Chinese Religion." In *Encyclopaedia Britannica*, 15th ed. (*Britannica 3*), *Macropaedia*, vol. 4, 1974: pp. 422a–428a.

Under the selected readings for each chapter, we have mentioned the pertinent section in the anthology of historical, descriptive, and analytical readings designed to accompany this text:

Thompson, Laurence G., ed. *The Chinese Way in Religion*. Belmont, CA: Wadsworth, 1973.

There is no doubt that in the field of Chinese religion, the proverbial "one book one would want to have on a desert island" is the following:

Yang, C. K. *Religion in Chinese Society*. Berkeley and Los Angeles: University of California Press, 1961.

CHAPTER 1: THE EARLY CHINESE WORLDVIEW

Chan, Wing-tsit. *A Source Book in Chinese Philosophy*. Princeton, NJ: Princeton University Press, 1963. See pertinent sections. Generous selections in reliable translation, with useful introductory remarks.

Fung, Yu-lan. *A History of Chinese Philosophy*. English translation by Derk Bodde, vol. 1. Princeton, NJ: Princeton University Press, 1952. This first volume deals with "The Period of the Philosophers (from the beginnings to circa 100 B.C.)." It is the standard work in the field to date.

Henderson, John B. *The Development and Decline of Chinese Cosmology*. New York: Columbia University Press, 1984. A detailed, sophisticated, lucidly written discussion of the Chinese traditional worldview, with intercultural comparisons.

Needham, Joseph. *Science and Civilization in China*. Cambridge, England: Cambridge University Press, 1954 to date. A multivolume work in progress. See especially vol. 2, *History of Scientific Thought*, 1956. This truly great work is one of the most impressive examinations ever undertaken of any civilization. Combines unparalleled erudition, brilliant creative imagination, and a sophisticated but lucid literary style.

Schwartz, Benjamin I. *The World of Thought in Ancient China*. Cambridge, MA: The Belknap Press of Harvard University Press, 1985. Sophisticated interpretive study.

CHAPTER 2: PRESCIENTIFIC THEORY AND RELIGIOUS PRACTICE

Burkhardt, V. R. *Chinese Creeds and Customs*. 3 vols. Hong Kong: South China Morning Post, Ltd., 1953–1958. Personal observations among the Chinese in Hong Kong and vicinity, with charming illustrations by the author. Originating as a column in the *South China Morning Post*, the style is popular and the articles are short.

Elliott, Alan J. A. *Chinese Spirit Medium Cults in Singapore*. London: London School of Economics and Political Science, Department of Anthropology, 1955. Report of field study by an anthropologist.

Forke, Alfred. *The World-Conception of the Chinese*. London: Arthur Probsthain, 1925. Also useful for the topic of Chapter 1.

Lessa, William A. *Chinese Body Divination.* Los Angeles: United World Academy and Fellowship, 1968. Comprehensive and copiously illustrated study by an anthropologist.

Smith, Richard J. *Fortune-Tellers and Philosophers: Divination in Traditional Chinese Society.* Boulder, CO: Westview Press, 1991. First comprehensive historical survey.

Wei, Tat. *An Exposition of the I-Ching or Book of Changes.* Taipei: Institute of Cultural Studies, 1970. Careful, detailed study. Author's naïveté in text-critical matters does not detract from the value of his interpretations and analyses. One can actually get a glimmering of understanding of this incredibly complicated work from Wei's exposition.

Wilhelm, Hellmut. *Change: Eight Lectures on the I Ching.* New York: Pantheon, published for the Bollingen Foundation, 1960. Still the most intelligible introduction.

Yoon, Hong-key. *Geomantic Relationships between Culture and Nature in Korea.* Taipei: Orient Cultural Service, 1976. As applicable to China as to Korea.

CHAPTER 3: THE FAMILY: KINDRED AND ANCESTORS

Ahern, Emily M. *The Cult of the Dead in a Chinese Village.* Stanford, CA: Stanford University Press, 1973. Most detailed study to date. The author, an anthropologist, worked in a village in northern Taiwan. There is some question about whether the practices there—particularly in regard to ancestral tablets—can be regarded as completely representative of the ancestral cult in general.

Chiang, Yee. *A Chinese Childhood.* New York: Norton, 1963. Charming reminiscences with illustrations by the author. Discusses what it was like to grow up in a wealthy lineage-family environment in the early twentieth century.

Groot, J. J. M. de. *The Religious System of China.* 6 vols. Leiden: E. J. Brill, 1892–1910; reprinted in Taipei by Literature House, 1964. Family religion as seen in mortuary rites is presented in great detail in the first three volumes.

Hsu, Francis L. K. *Under the Ancestors' Shadow.* London: Routledge & Kegan Paul, 1949. This study of a town in southwest China has become a "classic"; its theme is the all-pervasive influence of the ancestors.

Hu, Hsien Chin. *The Common Descent Group in China and Its Functions.* New York: Viking Fund, 1948 (Viking Fund Publications in Anthropology Number Ten). Covers the subject of *tsu,* with emphasis on its religious implications, in clear and detailed fashion.

Liu, Hui-chen Wang. "An Analysis of Chinese Clan Rules: Confucian Theories in Action." In *Confucianism in Action,* edited by Arthur F. Wright. Stanford, CA: Stanford University Press, 1959; reprinted in same editor's *Confucianism and Chinese Civilization.* New York: Atheneum, 1964.

Yang, C. K. *Religion in Chinese Society.* Berkeley and Los Angeles: University of California Press, 1961. Excellent analysis by sociologist.

CHAPTER 4: THE COMMUNITY: GODS AND TEMPLES

Baity, Philip Chesley. *Religion in a Chinese Town.* Taipei: Orient Cultural Service, 1975. An anthropological study of popular religion in northern

Taiwan, centering on Tamsui and vicinity. The author gives important theoretical analyses of various aspects of this religion, making functional distinctions of temples and suggestions with regard to the "genesis of the gods."

Burkhardt, V. R. *Chinese Creeds and Customs.* 3 vols. Hong Kong: South China Morning Post, Ltd., 1953–1958. The best account of popular religion in the Hong Kong area, written in popular style, with many illustrations.

Cohen, Alvin P. "Chinese Religion: Popular Religion." In *The Encyclopedia of Religion,* edited by Mircea Eliade, vol. 3, pp. 289a–296b. New York and London: Macmillan, 1987. Brief but comprehensive overview.

Day, Clarence B. *Chinese Peasant Cults; Being a Study of Chinese Paper Gods.* Shanghai: Kelly & Walsh, 1940; reprinted in Taipei by Ch'eng-wen, 1969. The paper gods are images produced for household use. This is a thorough study made in the field by a missionary scholar. It is well illustrated.

Dean, Kenneth. *Taoist Ritual and Popular Cults of Southeast China.* Princeton, NJ: Princeton University Press, 1993. One of the first personal investigations of religion on the mainland following the partial "opening up" of the People's Republic of China. Author is trained in the French school of Taoism and Sinology and has studied in Taiwan as well.

Goodrich, Anne Swann. *The Peking Temple of the Eastern Peak.* Nagoya: Monumenta Serica, 1964. Detailed study of the pantheon found in one of Peking's most famous temples. Copiously illustrated. This is one of the rare surviving temples belonging to the Total Perfection (Ch'üan-chen) Taoists.

Hodous, Lewis. *Folkways in China.* London: Arthur Probsthain, 1929. Deals with some of the major deities and the round of the festival year. The study is centered on the Foochow area of Fuchien province. Illustrated with photos.

Jordan, David K. *Gods, Ghosts, and Ancestors: Folk Religion in a Taiwanese Village.* Berkeley and Los Angeles: University of California Press, 1972. A much-cited field study by an anthropologist. Well-illustrated.

Maspero, Henri. "The Mythology of Modern China." In *Asiatic Mythology,* J. Hackin et al. New York: Crowell, n.d.; reprinted 1963. The author was a leading authority. For him, "modern China" is essentially the most recent millennium. The subject of his presentation is treated rather unsystematically, but it is written in an interesting style, with many illustrations.

Po, Sung-nien and David Johnson. *Domestic Deities and Auspicious Emblems: The Iconography of Everyday Life in Village China.* Berkeley: University of California, Chinese Popular Culture Project, publication No. 2, 1992. Profusely illustrated with color photos of an important collection of prints and explained by intelligent text.

Sangren, P. Steven. *History and Magical Power in a Chinese Community.* Stanford, CA: Stanford University Press, 1987. More than an anthropological community study, this is a sophisticated social scientific effort to interpret Chinese religion using certain contemporary theoretical ideas.

Thompson, Laurence G., ed. *The Chinese Way in Religion.* Belmont, CA: Wadsworth, 1973. See part 6: "Popular Religion."

Weller, Robert P. *Unities and Diversities in Chinese Religion.* Seattle: University of Washington Press, 1987. Another field study by an anthropologist. His work was done in a town in northern Taiwan. Small section of photos.

Yang, C. K. *Religion in Chinese Society.* Berkeley and Los Angeles: University of California Press, 1961. Best general exposition of the subject.

CHAPTER 5: THE STATE: EMPEROR AND OFFICIALS

Bilsky, Lester J. *The State Religion of Ancient China.* 2 vols. Taipei: Orient Cultural Service, 1975. Detailed account covering Western Chou through the mid-second century BCE.

Huang, K'uei-yen, and John K. Shryock. "A Collection of Chinese Prayers." *Journal of the American Oriental Society* 49 (1929): 128–155. Unique specimens, taken from an official liturgical manual.

Kong, Demao, and Ke Lan. *In the Mansion of Confucius' Descendants—an Oral History.* Beijing: New World Press, 1984. Translated from Chinese by Rosemary Roberts. Simply but eloquently told: an unprecedented inside account of the household and traditions of the Master's descendants in recent times. There is nothing like it to make "Confucianism" come alive. Illustrated with photos.

Meyer, Jeffrey F. *The Dragons of Tiananmen: Beijing as a Sacred City.* Columbia, SC: University of South Carolina Press, 1991. Much revised and improved version of author's earlier work, *Peking as a Sacred City,* published in Taipei in 1976. Deals with rituals, icons, and ritual places in the Ming and Ch'ing (and now People's Republic of China) center of power.

Moule, G. E. "Notes on the *Ting-chi,* or Half-Yearly Sacrifice to Confucius." *Journal of the North China Branch, Royal Asiatic Society* XXXIII (1900–1901): 37–73 (as misprinted; actually pp. 120–156). Unique description, complete with photos, drawings, plans, and musical score.

Palmer, Spencer J. *Confucian Rituals in Korea.* Berkeley and Seoul: Asian Humanities Press & Po Chin Chai Ltd., n.d. (1985). Informative text and 113 color plates. The rituals in Korea were of course closely similar to those in China; here we see them as preserved to the present day in South Korea.

Shryock, John K. *The Origin and Development of the State Cult of Confucius.* New York and London: Century, 1932. Still the only full-scale historical treatment.

Thompson, Laurence G., ed. *The Chinese Way in Religion.* Belmont, CA: Wadsworth, 1973. See Part 4: "Religion of the State."

Thompson, Laurence G. "Confucian Thought: The State Cult." In *The Encyclopedia of Religion,* edited by Mircea Eliade, vol. 4, pp. 36a–38b. New York and London: Macmillan, 1987. Brief summary.

Wechsler, Howard J. *Offerings of Jade and Silk.* New Haven and London: Yale University Press, 1985. The subtitle of this well-written book indicates its subject: *Ritual and Symbol in the Legitimation of the T'ang Dynasty.* In-depth historical study informed by anthropological and history of religions insights.

Williams, E. T. "The State Religion of China during the Manchu Dynasty." *Journal of the North China Branch, Royal Asiatic Society* XLIV (1913): 11–45. A good discussion of the imperial worship.

Yang, C. K. *Religion in Chinese Society.* Berkeley and Los Angeles: University of California Press, 1961. Masterly analysis.

For the best English-language introductions to Taoist religion, one should consult the following encyclopedia articles:

Baldrian, Farzeen (translation from French by Charles Le Blanc). "Taoism: An Overview." In *The Encyclopedia of Religion,* edited by Mircea Eliade, pp. 288b–306a, with extensive bibliography. New York and London: Macmillan, 1987. Lagerwey, John. "Taoism: The Taoist Religious Community." *Ibid.,* pp. 306a–317a; Boltz, Judith Magee. "Taoism: Taoist Literature." *Ibid.,* pp. 317a–329b.

Seidel, Anna K. "Taoism." In *Encyclopaedia Britannica,* 15th ed. (*Britannica 3*), *Macropaedia,* vol. 17, 1974: pp. 1032b–1044b; Strickmann, Michel. "Taoism, History of." *Ibid.,* pp. 1044b–1050b; Strickmann, Michel. "Taoist Literature." *Ibid.,* pp. 1051a–1055a.

For more specialized study, see the following:

Blofeld, John. *Beyond the Gods: Buddhist and Taoist Mysticism.* London: Allen & Unwin; New York: Dutton, 1974. A valuable work written in the author's lucid and interesting style. For Taoism, see the first three chapters.

Blofeld, John. *The Secret and Sublime: Taoist Mysteries and Magic.* London: Allen & Unwin, 1973. Entertainingly written account of the author's personal experiences, informed by his knowledge of the literary sources. A basic work for approaching Taoism on all levels.

Giles, Lionel. *A Gallery of Chinese Immortals.* London: John Murray, 1948. Wisdom of the East Series. Biographies of Taoist adepts taken from the Taoist Canon.

Girardot, Norman J. *Myth and Meaning in Early Taoism.* Berkeley, Los Angeles, London: University of California Press, 1983. A highly sophisticated study that brings certain Chinese mythological concepts into the company of world mythologies.

Goullart, Peter. *The Monastery of Jade Mountain.* London: John Murray, 1961. Unique autobiographical account of a sincere European Taoist. Rather naive and sentimental but contains valuable material.

Lagerwey, John. *Taoist Ritual in Chinese Society and History.* New York and London: Macmillan, 1987. By far the most detailed descriptions of Taoist liturgies available in English. The author is trained in the contemporary French school of Sinology with its special expertise in Taoism.

Lu, K'uan-Yü (Charles Luk). *Taoist Yoga: Alchemy and Immortality.* London: Rider & Co., 1970. Translation of a late nineteenth century text called *The Secrets of Cultivating Essential Nature and Eternal Life.* A good example of one of the most important concerns of Taoism. Well translated.

Luk, Charles (K'uan-Yü Lu). *The Secrets of Chinese Meditation.* London: Rider & Co., 1964. Deals clearly and well with techniques of various Buddhist and Taoist schools.

Maspero, Henri. Translated from French by Frank A. Kierman, Jr. *Taoism and Chinese Religion.* Amherst, MA: University of Massachusetts Press, 1981. The most extensive anthology of Taoist texts in translation, incorporating the studies of one of the preeminent Western pioneers.

Rawson, Philip, and Laszlo Legeza. *Tao: the Eastern Philosophy of Time and Change*. New York: Avon Books, 1973. Breaks new ground in showing the pervasiveness of Taoist ideas in Chinese art. Excellent introduction and 196 plates.

Robinet, Isabelle. English translation by Julian F. Pas and Norman J. Girardot. *Taoist Meditation: The Mao-shan Tradition of Great Purity*. Albany, NY: State University of New York Press, 1993. Rather technical; the author is the leading authority on the subject.

Saso, Michael, and David W. Chappell, eds. *Buddhist and Taoist Studies*, I. Honolulu: University Press of Hawaii, 1977. Contains four important studies of Taoism and a lengthy bibliography.

Schipper, Kristofer M. English translation by Karen C. Duval, Foreword by Norman J. Girardot. *The Taoist Body*. Berkeley, Los Angeles, London: University of California Press, 1992. Original French edition, 1982. To date the best summary of Taoism as a religion.

Thompson, Laurence G., ed. *The Chinese Way in Religion*. Belmont, CA: Wadsworth, 1973. See Part 2, "Taoism."

Thompson, Laurence G. "Taoism: Classic and Canon." In F. M. Denny and R. L. Taylor, eds., *The Holy Book in Comparative Perspective*, 204–223. Columbia, SC: University of South Carolina Press, 1985. Brief summary of history and contents of the *Tao Tsang*.

Ware, James R. *Alchemy, Medicine, and Religion in the China of A.D. 320: The Nei P'ien of Ko Hung (Pao-P'u Tzu)*. Cambridge, MA: M.I.T. Press, 1966. The text is one of the most important in the history of Taoism. The translation is vivid but perhaps a bit too free; unfortunately its lack of scholarly apparatus too often leaves the reader in the dark.

Wilhelm, Richard. Translated from the German translation by Cary F. Baynes. *The Secret of the Golden Flower*. New York: Harcourt Brace & World, 1931; revised edition, 1962. The title covers two basic texts coming out of two Taoist sects. Extensive commentary by C. G. Jung, the value of which depends on one's opinion of Jung's ideas and his understanding of Taoism— which he got mostly from Wilhelm.

Wu, Yao-yü. Translated from Chinese by Laurence G. Thompson; edited by Gary Seaman. *The Taoist Tradition in Chinese Thought*. Los Angeles: University of Southern California Center for Visual Anthropology, Ethnographics Press, 1991. Historical survey by a contemporary Chinese scholar with no Western biases.

CHAPTER 7: THREE WAYS TO ULTIMATE
TRANSFORMATION: (2) LITERATI TRADITION

For background on the Literati Tradition in both its ancient and medieval forms, one may consult the two articles by Wing-tsit Chan, "Confucian Thought: Foundations of the Tradition" and "Neo-Confucianism." In *The Encyclopedia of Religion*, edited by Mircea Eliade, vol. 4, pp. 15a–24a; 24a–36a. New York and London: Macmillan, 1987.

Bruce, J. Percy. *Chu Hsi and His Masters*. London: Arthur Probsthain, 1923. Despite its early date, this is still a valuable study of the subject.

Chan, Wing-tsit, trans. *Instructions for Practical Living and Other Neo-Confucian Writings by Wang Yang-ming.* New York: Columbia University Press, 1963. Definitive translation of the most important documents of the Hsin (Mind) School.

Chan, Wing-tsit, trans. *Reflections on Things at Hand: The Neo-Confucian Anthology Compiled by Chu Hsi and Lü Tsu-ch'ien.* New York: Columbia University Press, 1967. Copiously annotated and lucidly translated presentation of the *Chin Ssû Lu,* a classic summary of Li (the Principle) School thought.

Tang, Chün-i. "Religious Beliefs and Modern Chinese Culture, Part II: The Religious Spirit of Confucianism." *Chinese Studies in Philosophy* V, no. 1 (Fall 1973): 48–85. The author is an eminent scholar of our day; the essay is a personal testament.

Tang, Chün-i. "The Spirit and Development of Neo-Confucianism." In *Invitation to Chinese Philosophy,* edited by Arne Naess and Alastair Hannay, pp. 56–83. Oslo: Universitetsforlaget, 1972. Unexciting but reliable.

Taylor, Rodney L. *The Religious Dimensions of Confucianism.* Albany, NY: State University Press of New York, 1990. Collects in one place most of the author's pioneering essays in this field.

Tu, Wei-ming. *Confucian Thought: Selfhood as Creative Transformation.* Albany, NY: State University of New York Press, 1985. Collection of articles by the author, who represents a contemporary "Confucian" revival both in scholarship and in personal philosophy.

Tu, Wei-ming. *Humanity and Self-Cultivation: Essays in Confucian Thought.* Berkeley, CA: Asian Humanities Press, 1979. Collection of the author's articles dealing with various aspects of the Literati Tradition in a highly sophisticated manner.

Tu, Wei-ming. *Neo-Confucian Thought in Action: Wang Yang-ming's Youth (1472–1509).* Berkeley, Los Angeles, London: University of California Press, 1976. A deeply empathetic, sensitive spiritual biography.

Wu, Yao-yü. *The Literati Tradition in Chinese Thought.* Translated from Chinese by Laurence G. Thompson; edited by Gary Seaman. Los Angeles: University of Southern California Center for Visual Anthropology, Ethnographics Press, 1995. Unique historical treatment by contemporary Chinese scholar.

CHAPTER 8: THREE WAYS TO ULTIMATE
TRANSFORMATION: (3) BUDDHIST TRADITION

Blofeld, John. *Beyond the Gods: Buddhist and Taoist Mysticism.* London: Allen & Unwin; New York: Dutton, 1974. Informed by Blofeld's long and sustained involvement with Chinese religion; written in his lucid and interesting style.

Blofeld, John. *The Jewel in the Lotus: An Outline of Present Day Buddhism in China.* London: The Buddhist Society, 1948. Brief but good introduction to Chinese Buddhism. Broader coverage than the title indicates.

Blofeld, John. *The Wheel of Life.* London: Rider & Co., 1959. Autobiographical account of Buddhism as author observed and experienced it in pre–World War II days. Author was for many years a committed Buddhist in quest of enlightenment; his account is neither sentimental nor smug.

Chang, Chen-chi. *The Practice of Zen*. London: Rider & Co., 1960. Excellent exposition of the practice of yogic concentration as taught in Chinese Buddhism. Succinct and lucid.

Ch'en, Kenneth K. S. *Buddhism in China: A Historical Survey*. Princeton, NJ: Princeton University Press, 1964. Best historical treatment to date. Treats Buddhism primarily from the institutional point of view. Written in a lucid and nontechnical style.

Ch'en, Kenneth K. S. *The Chinese Transformation of Buddhism*. Princeton, NJ: Princeton University Press, 1973. The theme is the Sinification of Buddhism, mainly during the T'ang dynasty. Buddhist influences on Chinese culture are carefully considered. Written in a nontechnical style. The author is a leading authority.

Chen-hua. Translated by Denis C. Mair; edited by Chün-fang Yü. *In Search of the Dharma: Memoirs of a Modern Chinese Buddhist Pilgrim*. Albany, NY: State University of New York Press, 1992. Unique revelations of a monk caught in the turbulent currents of twentieth century politics and religion.

Ikeda, Daisaku. Translated from Japanese by Burton Watson. *The Flower of Chinese Buddhism*. New York and Tokyo: Weatherhill, 1986. The story of Buddhism in China until the great persecution of mid-ninth century, well told.

Johnston, Reginald F. *Buddhist China*. London: John Murray, 1913; reprinted in Taipei, 1976. Contains many interesting comparisons of Chinese Buddhism and non-Chinese religions. Valuable material on pilgrimages. Remarkably good "snapshots."

Kapleau, Philip, comp. and ed. *The Three Pillars of Zen*. Boston, MA: Beacon Press, 1967 (first published in Tokyo by John Weatherhill, 1965). The "three pillars" are teaching, practice, enlightenment. This is a collection of translations, with introductions and notes, that accurately represents the two basic schools of Zen or Ch'an. It is one of the comparatively few books in English on which one can rely for a true depiction of this form of Buddhism.

Kitagawa, Joseph M. and Mark D. Cummings, eds. *Buddhism and Asian History*. New York etc., 1989. Collection of articles extracted from the *Encyclopedia of Religion*, edited by Mircea Eliade. New York and London: Macmillan, 1987. For relevant articles see passim.

Luk, Charles (K'uan-Yu Lu). *The Secrets of Chinese Meditation*. London: Rider & Co., 1964. Deals clearly and well with the techniques of various Buddhist and Taoist schools.

Nakamura, Hajime. "Buddhism, Schools of: Mahayana Buddhism." In *The Encyclopedia of Religion*, edited by Mircea Eliade, vol. 2, pp. 456a–472b. New York and London: Macmillan, 1987. Concise information about the forms of Buddhist philosophy that were influential in China, by a leading authority.

Prip-Møller, J. *Chinese Buddhist Monasteries: Their Plan and Its Function As a Setting for Buddhist Monastic Life*. New York: Oxford University Press, 1937; reprinted by Hong Kong University Press, 1967. Monumental, masterly study by architect-Sinologist. A thorough exposition of all aspects of Buddhist monachism in early twentieth century China. Illustrated with 365 plates, plans, and elevations; notes and Chinese graphs used throughout.

Seckel, Dietrich. Translated by Ulrich Mammitzsch. *Buddhist Art of East Asia.* Bellingham, WA: Western Washington University, 1989. Author is the leading Western authority in this field.

Thompson, Laurence G., ed. *The Chinese Way in Religion.* Belmont, CA: Wadsworth, 1973. See Part 3, "Buddhism."

Weinstein, Stanley. "Buddhism, Schools of: Chinese Buddhism." In *The Encyclopedia of Religion,* edited by Mircea Eliade, vol. 2, pp. 482a–487b. New York and London: Macmillan, 1987. Brief information on what constituted a *tsung* ("school") in Chinese Buddhism.

Welch, Holmes. *The Practice of Chinese Buddhism, 1900–1950.* Cambridge, MA: Harvard University Press, 1967. The author, who was knowledgeable about the literature, interviewed Saṅgha refugees from mainland China while living in Hong Kong. The resulting work is a major study of a neglected subject, a good complement to the work of Prip-Møller listed above.

Xu Yün (Hsü-yün). Translated by Charles Luk. Revised and edited by Richard Hunn. *Empty Cloud: The Autobiography of the Chinese Zen Master Xu-yun.* Longmead, Shaftesbury, Dorset, England: Element Books Ltd., 1988. Precious revelations by the monk often revered as the leading Buddhist of China during this century.

Zürcher, Erik. "Buddhism in China." In *The Encyclopedia of Religion,* edited by Mircea Eliade, vol. 2, pp. 414a–421a. New York and London: Macmillan, 1987. An authoritative historical survey in small compass.

CHAPTER 9: THEIR SEPARATE WAYS: CULTS AND SECTS

Dunstheimer, Guillaume. "Some Religious Aspects of Secret Societies." In *Popular Movements and Secret Societies in China, 1840–1950,* edited by Jean Chesneaux, pp. 23–28. Stanford, CA: Stanford University Press, 1972. Analyzes the common elements in secret societies that are religious in nature.

Groot, J. J. M. de. *Sectarianism and Religious Persecution in China.* 2 vols. Leiden: E. J. Brill, 1901; republished in Taipei by Literature House, 1963, 2 vols. in 1. Extensive historical survey based on the author's translations of government documents. Includes also important essays on two sects personally investigated by author in late nineteenth century. Formidable evidence for author's thesis that the State has always persecuted sectarian forms of religion; marred (from the point of view of modern scholarship) by his obvious biases.

Jordan, David K., and Daniel L. Overmyer. *The Flying Phoenix: Aspects of Chinese Sectarianism in Taiwan.* Princeton, NJ: Princeton University Press, 1986. Combined talents of an anthropologist and a historian of religions, both of whom are specialists in Taiwanese religion, give us what is by far the most extensive, probing, and revealing study of spirit-writing cults.

Naquin, Susan. *Millenarian Rebellion in China: The Eight Trigrams Uprising of 1813.* New Haven, CT: Yale University Press, 1976. Painstaking investigation of an important case of religious sectarianism that erupted into secular history. Readers who find the book too long and detailed may profitably study the Introduction and Part 1, "Inspiration: The Organization and Ideology of White Lotus Sects," pp. 1–60.

Overmyer, Daniel L. "Boatmen and Buddhas: The Lo Chiao in Ming Dynasty China." *History of Religions* 17, nos. 3/4 (February–May, 1978): 284–302. Pioneering study of a religious sect of precontemporary times from the point of view of history of religions.

Overmyer, Daniel L. *Folk Buddhist Religion: Dissenting Sects in Late Traditional China.* Cambridge, MA: Harvard University Press, 1976. A pioneering study that presents much new material and shows the difference between religious sects and secret societies.

Plopper, Clifford H. *Chinese Religion Seen Through the Proverb.* Shanghai: China Press, 1926; recent reprint available. A rich repertory of popular beliefs revealed in proverbs. They are classified, explained, and have the Chinese texts appended.

Seaman, Gary. *Journey to the North: An Ethnohistorical Analysis and Translation of the Chinese Folk Novel Pei-Yu-Chi.* Berkeley, Los Angeles, London: University of California Press, 1987. In his introduction the translator discusses this "folk novel" and its probable origin in a spirit-writing cult connected with the sacred mountain Wu-tang Shan and its unexpected association with imperial politics during the Ming dynasty (1368–1644).

Seaman, Gary. *Temple Organization in a Chinese Village.* Taipei: Orient Cultural Service, 1978. First monographic study of a spirit-writing cult in Taiwan, with much else.

Shek, Richard. "Millenarianism: Chinese Millenarian Movements." In *The Encyclopedia of Religion,* edited by Mircea Eliade, vol. 9, pp. 532b–536b. New York and London: Macmillan, 1987. See also the bibliographic note appended to this summary article.

Suzuki, Teitaro, and Paul Carus, trans. *T'ai-shang Kan-ying P'ien.* Chicago: Open Court, 1906; reprinted at various times. A widely known popular tract of the *shan-shu,* or morality book, type.

Suzuki, Teitaro, and Paul Carus, trans. *Yin Chih Wen.* Chicago: Open Court, 1906; reprinted at various times. Another widely known morality text.

Thompson, Laurence G., ed. *The Chinese Way in Religion.* Belmont, CA: Wadsworth, 1973. See Part 6: "Popular Religion."

Thompson, Laurence G. "The Moving Finger Writes: A Note on Revelation and Renewal in Chinese Religion." *Journal of Chinese Religions* 10 (Fall 1982): 92–147. About *shan-shu* (morality tracts) produced by spirit-writing, with translation of one such text from Taiwan, and the explanations of spirit-writing by a spirit-writing medium.

Topley, Marjorie. "The Great Way of Former Heaven: A Group of Chinese Secret Religious Sects." *Bulletin of the School of Oriental and African Studies,* London University, vol. 26 (1963): 362–392.

CHAPTER 10: THE FESTIVAL YEAR

Aijmer, Göran. *The Dragon Boat Festival on the Hupei-Hunan Plain, Central China.* Stockholm: Ethnographical Museum of Sweden, 1964. This study by an anthropologist is subtitled "A Study in the Ceremonialism of the Transplantation of Rice." It is a rare attempt at serious analysis of a major Chinese festival. Speculative and highly interesting.

Bredon, Juliet, and Igor Mitrophanow. *The Moon Year*. Shanghai: Kelly & Walsh, 1927; reprinted in New York by Paragon in 1966. Details about religious and secular customs, written around the framework of the festival calendar. Popular style. "Snapshots."

Burkhardt, V. R. *Chinese Creeds and Customs*. 3 vols. Hong Kong: South China Morning Post, Ltd., 1953–1958. See particularly vol. 1 for the festival calendar.

Hodous, Lewis. *Folkways in China*. London: Arthur Probsthain, 1929. The round of the festival year and some major deities, with special reference to the Foochow area in Fuchien province.

Law, Joan (photographs), and Barbara E. Ward (text). *Chinese Festivals*. Hong Kong: South China Morning Post, Ltd., 1982. A look at the celebrations in Hong Kong, with authoritative text and beautiful color plates.

Thompson, Laurence G. "Chinese Religious Year." In *The Encyclopedia of Religion*, edited by Mircea Eliade, vol. 3, pp. 323a–328a. New York and London: Macmillan, 1987. A brief outline based on Taiwanese customs.

Wong, C. S. *A Cycle of Chinese Festivities*. Singapore: Malaysia Publishing House, Ltd., 1967. The festivals as celebrated in Malaysia by overseas Chinese, and their literary background.

CHAPTER 12: THE DISRUPTION OF TRADITION

Brière, O. Translated from French by Laurence G. Thompson. *Fifty Years of Chinese Philosophy, 1898–1950*. London: Allen & Unwin, 1956. Reprinted several times. A condensed outline of the subject, with emphasis on the tensions between traditional Chinese and imported Western views.

Bush, Richard C., Jr. *Religion in Communist China*. Nashville and New York: Abingdon Press, 1970. Thorough, careful, and objective study based on Communist sources. Lucidly presented.

Chan, Wing-tsit. *Religious Trends in Modern China*. New York: Columbia University Press, 1953. An authoritative survey based primarily on written sources.

Dietrich, Craig. *People's China: A Brief History*. Oxford and New York: Oxford University Press, 2d ed., 1993. A well-balanced and objective overview for background on religious matters.

Franke, Wolfgang. *A Century of Chinese Revolution, 1851–1949*. New York: Harper Torchbooks, 1970. Amid a plethora of books on nineteenth and twentieth century political history, this is a good, concise summary.

MacInnis, Donald E. *Religion in China Today: Policy and Practice*. Maryknoll, NY: Orbis Books, 1989. Update and considerable expansion of author's 1972 book, giving descriptive material as well as documents.

Pas, Julian F., ed. *The Turning of the Tide: Religion in China Today*. Hong Kong, Oxford, etc.: Hong Kong Branch of the Royal Asiatic Society and Oxford University Press, 1989. Fifteen articles by good scholars.

Thompson, Laurence G., ed. *The Chinese Way in Religion*. Belmont, CA: Wadsworth, 1973. See "Postscript: Religion under Communism."

Welch, Holmes. *Buddhism Under Mao.* Cambridge, MA: Harvard University Press, 1972. This work completes the trilogy on twentieth century Chinese Buddhism begun with the author's *The Practice of Chinese Buddhism, 1900–1950* (listed under readings for Chapter 8). It is a thorough study by the leading authority. Many plates.

Welch, Holmes. *The Buddhist Revival in China.* Cambridge, MA: Harvard University Press, 1968. Deals with the period of the twentieth century prior to the Communist victory in 1949. There is a section of photographs by Henri Cartier-Bresson. This careful, objective study indicates that the "revival" was more apparent than real.

Yang, C. K. *Religion in Chinese Society.* Berkeley and Los Angeles: University of California Press, 1961. See Chapters 13 and 14. The author has done personal fieldwork in the early days of the People's Republic and has written authoritative works on conditions in those days.

Index